Sunset

1982

COOK BOOK OF
FAVORITE RECIPES II

By the Editors of Sunset Books and Sunset Magazine

LANE
PUBLISHING CO.
MENLO PARK,
CALIFORNIA

Another Encore of Favorites

For more than half a century, *Sunset* Magazine and Books have published exciting, reliable recipes. Over the years, many of our readers have let us know how much they treasure the "cream" of this cornucopia—recipes they make over and over again to serve to delighted family and friends.

In 1969, we published a diverse collection of favorites that is now called FAVORITE RECIPES I. Available in a fresh printing as companion to this book, that collection has been a resounding success and is one of our most widely used cook books.

In the last year or so, we decided it was time once again to invite our readers to nominate—for a brand-new book—their more recent favorites from *Sunset*. After we made known our plans in *Sunset* Magazine, our offices were fairly flooded by the exuberant response. And here is the proud result—FAVORITE RECIPES II —presented with our warm thanks to those of you who helped us choose its contents. Packed with more than 400 recipes, this book reflects *Sunset's* most successful dishes of the 1970's.

We were pleased by the broad spectrum—from simple family dishes to more exotic entertaining fare—that presented itself in our readers' selections. We expect it will please you, too, as it meets virtually every cooking style or occasion that might call you to the kitchen.

A glance at the names of a few of the most frequently nominated recipes hints that this book soars beyond the ordinary. Be sure to try these: Dutch Baby, a spectacular brunch pancake on page 128; Fish-in-a-Fish, fillets embellished and whimsically wrapped in pastry, on page 73; Smoky Beef Salami, page 52; Super Nachos, scrumptious finger food from Mexico, page 10; Overnight Layered Green Salad, page 20; Not-just-any-chili Chili, a jazzy update of an American classic, page 45; and Chocolate Chip Cookies at Their Best (no exaggeration!), page 139.

It took us months to poll the votes—months of feeling continuously gratified by the mounting number of tried-and-true favorites. You can be assured that, no matter what you decide to cook from this book, it comes with rave reviews.

Special Thanks

For their cooperation in sharing props for use in photographs, we extend our appreciation to The Best of All Worlds; Cotton Works; Good Cooks & Company; McDermott's; Peet's Coffee & Tea, Inc.; Taylor & Ng; William Ober Co.; Williams Cutlery; Williams-Sonoma Kitchenware; and House of Today.

Cover: Selected from this collection of *Sunset's* most popular recipes, succulent Spinach-stuffed Game Hens (page 67) rest on their bed of colorful spinach-and-rice stuffing. Buttered baby carrots accompany the enticing little birds, and Pear & Almond Tart (page 141) makes a first-class finale. Photographed by Darrow M. Watt. Cover design by Zan Fox.

Book Editors:
Elaine R. Woodard
Susan Warton
Claire Coleman

Special Consultants:
Jerry Anne DiVecchio
Home Economics Editor,
Sunset Magazine

Annabel Post
Senior Editor, Sunset Magazine

Photo Editor: **Lynne B. Morrall**
Design: **Lea Damiano Phelps**
Illustrations: **Alan May**

Photographers

Glenn Christiansen: 42, 114, 138. **Norman A. Plate:** 18, 82. **Darrow M. Watt:** 26, 34, 39, 47, 66, 71, 74, 79, 122, 130, 143. **Tom Wyatt:** 135. **Nikolay Zurek:** 23, 31, 87, 90, 95, 119, 127.

Editor, Sunset Books: David E. Clark

First printing October 1982

Library of Congress Catalog Card Number: 82-81400.
ISBN 0-376-06944-9. Lithographed in the United States.

CONTENTS

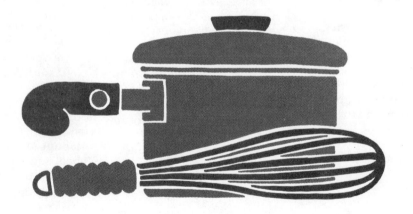

APPETIZERS

To spread, dip, or nibble

Bottomless Cheese Crock

Once this cheese crock is started, you can blend in leftovers whenever you have them to create a mellow spread that lasts almost indefinitely. To keep it smooth and moist, pour in olive oil and brandy each time you add to the crock.

4 cups (1 lb.) shredded sharp Cheddar cheese, softened
1 small package (3 oz.) cream cheese, softened
1 to 2 tablespoons olive oil
1 teaspoon *each* dry mustard and garlic salt
2 tablespoons brandy

In a large bowl, combine Cheddar cheese, cream cheese, oil, mustard, garlic salt, and brandy; beat until well blended. Pack into a container, cover, and refrigerate for a week before serving. Makes about 3 cups.

To add to the crock, use firm cheeses, such as Swiss, jack, and Cheddar. Shred and beat in, adding small amounts of olive oil or cream cheese for good consistency. Add 1½ teaspoons brandy, sherry, port, beer, or kirsch for each cup of cheese added.

Cover and refrigerate for several days before serving. Use every week or two, reserving some of the original mixture to keep the crock going.

Sesame Garlic Cheese Spread

For a quick nibble before dinner, offer crunchy raw vegetables with this garlic cheese spread. You can keep the spread refrigerated for up to a week; before serving, let it soften for half an hour.

1 teaspoon sesame seeds
1 small package (3 oz.) cream cheese, softened
½ cup ricotta cheese or small curd cottage cheese
1 tablespoon minced parsley
1 teaspoon garlic salt
    Assorted raw vegetables

In a small frying pan over medium heat, toast sesame seeds, shaking pan often, until golden (about 2 minutes); remove from heat and set aside.

In a bowl, beat cream cheese until smooth. Beat in ricotta, parsley, garlic salt, and sesame seeds.

If made ahead, cover and refrigerate for up to a week. Before serving, let stand at room temperature until softened (about 30 minutes).

Mound in a small serving bowl and serve with vegetables. Makes about 1 cup.

Dilled Shrimp Spread

For an especially attractive presentation, chill this simple make-ahead party hors d'oeuvre in a pretty mold—a fish-shaped one, if you like. Arrange crackers and crisp vegetables on the serving platter. The cool, refreshing shrimp spread is a natural choice for summer entertaining.

- 1 envelope (1 tablespoon) unflavored gelatin
- 3 tablespoons cold water
- 1 can (10¾ oz.) condensed cream of mushroom soup
- 2 small packages (3 oz. *each*) cream cheese
- ½ cup *each* mayonnaise, sour cream, chopped parsley, and diced celery
- ¼ cup thinly sliced green onions (including tops)
- 2 tablespoons lemon juice
- ¼ to ½ teaspoon liquid hot pepper seasoning
- ¼ teaspoon dill weed
- ½ pound small cooked shrimp

Place gelatin in a small bowl, stir in water, and let stand until softened (about 5 minutes).

In a 2-quart pan over medium heat, combine soup and gelatin mixture; cook, stirring, until gelatin is dissolved. Add cream cheese, stirring until melted; let cool.

Stir in mayonnaise, sour cream, parsley, celery, onions, lemon juice, hot pepper seasoning, dill, and shrimp. Spoon into a 6-cup mold. Cover and refrigerate until firm (about 4 hours).

To serve, unmold onto a serving platter. Makes 8 to 10 servings.

Caponata

Whether served as a first course, as part of an antipasto platter, or as a condiment for barbecued meats, caponata is a deliciously piquant offering. Our version of this thick eggplant-based relish is from Sicily.

- ½ cup olive oil or salad oil
- 2 cups diced celery
- 1 large eggplant (about 1½ lbs.), unpeeled, cut into ¾-inch cubes
- 1 large onion, chopped
- ⅓ cup red or white wine vinegar
- 1 teaspoon sugar
- 2 large tomatoes, peeled, seeded, and diced
- 1 cup water
- 1 tablespoon capers, drained
- ¼ cup sliced pimento-stuffed olives
- 1 can (2¼ oz.) sliced ripe olives, drained
- 2 tablespoons minced parsley
  Salt (optional)
  Crackers or crisp lettuce leaves

Heat oil in a wide frying pan over medium-high heat. Add celery and cook, stirring, until tender. With a slotted spoon, lift out celery and set aside.

Add eggplant to pan, reduce heat to medium, and cook, stirring, until lightly browned and tender. Add onion and continue cooking and stirring until onion is soft. With a slotted spoon, lift out eggplant and onion and set aside.

Add vinegar, sugar, tomatoes, and water to pan; cook, stirring, for 5 minutes. Return celery, eggplant, and onion to pan. Stir in capers, stuffed olives, ripe olives, and parsley; reduce heat and simmer, uncovered, for about 20 minutes. Season with salt to taste, if desired.

If made ahead, cool, cover, and refrigerate; serve at room temperature.

To serve, spread on crackers or spoon onto lettuce leaves. Makes 6 to 8 servings.

Chicken Liver Pâté

Though they make elegant hors d'oeuvres, pâtés are often remarkably simple and inexpensive to prepare. This one uses chicken livers and is flavored with brandy to approximate the flavor of the costly French *pâté de fois gras* (goose liver marinated in cognac and flavored with truffles). Serve the pâté on toast or lightly salted crackers.

- 1½ cups (¾ lb.) butter or margarine
- 1 pound chicken livers, halved
- ¼ pound mushrooms, chopped
- ¼ cup chopped parsley
- ¼ cup chopped shallots or green onions (white part only)
- ½ teaspoon *each* thyme leaves and salt
- 2 tablespoons brandy or Madeira
- ½ cup dry red wine

In a wide frying pan over medium heat, melt ½ cup of the butter. Add livers, mushrooms, parsley, shallots, thyme, and salt. Cook, stirring often, until livers are browned on all sides but still slightly pink in center.

In a very small pan over low heat, warm brandy and set aflame (*not* beneath an exhaust fan or near flammable items); pour over liver mixture and shake pan until flame dies. Add wine and heat to simmering. Let cool to room temperature.

In a blender or food processor, whirl liver mixture until puréed. Cut remaining 1 cup butter into chunks, add to liver purée, and whirl until smooth. Pour into a 4 to 5-cup serving bowl or several small containers. Cover and refrigerate until next day or for up to a week; freeze for longer storage. Makes 12 to 16 servings.

Crunchy Indian Snack

A distinctive appetizer idea comes from the spicy Indian snack called *Bombay chiura*. It's a crunchy mixture of lentils, split peas, rice, nuts, and sesame seeds, with raisins added for sweetness and texture. Use tortilla chips or potato chips to scoop up the mixture, or serve it plain as finger food.

(Continued on next page)

¼ cup *each* uncooked lentils, long-grain rice, and split peas

3 cups water

2 tablespoons salad oil

1 tablespoon sesame seeds

1 teaspoon *each* ground coriander and ground cumin

½ teaspoon ground turmeric

½ cup *each* roasted salted peanuts and cashews

¼ cup raisins

⅛ to ¼ teaspoon ground red pepper (cayenne)

¼ teaspoon ground cloves

1 teaspoon salt

Tortilla chips or potato chips (optional)

Rinse lentils, rice, and peas and drain well. Place in a 2 to 3-quart pan and add water; bring to a boil over high heat. Boil for 1 minute; then remove from heat, cover, and set aside for 10 minutes. Drain, rinse under cold water, and drain again; spread on paper towels and pat dry.

Heat oil in a wide frying pan over medium heat. Add lentils, rice, peas, sesame seeds, coriander, cumin, and turmeric. Cook, stirring, until mixture is toasted (10 to 15 minutes). Remove from heat and stir in nuts, raisins, pepper, cloves, and salt.

If made ahead, store airtight for up to a week. To serve, place lentil mixture in a bowl and surround with chips, if desired. Makes 2 cups.

Won Ton Crispies

(Pictured on page 31)

You'd swear they were deep-fried, but these crackerlike treats are just brushed with butter and quickly baked. Sprinkled with Parmesan cheese, they make unusual appetizers or accompaniments for soup or salad. Add onion or a favorite herb to the cheese for more flavor.

If you like, you can create a sweet variation by sprinkling the snacks with cinnamon sugar instead of cheese.

4 tablespoons butter or margarine

20 won ton skins or 5 egg roll skins

½ cup grated Parmesan cheese

Instant minced onion *or* any herb or herb blend (optional)

In a small pan over medium heat, melt butter. Brush some of the butter on a rimmed baking sheet.

Cut each won ton skin in half to make rectangles (or cut each egg roll skin into quarters, then cut each quarter in half to make 8 small rectangles). Arrange closely together, without overlapping, on baking sheet and brush tops with butter.

Sprinkle with cheese, then with onion, if desired. Bake, uncovered, in a 375° oven for 5 to 6 minutes or until golden. Repeat until all are baked. Makes 40 appetizers.

Freezer Cheese Balls

Coarsely chopped nuts conceal the smooth and tangy interior of this three-cheese appetizer. You can make the cheese balls ahead of time and freeze them; add the nut coating just before serving.

½ pound sharp Cheddar cheese, softened

1 large package (8 oz.) cream cheese or Neufchâtel cheese, softened

¼ pound blue cheese, softened

4 tablespoons butter or margarine, softened

1 clove garlic, minced or pressed

⅔ cup coarsely chopped walnuts or pecans

Assorted crackers or wafers

Shred Cheddar cheese or cut into small pieces. In large bowl of an electric mixer, combine Cheddar, cream cheese, blue cheese, and butter; beat until creamy. Add garlic and beat until blended.

Cover and refrigerate until firm enough to shape into balls (about 3 hours). Divide in half and shape each portion into a smooth ball. Wrap in plastic wrap, seal in a plastic bag, and refrigerate until needed. Freeze for longer storage; let frozen cheese balls stand at room temperature for 3 to 4 hours before continuing.

Sprinkle nuts on a sheet of wax paper and roll each ball in nuts, pressing in lightly. Serve with crackers. Makes 2 balls, each about 3 inches in diameter.

Creamy Parmesan Fondue

Fondue is an ever-popular party appetizer, and this one is an especially good choice for a busy hostess. It's easy and uncomplicated, and it feeds a sizable group.

You'll need fondue forks and a fondue pot or chafing dish for serving.

2 large packages (8 oz. *each*) cream cheese or Neufchâtel cheese

About 2 cups milk

2 small cloves garlic, minced or pressed

About 1½ cups (4½ oz.) grated Parmesan cheese

Salt

Freshly ground pepper or thinly sliced green onion (including top)

1 loaf (1 lb.) French bread, cut into 1-inch cubes

Put cream cheese in top of a double boiler and place over simmering water. As cheese melts, gradually stir in 2 cups of the milk until mixture is smooth. Add garlic and Parmesan cheese; stir until cheese is melted and sauce is thickened. Season with salt to taste; add more milk if needed to thin to good dipping consistency.

To serve, pour fondue into a ceramic fondue pot over a low alcohol flame or into a chafing dish over hot water. Sprinkle with pepper. Serve with bread cubes for dipping. Makes 12 to 16 servings.

Artichoke Nibbles

Bake marinated artichoke hearts in a spicy cheese and custard mixture to make these highly acclaimed hors d'oeuvres.

2 jars (6 oz. *each*) marinated artichoke hearts
1 small onion, finely chopped
1 clove garlic, minced or pressed
4 eggs
¼ cup fine dry bread crumbs
¼ teaspoon salt
⅛ teaspoon *each* pepper, oregano leaves, and liquid hot pepper seasoning
2 cups (8 oz.) shredded sharp Cheddar cheese
2 tablespoons minced parsley

Drain marinade from 1 jar of artichokes into a small frying pan. Drain other jar (reserve marinade for other uses). Chop all artichokes; set aside. Heat marinade in pan over medium heat; add onion and garlic and cook, stirring, until onion is soft.

In a bowl, beat eggs with a fork. Stir in bread crumbs, salt, pepper, oregano, hot pepper seasoning, cheese, parsley, artichokes, and onion mixture. Turn into a greased 7 by 11-inch baking pan.

Bake, uncovered, in a 325° oven for 30 minutes or until set when lightly touched. Let cool in pan, then cut into 1-inch squares. Serve warm or at room temperature. Or cover, refrigerate, and serve cold.

To reheat, bake, uncovered, in a 325° oven for 10 to 12 minutes or until heated through. Makes about 6 dozen appetizers.

Stuffed Cherry Tomato Halves

(Pictured on page 90)

Brilliant red cherry tomato halves are neat, bite-size containers for fillings such as seasoned cream cheese or guacamole. Each filling has its own garnish.

1 basket cherry tomatoes
   Cheese & Shrimp Filling *or* Guacamole Filling (recipes follow)

Remove stems from tomatoes; cut each in half crosswise. Scoop out and discard seed pockets. Lay, cut side down, on paper towels for about 30 minutes.

Prepare filling of your choice. With 2 spoons, pile about 1 teaspoon of the filling into each tomato half. If made ahead, refrigerate for up to 4 hours. Garnish as directed. Makes about 40 appetizers.

CHEESE & SHRIMP FILLING. In a small bowl, stir together 1 large package (8 oz.) **cream cheese,** softened, ¼ cup **catsup,** and 1 teaspoon **dill weed** until blended. Garnish each filled tomato with a **small cooked shrimp** (you'll need about 2 oz. *total*).

GUACAMOLE FILLING. Peel and remove pit from 1 large ripe **avocado.** In a small bowl, mash avocado coarsely with a fork. Stir in 4 teaspoons **lemon juice,** 1 tablespoon finely chopped **onion,** 1 clove **garlic,** minced or pressed, and ½ teaspoon **salt** until blended.

If desired, cook 6 strips **bacon** in a wide frying pan over medium heat until crisp; drain, let cool, then crumble and sprinkle over filled tomatoes.

Happy-hour Mushrooms

Mushroom lovers will flock to a plate of these savory stuffed

mushroom caps, broiled just until the jack cheese becomes bubbly.

10 medium-size mushrooms (about ½ lb. *total*)
6   tablespoons butter or margarine, softened
1   clove garlic, minced or pressed
3   tablespoons shredded jack cheese
2   tablespoons dry white or red wine
1   teaspoon soy sauce
⅓   cup fine cracker crumbs

Remove stems from mushrooms (reserve stems for other uses). In a small pan over medium heat, melt 2 tablespoons of the butter; brush over mushroom caps, coating thoroughly. In a small bowl, stir together remaining 4 tablespoons butter, garlic, and cheese until blended. Stir in wine, soy, and cracker crumbs until well blended.

Place mushrooms, cavity side up, on a rimmed baking sheet. Mound filling in mushrooms, pressing in lightly. Broil about 6 inches from heat until bubbly and lightly browned (about 3 minutes). Serve warm. Makes about 10 appetizers.

Shrimp Cheese Stack

Top seasoned cream cheese with tangy chili sauce and succulent little shrimp for this easy-to-make layered appetizer. Spread it on your favorite crackers.

2 large packages (8 oz. *each*) cream cheese, softened
2 tablespoons Worcestershire
¼ teaspoon grated lemon peel
1 tablespoon lemon juice
½ cup thinly sliced green onions (including tops)
⅛ teaspoon liquid hot pepper seasoning
1 bottle (12 oz.) tomato-based chili sauce
1 tablespoon prepared horseradish
¾ pound small cooked shrimp
   Assorted crackers

(Continued on next page)

In a bowl, beat cream cheese, Worcestershire, lemon peel, lemon juice, onions, and hot pepper seasoning until smooth. Spread on a 10 to 12-inch rimmed serving plate. (At this point, you may cover and refrigerate until next day.)

Just before serving, stir together chili sauce and horseradish in a small bowl; spread over cheese layer. Top with shrimp and serve with crackers. Makes 12 to 16 servings.

Pacific Crab Puffs

These nicely seasoned fried puffs are best when served piping hot. Offer them with a sour cream and mustard dip.

    Mustard Dip (recipe follows)
1½ cups baking mix (biscuit mix)
⅓   cup grated Parmesan cheese
¼   cup finely chopped green onions (including tops)
½   pound crabmeat
1   egg, lightly beaten
⅓   cup water
1   teaspoon Worcestershire
¼   teaspoon liquid hot pepper seasoning
    Salad oil

Prepare Mustard Dip and refrigerate.

In a bowl, combine baking mix, cheese, and onions. Shred crabmeat and add to cheese mixture. In another bowl, combine egg, water, Worcestershire, and hot pepper seasoning. Stir into crab mixture just until blended.

Pour oil into a 4-quart pan or electric frying pan to a depth of about 1½ inches. Heat to 375° on a deep-frying thermometer. Dropping in a teaspoon of the batter for each puff, cook 3 or 4 puffs at a time, turning as needed, until golden brown on all sides (1½ to 2 minutes).

Lift out with a slotted spoon and drain. Keep warm until all are cooked or, if made ahead,

cool, wrap, and freeze. To reheat, place frozen puffs on a baking sheet and bake, uncovered, in a 350° oven for 15 to 20 minutes or until heated through. Serve with dip. Makes about 3 dozen appetizers.

MUSTARD DIP. In a small bowl, combine ½ cup **sour cream**, 2 tablespoons **Dijon mustard**, and 1 teaspoon **lemon juice**; refrigerate.

Appetizer Mini-Quiches

When hearty finger-food is called for, try these individual quiches with pastry seasoned to match the filling you choose. Good warm or at room temperature, the quiches will delight a hungry crowd.

    Shrimp & Ripe Olive Filling, Bacon & Mushroom Filling, Ham & Green Chile Filling, *or* **Clam & Bacon Filling (recipes follow)**
    Seasoned Pastry (recipe follows)
5   **eggs**
1⅔ **cups sour cream**

Prepare filling of your choice; set aside.

Prepare Seasoned Pastry. On a lightly floured board, roll dough ¹⁄₁₆ inch thick. Using a 3-inch round cooky cutter, cut 42 circles, rerolling scraps as needed. Fit circles into bottoms and slightly up sides of lightly greased 2½-inch muffin cups.

Spoon filling equally into muffin cups. In a bowl, beat eggs lightly; add sour cream and stir until smooth. Spoon about 1 tablespoon of the sour cream mixture over filling in each muffin cup.

Bake in a 375° oven for 20 to 25 minutes or until filling puffs and tops are lightly browned. Let cool in pans for 5 minutes. Lift out and serve warm, or transfer to racks, let cool completely, and serve at room temperature.

If made ahead, wrap cooled quiches airtight and refrigerate until next day. To reheat, bake, uncovered, in a 350° oven for about 10 minutes. Makes 3½ dozen appetizers.

SHRIMP & RIPE OLIVE FILLING. In a bowl, combine ⅓ pound **small cooked shrimp,** coarsely chopped; 1 can (2¼ oz.) sliced **ripe olives,** drained; ⅓ cup chopped **green onions** (including tops); and 1⅔ cup (about 7 oz.) shredded **Swiss cheese.** Mix well.

Add a dash of **ground red pepper** (cayenne) to sour cream mixture before spooning into muffin cups.

BACON & MUSHROOM FILLING. In a wide frying pan over medium heat, cook 8 strips **bacon** until crisp; drain, let cool, then crumble. Set aside. In another frying pan, melt 1 tablespoon **butter** or margarine; add ¼ pound **mushrooms,** chopped, and cook until mushrooms are soft and liquid has evaporated.

In a bowl, combine bacon, mushrooms, ⅓ cup chopped **green onions** (including tops), and 1⅔ cups (about 7 oz.) shredded **Swiss or jack cheese.** Mix well.

HAM & GREEN CHILE FILLING. In a bowl, combine ¾ to 1 cup finely diced **cooked ham** (about 3 oz.), 3 to 4 tablespoons chopped canned **green chiles,** ¼ cup chopped **green onions** (including tops), and 1⅔ cups (about 7 oz.) shredded **jack cheese.**

CLAM & BACON FILLING. In a wide frying pan over medium heat, cook 3 strips **bacon** until crisp; drain, let cool, then crumble. In a bowl, combine bacon with 2 cans (6½ oz. *each*) chopped **clams,** drained well; ⅓ cup chopped **green onions** (including tops); and 1⅔ cups (about 7 oz.) shredded **Swiss cheese.** Mix well.

(Continued on page 10)

PARTY BEVERAGES

When you're entertaining, you'll want to set a festive mood with beverages that complement the foods you're serving. Here we feature some party drinks that satisfy a variety of entertaining needs. All three recipes can be made ahead if you're pressed for time, and the amounts are easily adjustable for the number of people you're expecting.

Banana Fruit Slush

Thirst-quenching and not too sweet, this fruit drink is an icy blend of puréed bananas, fruit juices, and lemon-lime soda. It's ideal for summer entertaining and for children's parties, or for when you want to offer an alternative to alcoholic beverages. The frozen fruit slush packs conveniently in empty milk cartons, and it keeps in the freezer for up to 6 months; when ready to serve, just thaw it and stir in the soda.

    6 cups water
 1½ cups sugar
    1 large can (12 oz.) frozen orange juice concentrate, thawed
    1 large can (46 oz.) pineapple-grapefruit juice
    5 medium-size bananas
    1 bottle (32 oz.) carbonated lemon-lime beverage or 1 bottle (28 oz.) club soda, chilled

In a large bowl, stir together water and sugar until sugar is completely dissolved. Add orange juice concentrate and pineapple-grapefruit juice; mix well.

In a blender or food processor, whirl bananas until puréed, then stir into juice mixture until well combined. Pour into 2 half-gallon freezer containers or clean milk cartons. Cover and freeze for 24 hours or up to 6 months.

To serve, let punch thaw at room temperature for about 3 hours or until slushy. Stir in lemon-lime beverage, breaking up any frozen chunks with a spoon; serve immediately. Makes about 6 quarts.

Chilled Citrus Sangría

Here's a bubbly, citrus-flavored sangría to serve at your next Mexican meal or outdoor party. The fresh juices of oranges, lemons, and limes mingle with dry red wine for an extra-refreshing taste sensation.

    2 bottles (750 ml. *each*) dry red wine
    4 cups fresh orange juice
    1 cup *each* fresh lime juice and fresh lemon juice
       About ½ cup sugar
    4 cups sparkling water or club soda, chilled
       Orange slices
       Ice

In a large bowl, combine wine, orange juice, lime juice, lemon juice, and ½ cup of the sugar. Add more sugar to taste, if desired. Cover and refrigerate until well chilled.

Just before serving, stir in sparkling water and garnish with orange slices. Serve over ice. Makes about 4 quarts.

Hot Cranberry Glögg

What's more appropriate for the holidays than warm cranberry-red wine glögg spiced with cinnamon, cardamom, and cloves? It can be heated and served as soon as it's made, or allowed to steep to enhance the flavor.

    4 cups cranberry-apple juice
    2 cups dry red wine
  ¾ cup *each* sugar and water
    1 whole cinnamon stick
    3 whole cardamom pods, lightly crushed
    4 whole cloves
       Thin orange slice, unpeeled
       About ½ cup *each* raisins and whole blanched almonds

In a glass or stainless steel bowl, combine juice, wine, sugar, water, cinnamon, cardamom, and cloves. (At this point, you may cover and refrigerate.)

Warm glögg in a pan over medium heat just until heated through. Float orange slice on top. To serve, keep warm over a candle or on an electric warming tray, if desired. Ladle into cups, adding raisins and almonds to individual servings. Makes 7 cups.

To make without wine, omit sugar and water and use 2 cups more cranberry-apple juice.

Add a dash of **garlic powder** to sour cream mixture before spooning into muffin cups.

SEASONED PASTRY. Prepare enough **pastry** for a double-crust 9-inch pie, using recipe on page 146 or pie crust mix. Add one of the following seasonings to dry ingredients, depending on filling you use: ¼ teaspoon **dill weed** for Shrimp & Ripe Olive Filling; ½ teaspoon **caraway seeds** for Bacon & Mushroom Filling; ½ teaspoon **chili powder** for Ham & Green Chile Filling; or 2 teaspoons **parsley flakes** for Clam & Bacon Filling.

Potstickers

The Chinese call them *guotie* (pronounced gwau-tyeh); the popular name for them in this country is "potstickers." By either name, the filled dumplings make a tasty and substantial first course.

> **Pork-Onion Filling, Beef-Ginger Filling,** *or* **Shrimp Filling (recipes follow)**
> **About 3 cups all-purpose flour**
> ¼ teaspoon **salt**
> 1 cup **water**
> **Chile Dipping Sauce (recipe follows)**
> **Salad oil**
> **About ½ cup regular-strength beef broth**

Prepare filling of your choice; set aside.

In a bowl, stir together 3 cups of the flour and salt; with a fork, gradually stir in water. Work mixture with your hands until dough holds together. On a floured board, knead dough until firm, satiny, and smooth (about 5 minutes), adding flour as needed to prevent sticking. Cover and let rest for 20 to 30 minutes.

Divide dough in half. Keeping one portion covered, roll remaining portion into a 14-inch circle ⅛ inch thick. Using a 3½ to 4-inch round cooky cutter or can

(with ends removed), cut circles in dough.

Dot each circle with about 2 teaspoons of the filling. To shape each potsticker, fold dough in half over filling. Pinch closed about ½ inch of curved edge; continue sealing, forming 3 tucks along dough edge, until entire curve is sealed.

Set potsticker down firmly, seam side up, so dumpling will sit flat. Cover lightly until all are shaped. Repeat procedure with remaining dough. (At this point, you may place potstickers in a single layer on a baking sheet and freeze until hard; then transfer to a heavy plastic bag, seal, and return to freezer for up to a month. Cook without thawing as directed below.)

Prepare Chile Dipping Sauce; set aside.

To cook, brush a 10 to 12-inch frying pan with oil and place over medium-high heat. Set potstickers, seam side up, in pan, without crowding. Cook until bottoms are dark golden brown (5 to 10 minutes). Pour in ¼ cup of the broth and immediately cover pan tightly. Reduce heat to low and cook for 10 minutes (15 minutes, if frozen).

With a wide spatula, remove potstickers and arrange, browned side up, on a serving platter. Keep warm. Repeat until all are cooked, using remaining broth.

Accompany with individual cups of dipping sauce. Makes about 4 dozen potstickers.

PORK-ONION FILLING. Cut about 1¼ pounds **boneless pork shoulder** or butt into ⅓-inch cubes. In a bowl, stir together pork, 2 tablespoons **soy sauce,** 1 tablespoon **honey,** 2 cloves **garlic** (minced or pressed), and ⅓ cup minced **green onions** (including tops).

Heat 1 tablespoon **salad oil** in a wide frying pan over medium heat. Add pork mixture and cook, stirring, until well browned. In a small bowl, mix

2 teaspoons **cornstarch** with 2 tablespoons **dry sherry.** Add to pork mixture and cook, stirring, until filling mixture boils and thickens. Season to taste with **salt** and **pepper.**

BEEF-GINGER FILLING. In a bowl, mix ¾ pound **lean ground beef;** 1 tablespoon minced **fresh ginger;** 1 **onion,** finely chopped; 1 cup chopped **bean sprouts;** ¼ teaspoon **ground red pepper** (cayenne); and ½ teaspoon **salt** until blended.

SHRIMP FILLING. Shell and devein about ½ pound medium-size (30–32 per lb.) raw **shrimp;** chop shrimp and combine in a bowl with ½ pound **ground pork;** 1 cup finely shredded **cabbage;** ¼ cup minced **green onion** (including tops); ¼ cup chopped **mushrooms;** 1 clove **garlic,** minced or pressed; ½ teaspoon **salt;** and 2 tablespoons **oyster sauce** or soy sauce. Mix well.

CHILE DIPPING SAUCE. In a bowl, combine ½ cup *each* **soy sauce** and regular-strength **beef broth,** ¼ cup **sesame oil** or salad oil, 2 tablespoons **white wine vinegar,** and about ½ teaspoon **hot chile oil** *or* 1 teaspoon liquid hot pepper seasoning. Mix well. Makes 1⅓ cups.

Super Nachos

The Mexican snack known as "nachos" can be as simple as cheese melted over tortilla chips, with chiles added for zip. Or it can be as hearty as our party version. Serve with Chilled Citrus Sangría (page 9) or beer.

8 cups Crisp-fried Tortilla Pieces (recipe follows) or corn-flavored chips

½ pound *each* lean ground beef and chorizo sausage, casing removed (or use only lean ground beef—1 lb. *total*)

1 large onion, chopped
Salt
Liquid hot pepper seasoning

1 or 2 cans (about 1 lb. *each*) refried beans

1 can (4 oz.) whole green chiles, seeded and chopped

2 to 3 cups (8 to 12 oz.) shredded jack cheese or mild Cheddar cheese

¾ cup prepared green or red taco sauce
Garnishes (suggestions follow)

Prepare Crisp-fried Tortilla Pieces; set aside.

Crumble beef and sausage into a wide frying pan over medium-high heat. Add onion and cook, stirring to break up meat, until meat is lightly browned. Spoon off fat; season to taste with salt and hot pepper seasoning.

Spread beans in a shallow 10 by 15-inch baking pan or ovenproof dish. Top evenly with meat mixture. Sprinkle with chiles and cheese, then drizzle with taco sauce. (At this point, you may cover and refrigerate until next day.)

Bake, uncovered, in a 400° oven for 20 to 25 minutes or until very hot throughout. Meanwhile, prepare garnishes of your choice.

Remove pan from oven and quickly garnish, mounding avocado dip and sour cream, if used, in center, and adding other garnishes as desired.

Then quickly tuck tortilla pieces just around edges of bean mixture and serve immediately. If desired, keep platter hot on an electric warming tray. Makes 10 to 12 servings.

CRISP-FRIED TORTILLA PIECES. Arrange 12 **corn tortillas** in a stack and cut into 6 equal wedges.

Pour **salad oil** into a deep 2 to 3-quart pan to a depth of about ½ inch. Heat to 350° to 375° on a deep-frying thermometer or until a piece of tortilla dropped into oil sizzles. Add tortilla pieces, a stack at a time, stirring to separate. Cook until crisp (1 to 1½ minutes); lift out with a slotted spoon and drain on paper towels. Repeat until all are cooked. If desired, sprinkle lightly with **salt.** If made ahead, store airtight. Makes about 8 cups.

GARNISHES. Prepare some or all of the following: 1 can (7¾ oz.) frozen **avocado dip,** thawed, or 1 medium-size avocado, peeled, pitted, and coarsely mashed; about ½ pint (1 cup) **sour cream;** about ¼ cup chopped **green onions** (including some tops); about 1 cup pitted **ripe olives;** 1 mild **red pickled pepper;** and **fresh coriander** (cilantro) or parsley sprigs.

Curry-glazed Sesame Wings

Chicken wings are a thrifty and delicious choice for appetizers, not to mention being fun to eat out-of-hand. For a picnic or informal dinner, try glazing them with a honey-sweetened curry sauce as they sizzle under the broiler or over hot coals. Then, just before serving the wings, dip them in toasted sesame seeds.

¼ cup sesame seeds

2 tablespoons butter or margarine, melted

½ cup honey

¼ cup prepared mustard

1 teaspoon *each* salt and curry powder

1 dozen chicken wings (about 2 lbs. *total*)

In a wide frying pan over medium heat, toast sesame seeds, shaking pan often, until golden (about 2 minutes); set aside.

In a small bowl, stir together butter, honey, mustard, salt, and curry powder until smooth; set aside.

Arrange chicken wings on a broiler pan and broil about 4 inches from heat (or cook on a grill about 6 inches above a solid bed of medium-glowing coals), turning once, for 15 minutes.

Baste wings with honey mixture and continue cooking, turning and basting occasionally, until done to your liking (10 to 15 more minutes).

Dip wings in sesame seeds and arrange on a serving platter. Makes 1 dozen appetizers.

Ginger-marinated Wings

The bold flavors of candied ginger and soy sauce give these chicken-wing appetizers an Oriental spirit. Wings can be messy, so be sure to have plenty of napkins on hand.

⅓ cup soy sauce

¼ cup lightly packed brown sugar

1 tablespoon cornstarch

2 tablespoons vinegar

3 tablespoons finely chopped candied ginger or 1 tablespoon finely chopped fresh ginger

1 large clove garlic, minced or pressed

1 dozen chicken wings (about 2 lbs. *total*)

In a small bowl, combine soy, sugar, cornstarch, vinegar, ginger, and garlic. Arrange chicken wings in a shallow bowl and pour marinade over top. Cover and refrigerate for 1 hour or up to 4 hours.

Lift out chicken wings, reserving marinade. Arrange wings on a broiler pan and broil about 4 inches from heat (or cook on a grill about 6 inches above a solid bed of medium-glowing coals), turning and basting thoroughly with marinade several times, until done to your liking (20 to 25 minutes). Makes 1 dozen appetizers.

SOUPS

Light or hearty, hot or cold

Chunky Gazpacho

(Pictured on page 34)

A night in the refrigerator allows this soup to develop its robust flavor. Offer it instead of a salad for a summery meal-opener.

1 large can (1 lb. 12 oz.) stewed tomatoes
1 medium-size green pepper, seeded and coarsely chopped
½ cup *each* diced celery and thinly sliced green onions (including tops)
¼ cup *each* chopped watercress and sliced pimento-stuffed green olives
2 cloves garlic, minced or pressed
¼ cup finely chopped parsley
3 tablespoons olive oil or salad oil
1 tablespoon red wine vinegar
1 teaspoon soy sauce
 Salt and pepper
 Grated Parmesan cheese

In a large bowl, combine tomatoes (break up any large pieces with a spoon) and their liquid, green pepper, celery, onions, watercress, olives, garlic, parsley, oil, vinegar, and soy. Stir well; season to taste with salt and pepper. Cover and refrigerate until next day or for up to 3 days.

Pass cheese to sprinkle over individual servings. Makes 4 to 6 servings.

Cucumber Cream

Cool and refreshing cucumbers are puréed with yogurt and sour cream to make an easy soup that requires no cooking. Serve it as a first course at dinner, or pair it with cheese and crackers for a light meal at any hour. Crunchy condiments are added at the table.

3 medium-size cucumbers, peeled and cut into cubes
1 clove garlic, halved
3 tablespoons *each* chopped parsley and chopped onion
1 cup regular-strength chicken broth
3 tablespoons white wine vinegar
1 pint (2 cups) plain yogurt, homemade (page 85) or purchased
½ pint (1 cup) sour cream
 Salt and pepper
 Condiments (suggestions follow)

In a blender or food processor, combine cucumbers, garlic, parsley, onion, broth, and vinegar; whirl until well blended. Pour about half the mixture into a container; set aside.

Add 1 cup of the yogurt and ½ cup of the sour cream to cucumber mixture in blender; whirl until smooth. Transfer to a large bowl. Pour reserved cucumber mixture into blender container and add remaining yogurt and sour cream. Whirl until smooth. Add to bowl and season to taste with salt and pepper. Cover and refrigerate until well chilled. Meanwhile, prepare condiments of your choice.

Stir soup well; season again with salt and pepper, if desired. Pass condiments to sprinkle over individual servings. Makes 6 to 8 servings.

CONDIMENTS. Prepare three or four of the following: seeded and chopped **tomatoes,** thinly sliced **green onions** (including tops), chopped **fresh mint leaves** or parsley, crisp crumbled **bacon, sunflower seeds,** or **seasoned croutons,** homemade (page 25) or purchased. Arrange in separate bowls.

Chilled Beet Soup

A generous dollop of sour cream sprinkled with diced apple accents this bright magenta soup, a perfect first course for a festive summer party.

 6 cups peeled and diced beets (about 7 medium-size)
 2 cans (14 oz. *each*) regular-strength chicken broth
 2 cups buttermilk
 1 teaspoon dill weed
 ¾ cup thinly sliced green onions (including tops)
    Salt and pepper
 1 large apple
 2 teaspoons lemon juice
    Sour cream

In a 4-quart pan over medium-high heat, combine beets and broth. Bring to a boil; cover, reduce heat, and simmer until tender when pierced (about 25 minutes).

In a blender or food processor, whirl half the beet mixture at a time until smooth. Transfer to a large bowl. Stir in buttermilk, dill, and onions; season to taste

with salt and pepper. Cover and refrigerate until well chilled.

Just before serving, ladle soup into small bowls. Core and dice apple; in a small bowl, mix apple with lemon juice. Pass apple and sour cream to spoon over individual servings. Makes 10 to 12 servings.

Curried Broccoli Soup

Slightly peppery-tasting broccoli is a perfect base for this cool, curried concoction. Garnish with sour cream and crunchy salted peanuts for a pleasing contrast.

 2 pounds broccoli
 2 cans (14 oz. *each*) regular-strength chicken broth
 3 tablespoons butter or margarine
 2 medium-size onions, chopped
 1½ teaspoons curry powder
    Sour cream
    Chopped salted peanuts

Cut off broccoli stems and coarsely chop; set aside. Cut flowerets into bite-size pieces.

In a 3-quart pan over high heat, bring 1 cup of the broth to a boil. Add about half the flowerets and cook, uncovered, until crisp-tender (3 to 4 minutes). Drain, reserving broth. Let broccoli cool, then cover and refrigerate.

Reduce heat to medium and melt butter in pan. Add onions and curry powder and cook, stirring, until soft. Stir in broccoli stems, remaining flowerets, and all remaining broth. Cover and cook until crisp-tender (about 12 minutes).

In a blender or food processor, whirl broccoli mixture, a portion at a time, until smooth. Transfer to a large bowl, cover, and refrigerate until well chilled.

To serve, ladle soup into small bowls and top with cooked flowerets. Pass bowls of sour cream and peanuts to spoon over individual servings. Makes 6 to 8 servings.

Creamy Herbed Walnut Soup

Cooking with herbs enhances the subtle, mellow flavor of walnuts in this cream soup; a last-minute addition of sherry provides extra sophistication.

 1½ cups chopped walnuts
 2 cups milk
 ½ bay leaf
 ¼ teaspoon *each* thyme leaves and dry basil
 2 tablespoons chopped parsley
 2 tablespoons butter or margarine
 1 medium-size onion, sliced
 ½ cup thinly sliced celery
 2 tablespoons all-purpose flour
 3 cups regular-strength chicken broth
 2 tablespoons dry sherry
    Salt and pepper
    Finely chopped chives or green onions (optional)

Place nuts in a 2-quart pan, cover with water, and bring to a boil over high heat. Cook for 3 minutes; then drain. Return nuts to pan and add milk, bay leaf, thyme, basil, and parsley. Heat to scalding; then cover and set aside for 20 minutes.

Meanwhile, in a 3-quart pan over medium heat, melt butter. Add onion and celery and cook for 5 minutes. Blend in flour and cook, stirring, until bubbly. Gradually pour in broth and continue cooking and stirring until soup boils. Reduce heat and simmer gently for 10 minutes.

Remove bay leaf and add milk mixture to soup. In a blender or food processor, whirl soup, a small amount at a time, until smooth. (At this point, you may cover and refrigerate until next day. Just before serving, reheat to simmering.)

Add sherry and season to taste with salt and pepper. To serve, pour into mugs or cups and garnish each serving with chives, if desired. Makes 6 to 8 servings.

Mushroom Velvet Soup

Offer mugs of this smooth, creamy soup to your guests for sipping before they come to the table.

    4   tablespoons butter or margarine
    ½   pound mushrooms, sliced
    1   medium-size onion, coarsely chopped
    ⅔   cup finely chopped parsley
    1   tablespoon all-purpose flour
    1   can (14 oz.) regular-strength beef broth
    ½   pint (1 cup) sour cream

In a wide frying pan over medium-high heat, melt butter. Add mushrooms, onion, and parsley and cook, stirring, until mushrooms are soft and juices have evaporated (about 5 minutes). Stir in flour and cook for 1 minute; then stir in broth. Bring to a boil, stirring.

In a blender or food processor, whirl half the soup with ½ cup of the sour cream until smooth. Repeat for remaining soup and sour cream. If made ahead, cool, cover, and refrigerate until next day.

Return soup to pan and cook, stirring, until heated through (do not boil). Makes 4 to 6 servings.

Creamy Pumpkin Soup

Ginger, nutmeg, and chopped onion blend with pumpkin for an intriguing holiday soup.

    2   tablespoons butter or margarine
    1   small onion, chopped
    1   tablespoon all-purpose flour
    1   cup canned pumpkin
    ¼   teaspoon *each* ground ginger and ground nutmeg
    2½ cups regular-strength chicken broth
    1   cup milk
    2   eggs
        Salt and pepper
        Chopped parsley
        Salted hulled pumpkin seeds

In a 3-quart pan over medium heat, melt butter. Add onion and cook, stirring, until soft. Stir in flour and cook until bubbly. Stir in pumpkin, ginger, and nutmeg; then gradually blend in broth. (At this point, you may cool, cover, and refrigerate until next day.)

Bring soup to simmering, then stir in milk. Reduce heat to low.

Meanwhile, in a small bowl, lightly beat eggs. Stir about ½ cup of the hot soup into eggs, then return egg mixture to pan. Cook, stirring, until heated through (do not boil). Season to taste with salt and pepper.

Ladle into a soup tureen or individual mugs or bowls; garnish with parsley. Pass pumpkin seeds to sprinkle over individual servings. Makes 4 to 6 servings.

Creamy Potato Bisque

(Pictured on page 18)

Sunset readers know a good idea when they see one—we were happily overwhelmed with votes for this creamy potato soup. Its several delicious flavor variations also generated lots of enthusiasm.

        About 6 tablespoons butter or margarine
    1   large onion, chopped
    1   cup chopped celery (including some tops)
    3   to 4 medium-size thin-skinned potatoes, peeled and cut into ½-inch cubes (4 cups *total*)
    ¼   cup finely chopped parsley
        About ½ teaspoon salt
        About ¼ teaspoon pepper
    4   cups regular-strength chicken broth or 4 chicken bouillon cubes dissolved in 4 cups water
    1   quart (4 cups) milk
    3   tablespoons cornstarch mixed with ¼ cup water
        Finely chopped parsley

In an 8 to 10-quart kettle over medium heat, melt 4 tablespoons of the butter; add onion and celery and cook, stirring occasionally, until onion is very soft (about 10 minutes).

Add potatoes, the ¼ cup parsley, ½ teaspoon of the salt, ¼ teaspoon of the pepper, and broth. Bring to a boil; cover, reduce heat, and simmer until potatoes are tender when pierced (about 30 minutes).

Stir in milk and cook, covered, until soup is heated through (do not boil). Stir cornstarch mixture and add to soup. Continue cooking and stirring until soup boils and thickens (about 5 minutes). Season with more salt and pepper, if desired.

Just before serving, pour into a soup tureen, float remaining butter (about 2 tablespoons) on top, and sprinkle with parsley. Makes 6 to 8 servings.

MUSHROOM & POTATO BISQUE. Follow recipe for Creamy Potato Bisque, stirring in ½ pound sliced **mushrooms** with broth.

SHRIMP BISQUE. Follow recipe for Creamy Potato Bisque, stirring in 1¼ pounds **small cooked shrimp** or 2 packages (12 oz. *each*) frozen shrimp, partially thawed, just before adding cornstarch mixture.

CRAB BISQUE. Follow recipe for Creamy Potato Bisque, adding 1 **bay leaf** with salt and pepper. Stir in 1 pound **crabmeat** just before adding cornstarch mixture.

MINCED CLAM BISQUE. Follow recipe for Creamy Potato Bisque, omitting the 4 tablespoons butter. Instead, use 5 strips **bacon,** cut into 1-inch pieces. In kettle over medium heat, cook bacon until limp (about 5 minutes). Add onion and celery and continue cooking as directed.

Stir in 4 cans (6½ oz. *each*) **minced clams** and their liquid just before adding milk.

Garden Fresh Vegetable Soup

Your garden patch is the best place to start this soup, inspired by Italy's many versions of minestrone. Ideal as an entrée, the soup is economical and easy to multiply for a crowd.

½ pound lean ground beef (optional)

4 strips bacon, diced (optional)

3 tablespoons butter or margarine (optional)

1 large onion, chopped

2 cloves garlic, minced or pressed

6 cups prepared fresh vegetables, such as diced or sliced carrots; chopped or sliced celery; green beans, cut into ¾-inch lengths; diced thin-skinned potatoes; peas; whole kernel corn, cut off cob; and sliced zucchini or crookneck squash

8 cups regular-strength beef broth

1 can (1 lb.) kidney beans, drained

½ teaspoon *each* dry basil, oregano leaves, and dry rosemary

1 can (8 oz.) tomato sauce

2 large tomatoes, seeded and chopped

⅔ cup elbow macaroni or spaghetti (broken into pieces)

2 cups shredded cabbage, spinach, or Swiss chard

Salt and pepper

Grated Parmesan cheese

Crumble beef, if desired, into a 5 to 6-quart kettle over medium heat. Add bacon, if desired. (If not using meat, melt butter in kettle.) Add onion, garlic, and prepared vegetables and cook, stirring, until meat is browned and onion is soft; drain any excess fat.

Add broth, kidney beans, basil, oregano, and rosemary. Bring to a boil; cover, reduce heat, and simmer for about 30 minutes.

Add tomato sauce, tomatoes, and macaroni. Continue cooking, covered, until macaroni is tender. (At this point, you may cool, cover, and refrigerate; reheat to continue.)

Add cabbage and cook, cov-ered, just until cabbage wilts (about 5 minutes). Season to taste with salt and pepper. Pass cheese to sprinkle over individual servings. Makes 8 servings.

Clam & Vegetable Chowder

One of the potatoes is cooked, then puréed to give body to this rich-tasting soup.

1 cup water

1 bottle (8 oz.) clam juice

2 large thin-skinned potatoes, peeled and diced

½ cup shredded mild process cheese spread

3 strips bacon, diced

3 medium-size onions, chopped

2 cloves garlic, minced or pressed

1 medium-size green pepper, seeded and chopped

1 can (about 1 lb.) tomatoes

2 teaspoons chili powder

2 cans (6½ oz. *each*) minced clams

Salt and pepper

In a 5-quart kettle over high heat, combine water, clam juice, and 1 of the potatoes. Cover and bring to a boil. Reduce heat to medium and cook until potato is very tender. Turn into a blender or food processor and whirl until smooth; stir in cheese and set aside.

Rinse and dry kettle; add bacon and cook over medium heat until crisp. Add onions, garlic, and green pepper; cook, stirring, until onions are soft (about 5 minutes).

Stir in tomatoes (break up with a spoon) and their liquid, chili powder, clams and their liquid, remaining diced potato, and puréed potato mixture. Cover, reduce heat, and simmer, stirring occasionally, until diced potato is tender when pierced (20 to 30 minutes). Season to taste with salt and pepper. Makes about 8 servings.

Pacific Oyster Stew

At the table, garnish this creamy oyster stew with buttery-crisp croutons, still warm from their oven-toasting.

2 jars (10 oz. *each*) Pacific oysters

4 tablespoons butter or margarine

About 1 cup unseasoned croutons

1 small onion, chopped

½ cup thinly sliced celery

1 tablespoon all-purpose flour

1 can (14 oz.) regular-strength chicken broth

1 pint (2 cups) half-and-half (light cream) or milk

Salt, pepper, and ground nutmeg

Pour oysters and their liquid into a wide frying pan over medium-high heat; cook just until edges curl. Cut oysters into bite-size pieces, then set aside with their liquid.

In a 3-quart pan over medium heat, melt butter. Spread croutons in a shallow baking pan; drizzle croutons with about half the butter and toast in a 350° oven for about 10 minutes.

Meanwhile, add onion and celery to remaining butter in pan and cook, stirring, until onion is soft. Stir in flour and continue cooking and stirring for 1 minute. Gradually pour in broth and cream and continue cooking and stirring until bubbly.

Add oysters and their liquid to onion mixture; season to taste with salt, pepper, and nutmeg. Pass croutons to spoon over individual servings. Makes 6 to 8 servings.

Lentil Vegetable Soup

For a protein boost, slice three or four frankfurters or smoked link sausages into this hearty soup as it simmers.

2 tablespoons salad oil
1 large onion, chopped
1 clove garlic, minced or pressed
3 carrots, sliced
2 stalks celery, sliced
½ teaspoon chili powder
5 cups regular-strength beef broth or 6 beef bouillon cubes dissolved in 5 cups water
1 cup lentils
1 can (about 1 lb.) stewed tomatoes
  Chopped parsley
  Grated Parmesan cheese

Heat oil in a 3 to 4-quart pan over medium-high heat. Add onion and garlic and cook, stirring, until onion is soft. Add carrots, celery, and chili powder and continue cooking and stirring for 1 to 2 more minutes. Add broth and lentils and bring to a boil; cover, reduce heat, and simmer until lentils are tender (about 35 minutes).

Just before serving, stir tomatoes into soup, then ladle into a tureen or wide soup bowls. Garnish with chopped parsley. Pass cheese to sprinkle over individual servings. Makes 4 to 6 servings.

Cuban Black Bean Soup

Generous spoonfuls of marinated rice and finely chopped onion provide a unique topping for a bold whole-meal soup. The recipe calls for 6 cups of cooked beans—the approximate yield from 1 pound of dried beans. Or use four 1-pound cans. To supplement the protein in the beans, round out the menu with broiled, cheese-covered corn tortillas.

  Marinated Rice (recipe follows)
¼ cup olive oil or salad oil
2 medium-size onions, finely chopped
2 medium-size green peppers, seeded and finely chopped
5 large cloves garlic, minced or pressed
  About 3 cups water
4 beef bouillon cubes
1½ teaspoons *each* ground cumin and oregano leaves
2 tablespoons vinegar
6 cups cooked or canned black or red beans, drained

At least 1 hour ahead, prepare Marinated Rice and refrigerate.

Heat oil in a 4 to 5-quart kettle over medium heat. Add onions, peppers, and garlic and cook, stirring, until onions and peppers are soft. Add 3 cups of the water, bouillon cubes, cumin, oregano, vinegar, and beans. Bring to a boil; cover, reduce heat, and simmer for 30 minutes; add more water, if desired, for thinner consistency.

Ladle soup into small bowls, adding a generous spoonful of the rice to each serving. Makes 6 to 8 servings.

MARINATED RICE. In a bowl, combine 1½ cups **cooked rice** with ⅓ cup finely chopped **mild white onion** or white part of green onions, and 3 tablespoons *each* **olive oil** and **white wine vinegar.** Cover and refrigerate for 1 hour or until next day.

Black Forest Pea Soup

Basic to German family cooking is the *Eintopf,* or one-dish meal. Often a stewlike combination of simmered meat or chicken and vegetables, it can also be a sturdy soup such as this one, fortified with thinly sliced sausage.

3 or 4 medium-size leeks
2 tablespoons butter or margarine
1 medium-size onion, chopped
2 medium-size carrots, thinly sliced
1 stalk celery, thinly sliced
1 medium-size thin-skinned potato, peeled and cut into ½-inch cubes
1 large smoked ham hock (about 1 lb.) or 1 meaty ham bone
1 package (12 oz.) green split peas, rinsed and drained
1 can (12 oz.) beer *or* 1½ cups regular-strength chicken broth
6 cups water
1 teaspoon marjoram leaves
¼ teaspoon ground allspice
⅛ teaspoon ground red pepper (cayenne)
1 pound garlic frankfurters or knackwurst, casings removed and thinly sliced
1 tablespoon white vinegar
¼ cup chopped parsley

Trim and discard root ends and tough outer leaves from leeks. Cut each leek in half lengthwise, rinse between layers, and thinly slice.

In a 6 to 8-quart kettle over medium heat, melt butter. Add leeks, onion, carrots, and celery and cook, stirring, until onion is soft.

Stir in potato, ham hock, peas, beer, water, marjoram, allspice, and pepper. Bring to a boil; cover, reduce heat, and simmer until ham and peas are very tender when pierced (2½ to 3 hours).

Remove ham hock; when cool enough to handle, remove and discard bone and fat. Break meat into chunks and return to soup; stir in frankfurters, vinegar, and parsley. Makes about 6 servings.

Soybean Minestrone

A versatile and economical source of protein, soybeans are especially well-suited for use in soups and stews, because of the way the beans absorb the flavors of the foods they're cooked with. Here, soybeans are used in a hearty vegetable soup.

- 3 tablespoons olive oil or salad oil
- ½ cup brown rice
- 1 large onion, chopped
- ¼ pound mushrooms, halved
- 1 cup thickly sliced carrots
- ½ cup *each* chopped green pepper and celery
- 1 large can (1 lb. 12 oz.) tomatoes
- 2 cans (about 15 oz. *each*) soybeans, rinsed and drained, or 2½ cups cooked soybeans
- 5 cups water
- 7 vegetable or beef bouillon cubes
- 1 teaspoon *each* dry rosemary, dry basil, and oregano leaves
- ½ teaspoon *each* thyme leaves and savory leaves
- ⅛ teaspoon ground red pepper (cayenne)
- 1 cup dry red wine (optional)
- 1 cup thickly sliced zucchini
- ½ cup chopped parsley
  Grated Parmesan cheese

Heat oil in a 4 to 5-quart kettle over medium-high heat. Add rice, onion, and mushrooms and cook, stirring, until golden.

Add carrots, green pepper, celery, tomatoes (break up with a spoon) and their liquid, soybeans, water, bouillon cubes, rosemary, basil, oregano, thyme, savory, and red pepper. Stir in ½ cup of the wine, if desired.

Bring to a boil; cover, reduce heat, and simmer, stirring occasionally, for 40 minutes. Add zucchini and cook until tender (about 8 minutes). Stir in remaining ½ cup wine, if desired, and sprinkle with parsley. Pass cheese to sprinkle over individual servings. Makes 8 to 10 servings.

Meatball Minestrone

Here's a satisfying meal in a bowl—you mix ground beef with spinach to make meatballs, then add them to a kettle of simmering vegetable soup with pasta. For a flavor variation, take a tip from the *Sunset* reader who adds garlic and a can of garbanzos to the minestrone.

- 1 package (10 oz.) frozen chopped spinach, thawed
- 1½ pounds lean ground beef
- ⅓ cup fine dry bread crumbs
- 1 egg
- 1 teaspoon salt
- ¼ teaspoon pepper
- 2 tablespoons salad oil
- 1 large onion, coarsely chopped
- 7 cups water
- 7 beef bouillon cubes
- 1 can (about 1 lb.) tomatoes
- 1 can (1 lb.) kidney beans
- ½ teaspoon *each* oregano leaves and dry basil
- 1 cup *each* sliced carrots and celery
- 1 cup elbow, bow-shaped, or twisted macaroni
  Grated Parmesan cheese

Squeeze out as much moisture from spinach as possible. In a large bowl, mix spinach, beef, crumbs, egg, salt, and pepper. Shape into 1-inch balls.

Heat oil in a 5-quart kettle over medium heat. When oil is hot, add meatballs, a portion at a time, and cook until browned on all sides. As meatballs are cooked, remove from pan with a slotted spoon and set aside.

Add onion to pan and cook, stirring, until soft (about 5 minutes). Stir in water, bouillon cubes, tomatoes (break up with a spoon) and their liquid, beans and their liquid, oregano, and basil. Bring to a boil; cover, reduce heat, and simmer for 10 minutes.

Add carrots and celery; cover and continue simmering for 10 more minutes. Stir in macaroni; cover and simmer until macaroni is tender (about 10 minutes). Add meatballs to soup and cook until heated through. Pass cheese to sprinkle over individual servings. Makes 4 to 6 servings.

Eggplant Supper Soup

Eggplant, tomatoes, and ground beef team up to give this soup its color and flavor.

- 2 tablespoons olive oil or salad oil
- 2 tablespoons butter or margarine
- 1 medium-size onion, chopped
- 1 pound lean ground beef
- 1 medium-size eggplant (about 1 lb.), diced
- 1 clove garlic, minced or pressed
- ½ cup *each* chopped carrot and sliced celery
- 1 large can (1 lb. 12 oz.) Italian-style tomatoes
- 2 cans (14 oz. *each*) regular-strength beef broth
- 1 teaspoon *each* salt and sugar
- ½ teaspoon *each* pepper and ground nutmeg
- ½ cup salad macaroni
- 2 tablespoons minced parsley
  Grated Parmesan cheese

Heat oil and butter in a 5-quart kettle over medium heat. Add onion and cook, stirring, until soft. Then crumble meat into kettle and cook, stirring to break up, until browned.

Add eggplant, garlic, carrot, celery, tomatoes (break up with a spoon) and their liquid, broth, salt, sugar, pepper, and nutmeg. Bring to a boil; cover, reduce heat, and simmer for about 30 minutes.

Add macaroni and parsley; cover and continue simmering until macaroni is tender (about 10 minutes). Pass cheese to sprinkle over individual servings. Makes 6 to 8 servings.

Chicken & Vegetable Supper Soup

A velvety smooth broth brimming with carrots, zucchini, rice, and plenty of chicken distinguishes this easily prepared soup. For an appealing spring or summer luncheon, serve it with a fruit salad and whole wheat rolls with butter and honey.

(Continued on page 19)

6 to 7 cups regular-strength chicken broth

½ cup rice

3 medium-size carrots, sliced ⅛ inch thick

3 stalks celery, sliced ¼ inch thick

2 small zucchini, sliced ¼ inch thick

6 tablespoons butter or margarine

6 tablespoons all-purpose flour

1 pint (2 cups) half-and-half (light cream) or milk

About 4 cups cooked chicken, cut into bite-size pieces

About ½ cup thinly sliced green onions (including some tops)

Cooked giblets, chopped (optional)

Salt and pepper

¼ cup minced parsley

In a 5-quart kettle over high heat, bring broth to a boil. Add rice; cover, reduce heat, and simmer for 10 minutes. Add carrots, celery, and zucchini; cover and simmer until vegetables are crisp-tender (about 10 more minutes).

Meanwhile, in a small pan over medium heat, melt butter. Blend in flour and cook, stirring, until bubbly. Gradually pour in half-and-half; then stir in about a cup of the broth from soup mixture. Continue cooking and stirring until sauce boils and thickens; then stir into soup mixture.

Add chicken, green onions, and giblets, if desired. Season to taste with salt and pepper. Cook just until heated through. Sprinkle with parsley. Makes about 6 servings.

A GOLDEN POOL of melted butter crowns rich and luscious Shrimp Bisque (page 14), one of several variations you can make from a simple potato soup. Offer a large tureen of the bisque as the centerpiece of a warming winter supper.

Italian Sausage & Bean Soup

Winter suppers call for hot, satisfying dishes like this soup, a combination of sausage and vegetables in a beefy broth.

About 1 pound mild Italian sausages, casings removed

1 clove garlic, minced or pressed

1 large onion, chopped

⅓ cup chopped parsley

2 medium-size carrots, thinly sliced

1 cup thinly sliced mushrooms

1 can (about 1 lb.) garbanzos

3 cups water

2 beef bouillon cubes

½ teaspoon ground sage

Salt and pepper

Crumble sausages into a 3-quart pan over medium-high heat. Cook, stirring to break up, until browned. Add garlic, onion, ¼ cup of the parsley, carrots, and mushrooms; cook, stirring, until onion is soft.

Add garbanzos and their liquid, water, bouillon cubes, and sage. Bring to a boil; cover, reduce heat, and simmer until carrots are tender when pierced (about 10 minutes). Season to taste with salt and pepper.

Skim and discard fat. Garnish with remaining parsley. Makes 3 or 4 servings.

Sopa de Guadalajara

Inspired by a dish called *sopa de frijoles* from the Mexican city of Guadalajara, this pork and bean soup is sturdy enough to serve as a main course. It improves on standing, so you can make it ahead of time; then, when ready to serve, accompany with hot tortillas, guacamole, and beer. For dessert, try fresh pineapple or a chilled caramel flan.

Look for jars of baby corn where gourmet foods are sold.

3½ to 4 pounds boneless pork shoulder

1 tablespoon salad oil

1 cup finely chopped onions

2 cloves garlic, minced or pressed

2 teaspoons chili powder

1 teaspoon *each* oregano leaves and cumin seeds

7 cups water

2 cans (14 oz. *each*) regular-strength beef broth

1 cup dried pinto or small red beans

4 cups thinly sliced carrots

Condiments (suggestions follow)

2 jars (about 4 oz. *each*) baby corn on the cob, drained

Salt and pepper

Trim and discard excess fat from pork; cut meat into 1 to 1½-inch cubes. Heat oil in a 5-quart kettle over medium-high heat; add meat and cook, stirring, until well browned on all sides. Push meat to side of pan, add onions and garlic, and cook, stirring, until onions are soft.

Stir in chili powder, oregano, cumin, water, broth, and beans. Bring to a boil; cover, reduce heat, and simmer until meat and beans are tender when pierced—about 1½ hours. (At this point, you may cool, cover, and refrigerate until next day.)

Skim and discard fat from broth. Bring to a boil over high heat and add carrots. Cover, reduce heat, and simmer until carrots are tender when pierced (about 30 minutes). Meanwhile, prepare condiments and set aside.

Stir in corn and season to taste with salt and pepper. Pass bowls of condiments to add to individual servings. Makes 6 to 8 servings.

CONDIMENTS. Prepare and arrange in separate bowls cherry tomatoes, halved; sliced green onions (including tops); chopped fresh coriander (cilantro); and sour cream. Also offer lime wedges and bottled green taco sauce.

SALADS

Fresh & leafy, molded, or marinated

Overnight Layered Green Salad

It's an overnight sensation—a salad that's completely assembled the day before you need it.

- 1 medium-size head iceberg lettuce, shredded
- ½ cup thinly sliced green onions (including tops)
- 1 cup thinly sliced celery
- 1 can (8 oz.) water chestnuts, drained and sliced
- 1 package (10 oz.) frozen peas
- 2 cups mayonnaise
- 2 teaspoons sugar
- ½ cup grated Parmesan cheese
- 1 teaspoon seasoned salt
- ¼ teaspoon garlic powder
- ½ to ¾ pound sliced bacon, crisply cooked, drained, and crumbled
- 3 hard-cooked eggs, chopped
- 2 medium-size tomatoes, cut into wedges

Spread lettuce evenly in a wide 3 to 4-quart glass serving bowl. Top with a layer each of onions, celery, water chestnuts, and peas. Spread evenly with mayonnaise. Sprinkle with sugar, cheese, salt, and garlic powder. Cover and refrigerate for several hours or until next day.

Just before serving, sprinkle with bacon and eggs. Arrange tomato wedges on top.

To serve, use a spoon and fork to lift out servings, scooping down to bottom of dish to include all layers. Makes 8 to 10 servings.

Crisp Spinach Salad

(Pictured on page 79)

Deep green spinach leaves contrast with water chestnuts and bean sprouts in this popular salad.

- 1½ pounds spinach
- ½ pound bean sprouts
- 1 can (8 oz.) water chestnuts, drained and sliced
- 5 strips bacon, crisply cooked, drained, and crumbled
- ⅔ cup salad oil
- ⅓ cup *each* sugar, catsup, red wine vinegar, and finely chopped onion
- 2 teaspoons Worcestershire
  Salt and pepper
- 2 hard-cooked eggs, sliced

Remove and discard tough spinach stems; tear leaves into bite-size pieces. In a large salad bowl, combine spinach, bean sprouts, water chestnuts, and bacon. Cover and refrigerate until well chilled.

In a small bowl or jar, stir together oil, sugar, catsup, vinegar, onion, and Worcestershire. If made ahead, cover and refrigerate.

Just before serving, stir dressing, add to salad, and toss gently until well mixed. Season to taste with salt and pepper; garnish with eggs. Makes about 8 servings.

Romaine Salad with Creamy Garlic Dressing

(Pictured on page 23)

Reminiscent of the famous Caesar salad, this favorite romaine salad calls for a few extra goodies: cherry tomato halves, diced avocado, and sliced green onions.

1 large head romaine lettuce
2 cloves garlic, minced or pressed
½ teaspoon salt
1 tablespoon lime or lemon juice
1 egg
⅓ cup mayonnaise
2 teaspoons Worcestershire or soy sauce
1 avocado
3 tablespoons grated Parmesan cheese
1 cup cherry tomatoes, halved
2 green onions (including tops), thinly sliced
⅔ cup seasoned croutons, homemade (page 25) or purchased

Tear lettuce into bite-size pieces (you should have about 12 cups). Cover and refrigerate until well chilled.

Combine garlic and salt in a small bowl and mash with back of a spoon into a paste; or mash with a mortar and pestle and transfer to a bowl. Mix garlic paste with lime juice; add egg and beat until foamy. Stir in mayonnaise and Worcestershire. If made ahead, cover and refrigerate.

Just before serving, peel, pit, and dice avocado. In a large salad bowl, combine avocado, lettuce, cheese, tomatoes, onions, and croutons. Stir dressing, pour over salad, and toss until well mixed. Makes 6 to 8 servings.

Hot Romaine & Bacon Salad

A wok is the ideal pan for making this marvelous wilted salad.

1 small head romaine lettuce
2 tablespoons *each* sugar and lemon juice
1 tablespoon catsup
½ teaspoon *each* Worcestershire and Dijon mustard
6 strips bacon, cut into ½-inch pieces
  Salad oil
1 medium-size onion, chopped
1 clove garlic, minced or pressed
1 cup cherry tomatoes, halved
  Salt and pepper

Tear lettuce into bite-size pieces (you should have about 10 cups); set aside. In a small bowl, mix sugar, lemon juice, catsup, Worcestershire, and mustard; set aside.

Place a wok or wide frying pan over high heat. When pan is hot, add bacon and cook, stirring, until crisp. Remove pan from heat, lift out bacon with a slotted spoon, and drain. Discard all but ¼ cup of the drippings or add enough oil to make ¼ cup.

Return pan to high heat. When drippings are hot, add onion and garlic and cook, stirring, for 30 seconds. Add lemon juice mixture and bring to a boil; then add lettuce and tomatoes and immediately remove from heat.

Stir salad, add bacon, and stir again. Turn into a bowl and season to taste with salt and pepper. Makes 4 to 6 servings.

Mayan Salad

Spicy entrées such as burritos, enchiladas, and other Mexican favorites call for cooling companions, and this refreshing fruit salad from the Yucatan is a good choice. It's a colorful medley of crisp greens, two kinds of citrus, and jicama.

8 cups lettuce (iceberg, red, or butter) or spinach, torn into bite-size pieces
1½ cups jicama, cut into thin strips, or sliced water chestnuts
1 medium-size mild red onion, cut into rings
1 grapefruit
2 oranges
½ pound cherry tomatoes, halved
  Cumin Dressing (recipe follows)
1 large avocado

In a large salad bowl, mix lettuce and jicama; arrange onion rings on top. Remove peel and white membrane from grapefruit and oranges; cut into sections and arrange over onions along with tomatoes. Cover and refrigerate for 1 to 2 hours. Meanwhile, prepare Cumin Dressing.

Just before serving, peel, pit, and slice avocado; arrange on salad. Add dressing and mix gently. Makes 6 to 8 servings.

CUMIN DRESSING. In a blender or food processor, combine 3 tablespoons **cider vinegar,** 2 tablespoons **lime juice,** 6 tablespoons **olive oil** or salad oil, 1 clove **garlic,** 1 teaspoon **cracked black pepper,** ½ teaspoon *each* **salt** and **ground cumin,** and ⅛ teaspoon **crushed red pepper.** Whirl at high speed until well blended.

Autumn Slaw

A sweet vinegar dressing adds zest to this crisp cabbage salad.

1 medium-size head cabbage (about 2 lbs.)
1 teaspoon salt
1¼ cups *each* sugar and water
1 cup vinegar
3 cups thinly sliced celery
1 large red or green bell pepper, seeded and chopped
½ cup thinly sliced green onions (including tops)
1 teaspoon *each* celery seeds and mustard seeds

(Continued on next page)

Core and finely shred cabbage. Place in a large bowl, sprinkle with salt, and let stand for 2 hours.

Meanwhile, in a small pan over high heat, combine sugar, water, and vinegar. Bring to a boil and cook for 2 minutes; let cool to room temperature.

Pour off any liquid from cabbage. Add celery, pepper, onions, celery seeds, and mustard seeds. Mix well, then add vinegar mixture and mix again. Cover and refrigerate for 24 hours.

To serve, lift salad from liquid with a slotted spoon. Makes 10 to 12 servings.

Piquant Carrot Salad

A perky dressing flavors this make-ahead vegetable salad, and carrots and green pepper rings add bright colors. The salad is a good choice for a picnic.

- 1½ pounds (about 8 medium-size) carrots, cut into ¼-inch-thick slanting slices
- 1 medium-size onion, cut into rings
- 1 small green pepper, seeded and cut into rings
- ¼ cup white wine vinegar
- 3 tablespoons *each* sugar and salad oil
- 1 tablespoon catsup
- ½ teaspoon *each* seasoned salt, celery seeds, Worcestershire, and Dijon mustard

Pour water into a 4-quart pan to a depth of 1 inch. Bring to a boil over high heat. Add carrots; cover, reduce heat to medium, and cook until just crisp-tender (about 10 minutes). Drain, rinse under cold water, and drain again. In a serving bowl, layer carrots with onion and pepper rings.

In a small bowl or jar, stir together vinegar, sugar, oil, catsup, salt, celery seeds, Worcestershire, and mustard. Pour over carrot mixture.

Cover and refrigerate for 4 hours or until next day, stirring several times. Makes 4 to 6 servings.

Roasted Sweet Pepper & Eggplant Salad

Mellow, nutty-flavored roasted bell peppers are the basis for this flavorful marinated salad. Use either red or green peppers or a combination of the two; when roasted, fully ripened red bell peppers will be sweeter and slightly more tender than green peppers.

- 6 large red or green bell peppers (about 2½ lbs. *total*)
- 1 medium-size eggplant (about 1 lb.)
- 6 tablespoons olive oil
- 3 medium-size onions (about 1 lb. *total*), thinly sliced
- 2 tablespoons red or white wine vinegar or lemon juice
- 1 teaspoon salt
  Pepper
- 1 or 2 large tomatoes, cut into wedges

Place whole peppers in a shallow pan and broil about an inch from heat, turning often with tongs, until well blistered and charred on all sides (about 30 minutes). Place peppers in a paper bag, seal, and let peppers sweat for 15 to 20 minutes to loosen skins.

Peel off skins, cut peppers lengthwise into quarters, and remove and discard seeds and stems. (At this point, you may cool, cover, and refrigerate for up to 2 days; freeze for longer storage.)

Cut peppers crosswise into ½-inch strips, place in a bowl, and set aside.

Peel eggplant, if desired, and cut into ½-inch-thick slices. Lightly brush both sides with about 2 tablespoons of the oil, then cut eggplant slices into ½-inch-wide strips. Place strips on a baking sheet and broil about 4

inches from heat, turning often, until very soft and well browned on all sides (about 20 minutes). Add to peppers and set aside.

Heat remaining oil in a wide frying pan over medium heat. Add onions and cook, stirring, until soft and golden (about 20 minutes). Add to pepper mixture with vinegar and salt; sprinkle with pepper to taste. Stir gently until mixed.

Cover and let stand for about 4 hours, or refrigerate for up to 3 days. Just before serving, garnish with tomato wedges. Makes 4 to 6 servings.

Asparagus & Shrimp Vinaigrette Salad

Graceful spears of fresh asparagus, cooked and cooled, are arranged on a bed of butter lettuce and topped with a shrimp dressing, creating an elegant salad for a dinner party.

- 1 hard-cooked egg
- 3 green onions (including tops), minced
- 1 tablespoon minced parsley
- ¼ teaspoon salt
- ⅛ teaspoon pepper
- ¼ cup white wine vinegar
- ½ cup olive oil
- ¼ pound small cooked shrimp
- 18 to 24 spears asparagus (about 1 lb. *total*)
  Butter lettuce leaves

In a bowl, mash egg. Add onions, parsley, salt, pepper, vinegar, oil, and shrimp; stir until well combined. If made ahead, cover and refrigerate until next day.

Snap off and discard tough ends from asparagus. In a wide frying pan, lay spears parallel

THE FRESHEST INGREDIENTS ensure delicious, crisp salads every time. For Romaine Salad with Creamy Garlic Dressing (page 21), you can even make your own fresh Seasoned Croutons (page 25).

...Asparagus & Shrimp Salad (cont'd.)

and pour in boiling water just to cover. Cook over high heat, uncovered, until stems are just tender (6 to 8 minutes). Drain, immerse immediately in cold water, and drain again. Cover and chill.

Just before serving, arrange several butter lettuce leaves on each of 6 individual salad plates. Lay 3 or 4 asparagus spears on lettuce and spoon shrimp dressing over each serving. Makes 6 servings.

Tangy Tomato Mold

Pimento-stuffed olives distinguish this quick-to-assemble, sparkling red tomato aspic.

2 **cans (about 1 lb.** *each*) **stewed tomatoes**
2 **envelopes (2 tablespoons** *total*) **unflavored gelatin**
2 **tablespoons sugar**
¼ **cup lemon juice**
  About 6 drops liquid hot pepper seasoning
1 **jar (2 or 3 oz.) pimento-stuffed green olives**
¼ **cup sliced green onions (including tops)**
1 **cup thinly sliced celery**
  Salad greens

Pour tomatoes into a 2-quart pan and break up any large pieces with a spoon. Sprinkle gelatin over tomatoes and let stand until softened (about 5 minutes). Stir in sugar, lemon juice, and hot pepper seasoning. Place over low heat and cook, stirring, until gelatin is dissolved.

Drain liquid from olives into a measuring cup and add water, if needed, to make ⅔ cup liquid. Slice olives and stir into gelatin mixture with olive liquid, onions, and celery. Turn into a 6 or 8-cup mold or 8 individual molds.

Refrigerate until firm (about 5 hours). Just before serving, unmold onto a serving plate and garnish with greens. Makes 8 servings.

Colorful New-Potato Salad

Frozen mixed vegetables look like confetti in this creamy potato salad.

2½ **pounds thin-skinned potatoes**
1 **package (10 oz.) frozen mixed vegetables**
2 **hard-cooked eggs**
3 **tablespoons** *each* **white wine vinegar and chopped parsley**
1½ **tablespoons** *each* **Dijon mustard and capers, drained**
1 **teaspoon** *each* **sugar and salt**
½ **teaspoon liquid hot pepper seasoning**
½ **pint (1 cup) sour cream**
½ **cup** *each* **thinly sliced green onions (including tops) and diced celery**

Pour water into a 3-quart pan to a depth of 1 inch. Add potatoes, cover, and bring to a boil over high heat. Reduce heat to medium and cook until tender when pierced (about 25 minutes). Let cool, then peel and cut into thin slices (you should have 6 cups). Place in a large salad bowl.

Cook mixed vegetables according to package directions; drain, rinse under cold water, and drain again. Add to potatoes and set aside.

In a small bowl, mash egg yolks; in another bowl, chop egg whites and set aside. Gradually add vinegar to yolks, stirring until smooth. Stir in parsley, mustard, capers, sugar, salt, hot pepper seasoning, and sour cream until smooth.

Add onions, celery, and reserved egg whites to potato mixture; pour dressing over all and mix gently. Cover and refrigerate for 4 hours or until next day. Makes about 8 servings.

Curried Rice Salad

Deviled eggs border a mound of flavorful seasoned rice for this attractive chilled salad. If you like, you can make it a whole-meal salad by adding cheese or bite-size pieces of cooked meat.

1 **package (8 oz.) chicken-flavored rice and vermicelli mix**
½ **teaspoon curry powder**
1 **jar (6 oz.) marinated artichoke hearts**
10 **pimento-stuffed green olives, sliced**
½ **cup chopped green pepper**
4 **green onions (including tops), sliced**
¼ **cup mayonnaise**
  Lettuce leaves
4 **to 6 deviled egg halves**

Brown rice mix according to package directions, stirring curry powder into butter called for on package. Cook as directed and let cool.

Meanwhile, drain artichoke hearts, reserving marinade. Cut artichokes into quarters and stir into rice mixture with olives, pepper, and onions.

In a small bowl, combine reserved artichoke marinade and mayonnaise, then gently stir into rice mixture. Cover and refrigerate for 6 hours or until next day.

To serve, arrange lettuce leaves on a serving plate and mound rice mixture on lettuce; garnish with egg halves. Makes 4 to 6 servings.

Cappelletti Pesto Salad

Piquant pesto sauce is often used on hot pasta or in soups. Here, though, it's mixed with oil and vinegar to make a lively dressing for a chilled pasta salad. You can use medium-size pasta in any shape that appeals to you.

- 8 ounces cappelletti or other medium-size fancy-shaped pasta
- ⅓ cup pesto sauce, homemade (page 105) or purchased
- ⅓ cup olive oil
- 2 tablespoons white wine vinegar

Cook cappelletti according to package directions. Drain, rinse under cold water, and drain again. Turn into a large bowl.

In a small bowl, stir together pesto sauce, oil, and vinegar; pour over pasta and stir gently. Cover and refrigerate for an hour or until next day. Makes 4 to 6 servings.

Tabbuli

Nutty-flavored and seasoned with mint and green onions, this Middle Eastern cracked wheat salad can be made several days ahead of time. At serving time, diners can scoop tabbuli onto crisp romaine leaves and top with tomato wedges to eat.

- 1 cup *each* bulgur wheat and cold water
- ½ cup *each* minced parsley and minced green onions (including tops)
- ¼ cup chopped green pepper
- ¼ cup chopped fresh mint or 2 tablespoons dry mint
- 1 large tomato, peeled and chopped
- ¼ cup *each* olive oil and lemon juice
  Salt
  Inner romaine lettuce leaves
  Tomato wedges

In a large bowl, combine bulgur and water and let stand for 1 hour; drain any remaining liquid.

(Continued on page 27)

CRISP CROUTONS FOR SOUP & SALAD

Don't toss out that day-old French bread—instead, use it to make your own crunchy seasoned croutons. About a third of a 1-pound loaf of French bread will give you 2 cups of croutons, flavored with the seasoning mixture of your choice.

Just as you'll want to sample the three flavor varieties, you may also want to experiment with the shapes and sizes of your croutons when you cut them. You can store the croutons in a covered jar at room temperature for several weeks.

Seasoned Croutons

(Pictured on page 23)

About ⅓ pound day-old French bread
4 tablespoons butter or margarine
Italian Herb & Cheese Seasoning, Herb & Onion Seasoning, or Garlic Seasoning (directions follow)

Cut bread into ½-inch cubes (you should have 2 cups). Spread cubes on a rimmed baking sheet and bake in a 300°

oven for 10 minutes. Remove from oven; reduce oven temperature to 275°.

In a wide frying pan or wok over medium heat, melt butter. Stir in seasoning mixture of your choice as directed. Add toasted bread cubes and stir to coat evenly.

Spread cubes on baking sheet and bake for 30 minutes or until crisp and lightly browned. Let cool completely. Store in a covered jar for up to 3 weeks. Makes 2 cups croutons.

Italian Herb & Cheese Seasoning. Stir into melted butter 1 teaspoon **Italian seasoning** or ¼ teaspoon *each* oregano, thyme, and marjoram leaves, and dry basil; and ½ teaspoon **Worcestershire.** Remove from heat and stir in 1 tablespoon grated **Parmesan cheese.**

Herb & Onion Seasoning. Stir into melted butter 1 teaspoon **onion powder** and ½ teaspoon *each* **dry basil, dry chervil,** and **oregano leaves.** Remove from heat.

Garlic Seasoning. Stir into melted butter 1 large clove **garlic,** minced or pressed, and 1 teaspoon **parsley flakes.** Remove from heat.

Add parsley, onions, pepper, mint, chopped tomato, oil, and lemon juice; stir gently until blended. Sprinkle with salt to taste. Cover and refrigerate until well chilled or for up to 3 days.

To serve, mound tabbuli in a serving bowl and surround with lettuce leaves and tomato wedges. Makes 6 to 8 servings.

Garbanzo & Walnut Salad

Coarsely mashed garbanzo beans and finely chopped walnuts mingle with a lemon-garlic dressing in this unusual Turkish salad.

1 can (about 1 lb.) garbanzos, drained
⅔ cup finely chopped walnuts
Lemon Dressing (recipe follows)
Inner romaine lettuce leaves

In a large bowl, mash garbanzos until they resemble coarse crumbs; stir in nuts. Prepare Lemon Dressing and add to garbanzo mixture, stirring until blended.

Spoon into center of a shallow bowl or plate and surround with lettuce leaves. Serve at room temperature. Makes about 6 servings.

LEMON DRESSING. In a small bowl, combine 6 tablespoons **lemon juice**; ¼ cup **olive oil** or salad oil; 2 cloves **garlic,** minced or pressed; and 1 teaspoon **salt.** Mix until well blended.

Antipasto Salad

(Pictured on page 119)

Here's a spirited salad to serve as a first course with an Italian meal or as a dinner salad with roasted or barbecued meats. To turn it into a luncheon entrée, double the amount of tuna and offer with bread sticks or crusty rolls.

1 jar (11 oz.) pickled mixed vegetables, drained
1 can (4 oz.) whole mushrooms, drained
1 can (6 oz.) medium-size pitted ripe olives, drained
2 jars (6 oz. *each*) marinated artichoke hearts
1 can (8 oz.) tomato sauce
½ teaspoon dry basil
1 can (7 oz.) solid pack tuna, drained
Butter lettuce leaves (optional)
Sliced salami
Fresh basil leaves

Cut pickled vegetables into bite-size pieces; place in a large bowl and add mushrooms and olives. Cut artichokes from 1 jar (reserve remaining jar for garnish) lengthwise into 2 or 3 pieces. Add artichoke pieces and their marinade to vegetable mixture. Stir in tomato sauce and dry basil. Distribute tuna over top and mix gently. Cover and refrigerate until next day or for up to 5 days.

Just before serving, line a large serving plate with lettuce leaves, if desired. Mix salad well; then lift vegetables out with a slotted spoon and arrange on plate. Drain marinade (reserve for other uses) from remaining artichokes, and garnish salad with artichokes, salami slices, and basil leaves.

Pass any remaining sauce to spoon over individual servings. Makes about 6 servings.

Chicken-Cantaloupe Salad

Spilling over each cantaloupe wedge are chunks of tender chicken, mandarin orange sections, and crunchy celery and almonds in a tart ginger-orange dressing. With hot rolls and butter, this main-dish salad makes a summery lunch or supper.

2 whole chicken breasts (about 2 lbs. *total*)
2 cups thinly sliced celery
1¼ cups slivered almonds
2 cans (11 oz. *each*) mandarin orange sections, drained
¾ cup *each* sour cream and mayonnaise
3 tablespoons finely minced preserved or candied ginger
2 tablespoons lemon juice
½ teaspoon salt
1 teaspoon grated orange peel
Dash of ground nutmeg
3 medium-size cantaloupes, chilled well

Place chicken breasts in a 3 to 4-quart pan and pour in enough water to cover. Bring to a boil over high heat; cover, reduce heat, and simmer until tender when pierced (15 to 20 minutes). Let cool in broth, then lift out chicken; remove and discard skin and bones. Cut meat into bite-size pieces.

In a large bowl, combine chicken, celery, nuts, and orange sections. In a small bowl, stir together sour cream, mayonnaise, ginger, lemon juice, salt, orange peel, and nutmeg.

Mix just enough of the dressing with chicken mixture to bind; cover and refrigerate chicken salad and remaining dressing separately until well chilled.

Just before serving, cut each cantaloupe into thirds; scoop out and discard seeds. Place on individual salad plates and spoon chicken salad over each cantaloupe wedge. Pass remaining dressing at the table. Makes 9 servings.

Overnight Layered Chicken Salad

(Pictured on facing page)

A creamy curry-flavored dressing accents layers of crisp vegetables

(Continued on page 29)

STRIKINGLY DISPLAYED in a glass salad bowl, Overnight Layered Chicken Salad (recipe on this page) is an attractive entrée for an outdoor lunch—from its shredded lettuce bottom to its tomato-garnished top.

FRESH BUTTERMILK DRESSINGS

Why use a bottled salad dressing, when you can make your own fresh one in minutes? With these three versatile dressings, you can create your favorite flavor combination by varying the seasonings on a basic buttermilk-and-mayonnaise formula. The result is a thick, creamy, fresh-tasting dressing that can enhance all kinds of green salads. If you like, you can trim calories by substituting imitation mayonnaise for the real thing.

The first recipe requires the use of a blender or food processor; each of the others can be stirred together in a bowl.

Green Goddess Buttermilk Dressing

Here's a buttermilk variation of the dressing made famous by the Palace Hotel in San Francisco.

- 6 tablespoons buttermilk
- ¼ cup *each* coarsely chopped green onions (including tops), parsley, and watercress
- ½ teaspoon dry tarragon
- 2 teaspoons lemon juice
- ½ teaspoon anchovy paste
- ½ cup mayonnaise
  Salt and pepper

In a blender or food processor, combine buttermilk, onions, parsley, watercress, tarragon, lemon juice, and anchovy paste. With motor on low speed (or with on-off bursts of food processor), whirl until vegetables are finely chopped. Add mayonnaise and whirl just until blended. Season to taste with salt and pepper. If made ahead, cover and refrigerate for up to 10 days. Makes about 1 cup.

Thousand Island Buttermilk Dressing

A profusion of assertive ingredients—finely chopped dill pickle, chili sauce, horseradish, minced onions, and liq-uid hot pepper seasoning—combine to make this spirited dressing.

- ¼ cup tomato-based chili sauce
- 1 tablespoon instant minced onion
- 2 tablespoons minced dill pickle
- ½ teaspoon *each* grated lemon peel and prepared horseradish
- ½ cup mayonnaise
- 1 hard-cooked egg, chopped (optional)
- 4 to 6 tablespoons buttermilk
  Garlic salt, pepper, and liquid hot pepper seasoning

In a bowl, combine chili sauce, onion, pickle, lemon peel, horseradish, mayonnaise, and egg, if desired. Stir in buttermilk until dressing is of desired consistency. Season to taste with garlic salt, pepper, and hot pepper seasoning. If made ahead, cover and refrigerate for up to 10 days. Makes 1 cup.

Herbed Buttermilk Dressing

You can vary this dressing by adding Roquefort cheese.

- 1 cup buttermilk
- 2 tablespoons *each* chopped parsley and instant minced onion
- ¼ teaspoon *each* dry basil, dry rosemary, oregano leaves, and savory leaves
- 1 clove garlic, minced or pressed
- 1 cup mayonnaise
  Salt and pepper
- 1 cup crumbled Roquefort or other blue-veined cheese (optional)

In a bowl, combine buttermilk, parsley, onion, basil, rosemary, oregano, savory, and garlic; let stand for 5 minutes. Then, with a wire whisk, beat in mayonnaise. Season to taste with salt and pepper. If made ahead, cover and refrigerate for up to 10 days.

Just before serving, stir in cheese, if desired. Makes about 2 cups.

and chicken for this crunchy luncheon entrée. Garnish the make-ahead salad with Spanish peanuts and cherry tomato halves.

- 6 **cups shredded iceberg lettuce**
- ¼ **pound bean sprouts**
- 1 **can (8 oz.) water chestnuts, drained and sliced**
- ½ **cup thinly sliced green onions (including tops)**
- 1 **medium-size cucumber, thinly sliced**
  About 4 cups cooked chicken, cut into 2 to 3-inch strips
- 2 **packages (6 oz. *each*) frozen pea pods, thawed**
- 2 **cups mayonnaise**
- 2 **teaspoons curry powder**
- 1 **tablespoon sugar**
- ½ **teaspoon ground ginger**
- ½ **cup Spanish peanuts**
- 12 **to 18 cherry tomatoes, halved**

Spread lettuce evenly in a wide 4-quart glass serving bowl. Top with a layer each of bean sprouts, water chestnuts, onions, cucumber, and chicken. Pat pea pods dry and arrange on top.

In a small bowl, stir together mayonnaise, curry powder, sugar, and ginger. Spread mayonnaise mixture evenly over pea pods. Cover and refrigerate for several hours or until next day.

Just before serving, garnish with nuts and tomato halves. To serve, use a spoon and fork to lift out servings, scooping down to bottom of dish to include all layers. Makes 10 to 12 servings.

Shanghai Tofu & Peanut Salad

(Pictured on page 31)

Though Chinese cooks typically serve this salad as a side dish, it also makes a good main course for a meatless lunch. Lightly sweet dressing, spiced with cayenne, coats the chilled tofu, crisp vegetables, and coarsely chopped peanuts.

- 1 **package (1 lb.) medium-firm tofu (bean curd)**
  Salad oil
  Sesame Dressing (recipe follows)
- ¾ **pound bean sprouts**
- 1 **medium-size cucumber**
- 1 **cup shredded carrots**
- 3 **green onions (including tops), thinly sliced**
- ¾ **cup coarsely chopped salted peanuts**
  Fresh coriander (cilantro) sprigs
  Green onions, sliced diagonally into ¼-inch pieces

Cut tofu crosswise into 1-inch-thick slices. Let drain in a colander for 15 minutes, then place between paper towels and gently press out excess water. Place tofu on a rack in a shallow rimmed baking pan and brush all surfaces with oil.

Bake in a 350° oven for 20 minutes. Let cool, then cut into ¼ by ¼ by 1-inch strips. Prepare Sesame Dressing and add tofu, stirring gently to coat. Cover and refrigerate for 30 minutes or up to 24 hours.

Meanwhile, fill a 4-quart pan half-full with water. Bring to a boil over high heat. Add bean sprouts and cook for 10 seconds; then drain, rinse under cold water, and drain again. Cover and refrigerate.

Peel cucumber, if desired, and cut in half lengthwise. Scoop out and discard seeds, if large, and slice thinly; cover and refrigerate.

Just before serving, combine tofu and dressing, bean sprouts, cucumber, ⅔ cup of the carrots, thinly sliced onions, and nuts in a large salad bowl; toss gently. Garnish with remaining carrots, coriander, and diagonally sliced onions. Makes 4 to 6 servings.

SESAME DRESSING. In a bowl, stir together ¼ cup **white wine vinegar**, 2 tablespoons *each* **sugar** and **salad oil**, 1 tablespoon **soy sauce**, 1½ teaspoons **sesame oil**, ¾ teaspoon **salt**, and ¼ teaspoon **ground red pepper** (cayenne).

Salad-in-a-Boat

Highly recommended by *Sunset* readers, this spectacular-looking entrée belies its simplicity and offers intriguing texture and flavor contrasts: a crackling, chewy crust and a layer of crisp vegetable crowned with a cool, creamy salad.

- ⅔ **cup water**
- 5 **tablespoons butter or margarine**
- ¼ **teaspoon salt**
- ⅔ **cup all-purpose flour**
- 3 **eggs**
  Chicken & Pea Pod Salad, Egg & Spinach Salad, *or* Chilled Fish & Carrot Salad (recipes follow)

In a 2-quart pan over high heat, combine water, butter, and salt. Bring to a boil, stirring, and cook until butter is melted. Remove pan from heat and add flour all at once. Beat with a wire whisk until smooth.

Reduce heat to medium and return pan to heat. Cook, stirring rapidly, until a ball forms in middle of pan and a film forms on bottom of pan (about 1 minute). Remove from heat and beat in eggs, one at a time, until batter is smooth and glossy. Spoon into a greased 9-inch spring-form pan. Spread evenly over bottom and up sides of pan.

Bake in a 400° oven for 40 minutes or until puffy and browned. Turn off oven. With a wooden pick, prick crust in 10 to 12 places and let dry in closed oven for about 10 minutes; then remove from oven and let cool completely. Remove from pan.

If made ahead, cover loosely with foil and store at room temperature until next day. For longer storage, wrap completely in foil and freeze. Recrisp crust (thaw completely, if frozen), uncovered, in a 400° oven for 10 minutes. Let cool.

Prepare salad of your choice and fill crust as directed. To serve, cut into thick wedges. Makes 4 to 6 servings.

(Continued on next page)

CHICKEN & PEA POD SALAD.

In a large bowl, combine 3 cups **cooked chicken,** cut into bite-size pieces; 1 can (8 oz.) **water chestnuts,** drained and sliced; ½ cup thinly sliced **green onions** (including tops); and 2 hard-cooked **eggs,** coarsely chopped.

In a small bowl, stir together ½ pint (1 cup) **sour cream,** 1 teaspoon **lime juice,** 2 teaspoons *each* **sugar** and **curry powder,** and ½ teaspoon **ground ginger.** Stir into chicken mixture; season to taste with **salt** and **pepper.** If made ahead, cover and refrigerate for up to 24 hours.

Remove tips and strings from ¼ pound **Chinese pea pods.** Fill a 2-quart pan half-full with water. Bring to a boil over high heat. Add pea pods and cook for 1½ minutes. Drain, rinse under cold water, drain again, and pat dry.

To serve, line bottom and sides of crust with pea pods. Pile chicken salad on top and garnish with chopped fresh **coriander** (cilantro) or parsley.

EGG & SPINACH SALAD.

In a large bowl, combine 12 hard-cooked **eggs,** coarsely chopped; 3 **green onions** (including tops), thinly sliced; and 1 cup thinly sliced **celery.**

In a small bowl, stir together ½ cup **mayonnaise,** 1 teaspoon *each* **Dijon mustard** and **mustard seeds,** and ¼ teaspoon **ground cumin;** gently stir into egg mixture. Season to taste with **salt** and **pepper.** If made ahead, cover and refrigerate for up to 24 hours.

To serve, line crust with about 1½ cups small **spinach leaves** (or coarsely shredded large leaves). Pile egg salad over spinach and garnish with 8 to 10 **cherry tomatoes,** halved.

CHILLED FISH & CARROT SALAD.

In a large bowl, combine about 1 pound cold **cooked fish fillets** (such as red snapper, rock cod, or salmon), cut into bite-size pieces; 1 cup frozen **peas,** thawed and drained well; ½ cup thinly sliced **green onions** (including tops); 1 hard-cooked **egg,** coarsely chopped; and ¼ pound **small cooked shrimp** (reserving a few for garnish).

In a small bowl, stir together ½ cup **mayonnaise,** 2 tablespoons tomato-based **chili sauce,** 2 teaspoons **lemon juice,** 1 teaspoon **prepared horseradish,** and ½ teaspoon grated **lemon peel.** Gently stir into fish mixture; season to taste with **salt** and **pepper.** If made ahead, cover and refrigerate for up to 24 hours.

To serve, line crust with about 1 cup coarsely shredded **carrots.** Pile fish salad over carrots and garnish with reserved shrimp and 5 or 6 **lemon wedges.**

Holiday Salad Bowl

Rich red grapes and bright pomegranate seeds decorate this unique fruit and vegetable salad.

¼ cup slivered **almonds**
3 medium-size **oranges,** peeled and sliced
1 small mild white **onion,** thinly sliced
1 cup halved and seeded red **grapes**
1 medium-size **cucumber,** thinly sliced
¼ cup golden **raisins**
  Lime Dressing (recipe follows)
1 **pomegranate** (optional)
4 cups shredded **spinach**

Spread almonds in a shallow pan and toast in a 350° oven for 8 minutes or until lightly browned; set aside.

In a bowl, combine oranges, onion, grapes, cucumber, and raisins. Cover and refrigerate for up to 6 hours. Meanwhile, prepare Lime Dressing. If desired, cut pomegranate in half, removing and reserving seeds.

Just before serving, combine spinach, orange mixture, and almonds in a large salad bowl. Pour dressing over salad and mix well. Garnish with pomegranate seeds, if desired. Makes 6 to 8 servings.

LIME DRESSING. In a small bowl, stir together ¼ cup *each* **salad oil** and **lime juice;** 1 clove **garlic,** minced or pressed; 1 teaspoon *each* **curry powder** and **paprika;** and ¼ teaspoon **ground red pepper** (cayenne). Season with **salt** to taste.

Strawberry Cream Layered Salad

When you cut this salad into squares, three pretty layers of fruit and sour cream appear.

1 package (3 oz.) strawberry-flavored **gelatin**
½ cup boiling **water**
2 medium-size **bananas**
1 package (10 oz.) frozen sweetened **strawberries,** thawed
1 can (8 oz.) crushed **pineapple,** drained well
1 cup coarsely chopped **walnuts**
½ pint (1 cup) **sour cream**
  Lettuce leaves

In a small bowl, dissolve gelatin in boiling water. In a large bowl, mash bananas and combine with strawberries and their juice, pineapple, and nuts. Add gelatin.

Pour half the mixture into an 8-inch square baking dish; cover and refrigerate until firm (about 1½ hours). Cover remaining banana mixture and let stand at room temperature.

Spread refrigerated portion evenly with sour cream, then spoon remaining banana mixture over sour cream layer. Cover and refrigerate until firm (at least 4 hours).

To serve, arrange lettuce leaves on 6 individual salad plates. Cut layered salad into 6 portions and arrange on lettuce. Makes 6 servings.

COOL AND REFRESHING Shanghai Tofu & Peanut Salad (page 29) combines the nutty crunch of peanuts, the crispness of fresh vegetables, and the silky smoothness of tofu. This Chinese-style salad pairs perfectly with Won Ton Crispies (page 6).

SANDWICHES & PIZZA

Savory specialties to eat out-of-hand

Chicken Supper Sandwiches

Buttery, toasted English muffins are the foundation of these robust hot chicken-and-tomato sandwiches. Don't forget to provide knives and forks—you'll need them!

- 1 whole chicken breast (about 1 lb.)
- 4 strips bacon
- 2 English muffins, split, toasted, and buttered
- 4 slices mild red onion
- 1 large tomato, peeled and cut into 4 thick slices
- ½ cup shredded Cheddar cheese

Pour water into a 2-quart pan to a depth of 1 inch. Add chicken and bring to a boil; cover, reduce heat, and simmer until meat near bone is no longer pink when slashed (about 15 minutes). Drain, remove and discard skin and bones, and slice.

Meanwhile, cut bacon strips in half crosswise. In a small pan over medium heat, partially cook bacon to remove most of the drippings (bacon should still be limp); drain well.

Arrange chicken over muffin halves; top each with an onion slice and a tomato slice. Sprinkle evenly with cheese and top with 2 bacon pieces.

Broil about 6 inches from heat until cheese is bubbly and bacon is crisp (3 to 5 minutes). Makes 2 servings (2 open-faced sandwiches *each*).

Swiss Crabwiches

These broiled sandwiches are just right for a special brunch or luncheon.

- ¼ cup *each* slivered almonds, sour cream, and mayonnaise
- 1 teaspoon *each* dry mustard and lemon juice
- ¼ teaspoon garlic powder
- ⅛ teaspoon *each* pepper and ground nutmeg
- ¼ pound sliced bacon, crisply cooked, drained, and crumbled
- ¾ pound crabmeat
- 6 to 8 green onions (including tops), thinly sliced
- 2 cups (8 oz.) shredded Swiss cheese
- 4 Kaiser or French rolls, split, buttered, and toasted

32

Spread almonds in a shallow pan and toast in a 350° oven for about 8 minutes or until lightly browned; let cool.

In a bowl, combine sour cream, mayonnaise, mustard, lemon juice, garlic powder, pepper, and nutmeg until well blended. Stir in bacon, almonds, crabmeat, onions, and cheese.

Spread about ⅓ cup of the mixture on each roll half. Place on a rimmed baking sheet and broil about 6 inches from heat until golden brown (about 5 minutes). Makes 4 servings (2 open-faced sandwiches *each*).

Monterey Bacon Hero

Here's a sophisticated version of the classic "BLT," made on a loaf of French bread.

- ½ **cup mayonnaise**
- ⅓ **cup sour cream**
- 2 **teaspoons Dijon mustard**
- 1 **green onion (including top), thinly sliced**
- ¼ **teaspoon Worcestershire**
- ⅛ **teaspoon garlic powder**
  Salt and pepper
- 1 **loaf (1 lb.) French bread *or* 6 to 8 French rolls**
  About 4 ounces alfalfa sprouts
- 1 **large avocado**
- 1 **tablespoon lemon juice**
- ½ **pound sliced bacon, crisply cooked and drained**
- ½ **pound jack cheese, thinly sliced**
- 2 **medium-size tomatoes, sliced**
- 8 **to 10 pitted ripe olives, sliced**

In a small bowl, combine mayonnaise, sour cream, mustard, onion, Worcestershire, and garlic powder. Season to taste with salt and pepper.

With a serrated knife, slice bread in half horizontally. If desired, scoop out some of the bread from each half and reserve for other uses. Spread cut sides of bread with mayonnaise mixture and sprinkle sprouts over bottom half.

Peel, pit, and slice avocado; sprinkle with lemon juice to prevent darkening. Arrange avocado evenly over sprouts; then top with bacon, cheese, tomatoes, and olives. Cover with top half of bread.

To serve, cut loaf into individual portions. Makes 6 to 8 servings.

Lamb Pocket Bread Sandwiches

For a Middle Eastern sandwich treat, stuff halves of pocket bread with marinated onions and lamb, vegetables, and yogurt. Pocket bread (also called peda or pita) is available in many supermarkets and in Middle Eastern food stores.

- ½ **cup lemon juice**
- ¼ **cup olive oil or salad oil**
- 1 **teaspoon *each* chopped fresh coriander (cilantro) and ground cumin**
- ½ **teaspoon *each* black pepper and ground turmeric**
- ¼ **teaspoon crushed red pepper**
- 2 **pounds lean boneless lamb (shoulder or leg), cut into ¾-inch cubes**
- 2 **large onions, thinly sliced and separated into rings**
- 6 **pocket breads**
- 12 **to 24 small romaine spears**
- 3 **medium-size tomatoes, cut into thin wedges**
- ½ **pint (1 cup) plain yogurt, homemade (page 85) or purchased**

In a small bowl, combine lemon juice, oil, coriander, cumin, black pepper, turmeric, and red pepper. Place lamb and onion rings in separate bowls. Pour half the lemon juice-oil marinade over lamb and remaining half over onions. Cover each bowl and refrigerate for 2 to 4 hours, stirring occasionally.

Lift meat from marinade and drain briefly, reserving marinade. Thread meat on sturdy metal skewers and place on a lightly greased grill 4 to 6 inches

above a solid bed of glowing coals.

Cook, turning and basting with reserved marinade, for 12 to 15 minutes or until lamb is well browned on all sides but still pink in center when slashed.

Meanwhile, cut pocket breads in half and wrap tightly in foil. Place at edge of grill (*not* directly over coals) and warm for about 10 minutes; turn often.

To serve, lift onions from marinade with a slotted spoon and place in a bowl. Stuff each pocket with 1 or 2 romaine spears, 5 or 6 lamb cubes, several onion rings, some tomato wedges, and a dollop of yogurt. Makes 6 to 12 servings.

Armenian Roast Beef Sandwiches

(Pictured on page 34)

These unique rolled-up roast beef sandwiches take liberties with crunchy Armenian cracker bread. Start with a crisp bread round, moistened with water; let it stand until it's soft and pliable. Then fill, roll up, and cut into individual portions.

Look for the cracker bread in supermarkets, delicatessens, or markets specializing in international foods.

- 1 **Armenian cracker bread (14 inches in diameter)**
- 1 **small package (3 oz.) cream cheese, softened, or 1 package (4 oz.) whipped cream cheese**
- 1 **tablespoon prepared horseradish**
- ¼ **teaspoon pepper**
  About 1 tablespoon milk
- ⅓ **to ½ pound roast beef, very thinly sliced**
- 12 **to 15 large spinach leaves *or* 1 cup alfalfa sprouts**
- 2 **medium-size tomatoes, sliced paper thin**

To soften cracker bread, hold round of bread under a gentle spray of cold water for about 10

seconds on each side or until well moistened. Place between clean damp cloth towels. Let stand until soft and pliable (about 1 hour—time depends on freshness and thinness). Check often; if round still seems crisp in spots, sprinkle with more water.

Meanwhile, in a bowl, beat cream cheese until light and fluffy. Stir in horseradish, pepper, and 1 tablespoon of the milk. Add more milk, if necessary, so cheese mixture will spread easily.

Spread softened bread round with cheese mixture and top with beef. Arrange spinach leaves over beef; then cover with tomato slices.

Roll up jelly roll style (if you have a broken edge on bread, start rolling from that point). If made ahead, cover with damp paper towels, wrap airtight, and refrigerate for up to 2 hours.

To serve, cut roll with a serrated knife into 12 thick slices. Makes 6 servings (2 slices *each*).

Mexican Flank Steak Sandwiches

For a south-of-the-border picnic, layer large tortillas with succulent strips of barbecued steak and zesty homemade tomato salsa. Then just roll the tortillas up and eat them out of hand.

Marinate the meat ahead of time and carry it to the picnic site, along with the prepared salsa, avocado, and tortillas. About 15 minutes before you're ready to eat, barbecue the steak.

PLUMP PINWHEELS of color will brighten your picnic when you serve Armenian Roast Beef Sandwiches (page 33). To round out a summer banquet on the grass, offer fresh fruit, Chunky Gazpacho (page 12), and Buttery Lemon Squares (page 140).

Tomato Salsa (recipe follows)
1 **flank steak (about 1½ lbs.)**
¼ **cup** *each* **olive oil and white wine vinegar**
½ **teaspoon** *each* **salt and oregano leaves**
⅛ **teaspoon pepper**
3 **cloves garlic, minced or pressed**
12 **large flour tortillas (about 10 inches in diameter)**

Prepare Tomato Salsa and refrigerate.

Place meat in a shallow, close-fitting container. In a small bowl, combine oil, vinegar, salt, oregano, pepper, and garlic. Pour over meat, cover, and refrigerate for at least 6 hours or until next day; turn steak over several times.

To cook, lift steak from marinade, drain briefly, and place on a lightly greased grill 4 to 6 inches above a solid bed of glowing coals. Cook, turning once, for 5 to 8 minutes per side for rare or until done to your liking when slashed. Slice diagonally across the grain into thin strips.

Meanwhile, place tortillas, one at a time, directly on grill and heat, turning once, for about 30 seconds per side or until soft and hot. Stack tortillas and wrap in a dampened cloth or in foil to keep warm.

To serve, arrange meat strips down center of each tortilla. Spoon salsa over meat and roll up. Makes about 6 servings.

TOMATO SALSA. In a small container with a lid, combine 2 medium-size **tomatoes,** peeled, seeded, and finely chopped; 3 **green onions** (including tops), finely chopped; 2 tablespoons seeded and chopped canned **green chiles;** 2 tablespoons chopped **fresh coriander** (cilantro); ½ teaspoon **salt;** and 1 tablespoon **olive oil.**

Cover and refrigerate for 6 hours or until next day. Just before serving, peel, pit, and dice 1 **avocado** and gently mix into salsa.

Chimichangas

Chimichangas! There's nothing quite like this specialty from the Mexican state of Sonora, just south of the border. We offer three choices for fillings—experiment to find your favorite for these crispy, golden brown tortilla packages.

All of the fillings can be made ahead; when you're ready to serve, assemble the tortilla bundles and fry them. Or you can freeze the fried chimichangas and reheat them in the oven.

Two or three chimichangas make a serving. Complete the menu with cold beer, crisp green salad, and fresh fruit.

Green Chile & Tomato Relish (recipe follows)
Beef & Bean, Spicy Pork, *or* **Chicken & Raisin Filling (recipes follow)**
12 **flour tortillas, at room temperature**
Salad oil
About 1½ cups guacamole, purchased or homemade
About 1½ cups sour cream

Prepare Green Chile & Tomato Relish; cover and refrigerate. Prepare filling of your choice.

Place about ¼ cup of the filling in center of each tortilla. Fold one edge partially over filling, then fold in sides. Starting from folded edge, roll up and secure with wooden picks. (If tortillas are too brittle to roll, lightly moisten with water, wrap in foil, and heat in a 350° oven until warm and pliable.)

Pour salad oil into a wide frying pan to a depth of ¾ inch; place over medium-high heat until oil reaches 370° on a deep-frying thermometer. Add chimichangas, 3 or 4 at a time, and fry, turning, until golden on all sides (about 1½ minutes total). Remove with tongs, drain on paper towels, and keep warm until all are cooked.

If made ahead, let cool, wrap

airtight, and freeze. To reheat, place frozen chimichangas in a single layer in a shallow rimmed baking pan. Bake, uncovered, in a 350° oven for about 25 minutes or until heated through.

At the table, pass individual bowls of relish, guacamole, and sour cream to spoon over chimichangas. Makes 4 to 6 servings.

GREEN CHILE & TOMATO RELISH. In a bowl, combine 1 pound (about 4 medium-size) tomatoes, peeled and diced, 1 can (4 oz.) diced **green chiles,** ½ cup chopped **onion,** 1 tablespoon **white vinegar,** 1 teaspoon **sugar,** ½ teaspoon **salt,** and ¼ teaspoon **pepper.** Mix well. Cover and refrigerate.

BEEF & BEAN FILLING. Heat 1 tablespoon **salad oil** in a wide frying pan over medium heat. Add ¾ pound lean **ground beef** and cook, stirring to break up meat, until lightly browned. Add 1 large **onion,** chopped; 1 large **green pepper,** seeded and chopped; and 1 clove **garlic,** minced or pressed; cook, stirring, until onion is soft.

Reduce heat to medium-low and stir in ½ teaspoon *each* **salt** and **ground cumin,** 2 tablespoons **chili powder,** ⅛ teaspoon **ground red pepper** (cayenne), and ½ cup canned **refried beans.** Cook, stirring constantly, until heated through. Fold in 1 cup (4 oz.) shredded **jack cheese;** let cool. If made ahead, cover and refrigerate until next day.

SPICY PORK FILLING. Trim excess fat from 2 pounds **pork shoulder;** bone and cut into ½-inch cubes. Heat 2 tablespoons **salad oil** in a wide frying pan over medium-high heat. Add pork and cook until lightly browned. Stir in 2 medium-size **onions,** chopped; 2 cloves **garlic,** minced or pressed; and 1 large **green pepper,** seeded and chopped; cook, stirring, until onions are soft.

Add ½ teaspoon *each* **salt** and **oregano leaves,** ¼ cup chopped **fresh coriander** (cilantro) or 1 tablespoon dry cilantro leaves, 1 can (4 oz.) diced **green chiles,** and 2 tablespoons **water.** Cover, reduce heat to low, and cook, stirring occasionally, until pork is fork-tender and liquid has evaporated (about 35 minutes); let cool.

If made ahead, cover and refrigerate until next day.

CHICKEN & RAISIN FILLING. Pour **water** into a large pan to a depth of 1 inch; add 2 whole **chicken breasts** (about 1½ lbs. *total*), split. Bring to a boil; cover, reduce heat, and simmer until tender (about 15 minutes). Remove breasts from broth and let cool; set aside ½ cup of the broth (reserve remaining broth for other uses).

Heat 2 tablespoons **salad oil** in a wide frying pan over medium heat. Add 1 large **onion,** chopped, and 1 clove **garlic,** minced or pressed; cook until onion is soft. Remove from heat.

Remove and discard bones and skin from chicken breasts; shred chicken and add to onion mixture. Stir in 2 small **dried hot red chiles,** seeded and crushed; reserved ½ cup broth; ½ teaspoon **salt;** ¼ cup chopped **fresh coriander** (cilantro) or 1 tablespoon dry cilantro leaves; and ¾ cup **raisins.**

Cover and cook over low heat, stirring, until liquid has evaporated (about 10 minutes); let cool. If made ahead, cover and refrigerate until next day.

Vegetable Burritos

Garden-fresh vegetables, two kinds of cheese, and Mexican seasonings mingle inside a burrito that makes a complete meal in itself. Offer a choice of condiments to spoon over the filling before rolling up the tortillas.

- 2 tablespoons salad oil
- 1 large onion, thinly sliced
- 2 cloves garlic, minced or pressed
- ½ pound mushrooms, sliced
- 1 large green pepper, seeded and cut into thin strips
- 2 medium-size carrots, thinly sliced
- 4 medium-size zucchini, cut into ½-inch-thick slices
- 2 large tomatoes, peeled and cut into ½-inch-thick wedges
- 1 can (7 oz.) diced green chiles
- 1 can (2¼ oz.) sliced ripe olives, drained
- 1 teaspoon *each* chili powder and salt
- ½ teaspoon *each* ground cumin and oregano leaves
- 1½ cups (6 oz.) shredded Cheddar cheese
- 1½ cups (6 oz.) shredded jack cheese
- 8 to 12 warm flour tortillas
  Bottled taco sauce (optional)
  Condiments: About 1 cup *each* guacamole (purchased or homemade), sour cream, thinly sliced green onions (including tops), and roasted salted sunflower seeds

Heat oil in a wide frying pan over medium heat. Add onion and garlic; cook, stirring, until soft. Stir in mushrooms, green pepper, carrots, zucchini, tomatoes, chiles, olives, chili powder, salt, cumin, and oregano. Bring to a boil; cover, reduce heat, and simmer for 10 to 12 minutes.

Uncover, increase heat, and gently boil, stirring occasionally, until vegetables are tender and all the liquid has evaporated (about 10 more minutes).

Stir half the Cheddar cheese and half the jack cheese into vegetables. Turn into a shallow baking dish and sprinkle with remaining Cheddar and jack cheeses. Broil 6 inches from heat until cheese is melted.

Spoon some of the vegetable mixture down center of each tortilla, and sprinkle with taco sauce, if desired. Serve condiments in separate bowls to spoon over top; roll up tortilla to eat. Makes 4 to 6 servings.

Flaky Mushroom Turnovers

For a meatless meal, serve flaky turnovers filled with tender mushrooms in sherry sauce. Offer them with your favorite hot soup, assorted cheeses, and crisp raw vegetables.

- 2 tablespoons butter or margarine
- 1 clove garlic, minced or pressed
- 1 large onion, thinly sliced
- 1 pound mushrooms, thinly sliced
- 1 large carrot, shredded
- 1 teaspoon marjoram or thyme leaves
- 2 teaspoons cornstarch
- ¾ cup regular-strength chicken broth
- 2 tablespoons dry sherry or regular-strength chicken broth
  Salt and pepper
- 1 package (10 oz.) frozen patty shells, thawed

In a wide frying pan over medium heat, melt butter. Add garlic and onion and cook, stirring, until onion is soft and golden (about 10 minutes). Add mushrooms, carrot, and marjoram; cook until juices have evaporated.

In a bowl, combine cornstarch, the ¾ cup chicken broth, and sherry; stir into mushroom mixture. Cook, stirring, until sauce boils and thickens. Season to taste with salt and pepper. Let mixture cool completely.

On a lightly floured board, roll each patty shell into a 7½-inch circle. Place ½ cup of the mushroom filling on half of each pastry circle. Lightly moisten edges of pastry with water and fold pastry over filling to enclose. With a fork, press edges together. Prick tops and arrange turnovers on a baking sheet. (At this point, you may cover and refrigerate until next day.)

Bake, uncovered, in a 400° oven for 30 to 35 minutes or until browned and puffy. Serve hot or at room temperature. Makes 6 servings.

Chinese Filled Buns

Fill these yeast buns with either a pork or beef mixture.

- 1 loaf (1 lb.) frozen bread dough
- 2 cloves garlic, minced or pressed
- ½ teaspoon grated fresh ginger or ¼ teaspoon ground ginger
- 4 teaspoons sugar
- 4 tablespoons soy sauce
- 1½ pounds boneless pork butt or shoulder, cut into ½-inch cubes
- 1 tablespoon *each* cornstarch and dry sherry
- ¼ cup water
- 1 tablespoon salad oil
- 1 medium-size onion, finely chopped
  About 2 tablespoons butter or margarine, melted

Remove bread dough from package and thaw as directed, covering with a damp cloth, just until dough is pliable (1 to 2 hours at room temperature).

Meanwhile, in a bowl, combine garlic, ginger, 2 teaspoons of the sugar, and 2 tablespoons of the soy. Pour over pork cubes and mix until well blended.

In a small bowl, combine remaining 2 teaspoons sugar and cornstarch; stir in sherry, water, and remaining 2 tablespoons soy; set aside.

Heat oil in a wide frying pan or wok over high heat. When oil is hot, add pork mixture and cook, stirring, until browned (about 5 minutes). Add onion and continue cooking and stirring until onion is soft (about 2 more minutes). Stir cornstarch mixture and add to pan. Cook, stirring, until sauce boils and thickens (about 30 seconds). Skim off and discard any fat. Let cool.

With a lightly floured knife, cut thawed bread in half lengthwise; then cut each half into 8 equal pieces. Roll each piece into a ball. On a lightly floured board, roll each ball into a 4½-inch circle.

Place about 2 tablespoons of the filling in center of each circle; gather edges of dough up around filling, being careful not to stretch dough. Pleat excess dough and tightly pinch edges together to seal in filling. Place buns, pinched side down, about 2 inches apart on a greased baking sheet. Cover lightly and let rise in a warm place until puffy and light (about 20 minutes).

Brush each bun with melted butter. Bake in a 350° oven for about 20 minutes or until golden brown. Serve warm or at room temperature. Makes 8 servings.

CURRY BEEF FILLING. In a large bowl, combine 1 teaspoon **curry powder,** ⅛ teaspoon **ground red pepper** (cayenne), ½ teaspoon **sugar,** 2 tablespoons **soy sauce,** 1 teaspoon grated fresh **ginger** or ½ teaspoon ground ginger, and 2 cloves **garlic,** minced or pressed. Thinly slice 1½ pounds **boneless beef** (such as top round) and cut into 1-inch squares. Add to soy mixture, stirring until coated.

In a small bowl, combine 1 teaspoon **curry powder** and 1 tablespoon **cornstarch.** Mix in 2 tablespoons *each* **water** and **soy sauce;** set aside.

Cook as directed for pork filling, but decrease browning time for meat from 5 to 2 minutes and add 1 small **onion,** chopped.

Italian Sausage Pizza

(Pictured on page 39)

Of all the Italian dishes to cross the Atlantic, none has inspired such devotion in the United States as pizza. Try this traditional recipe and you'll see why.

(Continued on next page)

1 **package active dry yeast**
1 **cup warm water** (about 110°)
½ **teaspoon salt**
2 **teaspoons olive oil**
  About 3½ cups all-purpose flour
  Tomato Sauce (recipe follows)
5 **mild Italian sausages** (about 1 lb. *total*)
  Olive oil or salad oil
½ **green pepper, seeded and cut into thin strips**
3 **cups** (12 oz.) **shredded mozzarella cheese**

In a large bowl, dissolve yeast in warm water; let stand until soft (about 5 minutes). Stir in salt and the 2 teaspoons olive oil. Gradually mix in 3 cups of the flour to form a soft dough. Turn dough out onto a floured board and knead until smooth and elastic (about 5 minutes), adding remaining flour as needed. Turn dough over in a greased bowl; cover and let rise in a warm place until doubled (about 1 hour).

Meanwhile, prepare Tomato Sauce and set aside. Remove casings from sausages. Crumble meat into a wide frying pan over medium heat and cook, stirring to break up, until browned. With a slotted spoon, remove meat and drain well; set aside.

Punch dough down and knead on a lightly floured board to shape into a smooth ball. Divide dough in half and roll each piece on a floured board until about ¾ inch thick. Gently pull each portion into an oval 12 to 14 inches long and 8 to 10 inches wide.

Place each oval on a greased baking sheet and brush generously with oil. Spread each with half the sauce, then top with half the sausage and half the pepper strips. Sprinkle each with half the cheese. Place one baking sheet at a time on lowest rack of a 500° oven. Bake for 12 to 15 minutes or until crust is browned.

Makes about 8 servings.

TOMATO SAUCE. In a 4-quart pan over medium heat, combine 3 cans (about 1 lb. *each*) **Italian-style tomatoes** (break up with a spoon) and their liquid, 1 can (6 oz.) **tomato paste**, 1 clove **garlic**, minced or pressed, 1 teaspoon **dry basil**, and ½ teaspoon *each* **dry rosemary** and **oregano leaves**; bring to a boil.

Continue to boil, stirring occasionally, until sauce thickens and is reduced to about 2 cups.

Spokane Pizza

Spokane, Washington, is the origin of this unusual spicy pizza.

1 **pound lean ground beef**
1 **medium-size onion, chopped**
1 **teaspoon garlic salt**
1 **can** (4 oz.) **diced green chiles**
½ **cup tomato-based chili sauce or catsup**
5 **flour tortillas**
2 **tablespoons butter or margarine, melted**
1 **can** (about 1 lb.) **refried beans**
1 **can** (2¼ oz.) **sliced ripe olives, drained**
2 **cups** (8 oz.) **shredded mozzarella or jack cheese**
½ **cup grated Parmesan cheese**
1 **medium-size firm ripe avocado**
  Bottled taco sauce or chile salsa
  Sour cream

Crumble beef into a wide frying pan over medium heat and cook, stirring to break up, until browned. Add onion and cook until soft. Stir in garlic salt, green chiles, and chili sauce until blended; set aside.

Brush tortillas on both sides with butter and overlap in a 14-inch pizza pan. Broil about 3 inches from heat until lightly browned and crisp (3 or 4 minutes).

Spread beans over tortillas and top with meat mixture. Distribute olives over meat and sprinkle evenly with mozzarella and Parmesan cheeses. Bake on lowest rack of a 450° oven for about 10 minutes or until cheese is melted and bubbly.

Meanwhile, peel, pit, and slice avocado; arrange on pizza. To serve, cut into wedges. At the table, pass taco sauce and sour cream to spoon over individual servings. Makes 4 to 6 servings.

Zucchini Pizza Pie

Zucchini forms the foundation for this no-bread pizza.

  About 1½ pounds zucchini
2 **eggs**
1 **cup** (4 oz.) *each* **shredded mozzarella cheese and sharp Cheddar cheese**
1 **pound lean ground beef**
¼ **teaspoon** *each* **salt and garlic salt**
1 **medium-size onion, chopped**
1 **can** (8 oz.) **tomato sauce**
2 **teaspoons oregano leaves**
1 **green pepper, seeded and cut into thin strips**
¼ **pound mushrooms, sliced**
⅓ **cup grated Parmesan cheese**

Shred zucchini (you should have 4 cups, lightly packed); squeeze out any moisture.

In a large bowl, beat eggs lightly; stir in zucchini and ½ cup *each* of the mozzarella and Cheddar cheeses. Press zucchini mixture into a greased 10 by 15-inch pan. Bake in a 400° oven for about 10 minutes.

Meanwhile, crumble beef into a frying pan over medium heat and cook, stirring to break up meat, until browned. Sprinkle with salt and garlic salt. Add onion and cook until soft. Drain off and discard drippings; then stir in tomato sauce and oregano.

Spoon meat mixture over zucchini crust. Arrange pepper strips and mushrooms on top; sprinkle with Parmesan and remaining ½ cup *each* mozzarella and Cheddar cheeses. Bake on lowest rack of a 400° oven for about 30 minutes or until cheeses are bubbly. Makes 6 servings.

HOT AND CHEESY—that's how pizza should be. And you don't have to visit a pizzeria to enjoy this tempting treat—just make our Italian Sausage Pizza (page 37).

MEATS

Beef, veal, lamb & pork

Bay Steak

You won't have to say a word—the rich aroma of barbecued steak basted with crumbled bay leaves and garlic in oil will call them to dinner. Additional bay leaves scattered on the grill contribute to the fragrance; for a dramatic effect, make a basting brush from a cluster of bay leaves bound together on a twig.

3 to 5 small cloves garlic
1 sirloin or porterhouse steak (about 4 lbs.), cut 2 inches thick
⅓ cup olive oil
8 to 10 bay leaves
  Salt

Sliver 1 or 2 cloves of the garlic. Cut small gashes in steak and insert garlic slivers. Mince or press remaining cloves garlic and combine with oil in a small bowl; crumble 2 of the bay leaves and add to oil mixture.

Place steak on a grill 4 to 6 inches above a solid bed of glowing coals. Cook, turning once, for about 15 minutes on each side for rare meat or until done to your liking when slashed. Brush steak often with oil mixture. As meat cooks, scatter bay leaves on grill. Season with salt to taste. Makes 6 to 8 servings.

Rolled Flank Steak (Braciola)

This dish is like a neatly packaged Italian picnic—it's a butterflied flank steak wrapped around bacon, salami, provolone, Parmesan, and hard-cooked eggs. Serve the meat rolls hot with Neapolitan Gravy, or chill, slice thinly, and use as cold cuts.

2 large flank steaks (1½ to 2 lbs. *each*)
¼ cup grated Parmesan cheese
10 strips bacon
8 thin slices provolone cheese
12 thin slices salami
6 hard-cooked eggs
2 tablespoons salad oil
  Neapolitan Gravy (page 49)

Trim and discard excess fat from steaks. Split each steak horizontally through center, leaving one edge attached. Open and place between 2 sheets of plastic wrap on a cutting board. With a smooth mallet, pound meat until evenly flattened, especially at center ridge. Discard top piece of wrap. Evenly sprinkle meat with Parmesan cheese.

In a wide frying pan over medium heat, cook bacon just until limp. Arrange 5 strips of the bacon across each steak and cover with 4 slices of the provolone cheese. Near one edge, arrange 6 slices of the salami and top with 3 of the hard-cooked eggs.

Using plastic wrap to help lift meat, roll up meat as tightly as possible, enclosing filling. With cord, tie each roll lengthwise, tucking in ends; then tie around each roll in 6 to 8 places.

Heat oil in an 8-quart kettle over medium heat. Add meat rolls, one at a time, and cook until well browned on all sides. Pour in Neapolitan Gravy. Bring to a boil; cover, reduce heat, and simmer until tender when pierced (about 3 hours). Lift out meat; skim and discard fat from sauce.

To serve hot, cut rolls into ½-inch-thick slices and pass sauce to spoon over individual servings. Or cool, cover, and refrigerate rolls; cut into thin slices and serve cold. Makes 10 to 12 servings.

Beef Pot Roast with Lima Beans

The beauty of casserole cookery is that it allows busy cooks to serve savory entrées with maximum ease and minimum cleanup. You can bake and serve this oven pot roast in the same container.

  1 **beef chuck roast (about 4 lbs.)**
  1 **envelope dry onion soup mix (amount for 4 servings)**
  1 **can (10½ oz.) condensed Scotch broth or beef soup with vegetables and barley**
  1½ **cups water**
  3 **medium-size carrots**
  1 **package (10 oz.) frozen baby lima beans, thawed**

Place beef in a 5-quart casserole. In a large bowl, combine onion soup mix, broth, and water; pour over meat. Bake, covered, in a 425° oven for 1 hour.

Meanwhile, cut carrots into 1-inch chunks. Remove casserole from oven and stir carrots into

cooking liquid. Return to oven and bake, covered, for 1¼ more hours or until meat is tender when pierced; add more water if needed.

Skim and discard fat from juices. Stir lima beans into juices. Return casserole to oven and continue baking, covered, for 25 more minutes or until beans are tender. Makes 6 to 8 servings.

Oven-simmered Beef Brisket

You'll put this marinated beef brisket high on your list of no-fuss entrées. Serve it hot with gravy; or omit the gravy, chill the meat, and offer thin slices for lunch with bread, butter, and mustard.

  1 **beef brisket (about 4 lbs.)**
  2½ **cups sweet vermouth or apple juice**
  ½ **cup soy sauce**
  ¼ **cup salad oil**
  2 **bay leaves**
  1 **clove garlic, minced or pressed**
  1 **large onion, chopped**
  ½ **teaspoon ground ginger**
  ¼ **teaspoon pepper**
  ¼ **cup *each* cornstarch and water**

Trim and discard excess fat from meat; place meat in a roasting pan. In a large bowl, combine vermouth, soy, oil, bay, garlic, onion, ginger, and pepper; pour over meat. Cover and refrigerate until next day.

Leave meat in marinade and bake, covered, in a 350° oven for 3 hours or until tender when pierced. Transfer meat to a serving platter. Skim and discard fat from pan juices; discard bay leaves.

To serve hot, combine cornstarch and water in a small bowl; stir into juices. Cook, stirring, over medium heat until mixture thickens; pass gravy to spoon over individual servings.

To serve cold, omit cornstarch and water. Let meat cool in pan juices, cover, and refrigerate for up to 2 days. Lift out meat and thinly slice. Makes 8 to 10 servings.

Tomato Beef

Tender strips of beef and crisply cooked vegetables are coated with a curry-flavored sauce for this easy Cantonese dish. Serve with steamed rice.

  ¾ **pound boneless lean beef**
  2 **teaspoons *each* cornstarch and soy sauce**
  1 **tablespoon *each* dry sherry and water**
  ¼ **teaspoon salt**
  ¼ **cup salad oil**
      Cooking Sauce (recipe follows)
  ½ **teaspoon minced fresh ginger or ¼ teaspoon ground ginger**
  1 **clove garlic, minced or pressed**
  2 **large stalks celery, cut into ¼-inch-thick slanting slices**
  1 **medium-size onion, cut into wedges with layers separated**
  1 **green pepper, seeded and cut into 1-inch squares**
  3 **medium-size tomatoes, each cut into 6 wedges**

Cut beef with the grain into 1½-inch-wide strips. Cut each strip across the grain into ⅛-inch-thick slanting slices. In a small bowl, combine cornstarch, soy, sherry, water, and salt. Add beef, stirring to coat; then stir in 1½ teaspoons of the oil and let stand for 15 minutes.

Meanwhile, prepare Cooking Sauce and set aside.

Heat a wok or wide frying pan over high heat. When pan is hot, add 2 tablespoons of the oil. When oil is hot, add ginger and garlic and stir once. Add beef mixture and cook, stirring, until meat is browned on outside but still pink inside (about 1½ minutes); remove from pan and set aside.

Add remaining 1½ table-

spoons oil to pan. When oil is hot, add celery and onion; cook, stirring, for 1 minute. Add green pepper and continue cooking and stirring for 1 more minute, adding a few drops of water if needed. Add tomatoes and cook, stirring, for 1 more minute.

Return meat to pan. Stir cooking sauce, add to pan, and cook, stirring, until sauce boils and thickens. Makes 4 servings.

COOKING SAUCE. In a small bowl, combine 1 tablespoon *each* **soy sauce, Worcestershire,** and **cornstarch;** 3 tablespoons **catsup;** 1 teaspoon **curry powder;** and ½ cup **water.** Stir until blended.

Green Chile Beef Stew

Tomatoes and green chiles join forces to flavor this meat stew. Top it all off with avocado, sour cream, and a squeeze of lime juice.

- 2 **tablespoons lard or salad oil**
- 2 **pounds beef stew meat (brisket, if available)**
- 2 **large onions, thinly sliced**
- 1 **can (4 oz.) whole green chiles, seeded and chopped**
- 1 **can (about 1 lb.) Italian-style tomatoes**
- 1 **cup regular-strength chicken broth**
  Salt
- 1 **avocado**
  Sour cream
- 2 **limes, cut into wedges**

In a 5-quart kettle over medium-high heat, melt lard. Add meat, a portion at a time, and cook until browned; lift out meat and place in a bowl.

YOU'LL NEED A KNIFE AND FORK to eat a Giant Flour Tortilla Taco (page 45). The crisp shell of this Mexican extravaganza is a large flour tortilla, quickly fried and shaped into an edible envelope.

Add onions to pan and cook, stirring, until soft. Return meat and juices to pan; add chiles, tomatoes (break up with a spoon) and their liquid, and broth. Bring to a boil; cover, reduce heat, and simmer until meat is tender when pierced (about 2½ hours). Season with salt to taste.

Peel, pit, and dice avocado. Spoon stew into soup bowls; pass avocado and sour cream to spoon over individual servings, and lime wedges to squeeze over top. Makes 4 to 6 servings.

Singapore Satay

Served on delicate china in Southeast Asia's finest restaurants or from a bamboo splinter at a sidewalk vendor's stall, *satay* (sah-tay) is the unofficial national dish of Singapore, Malaysia, and Indonesia.

- 2 **tablespoons** *each* **curry powder and sugar**
- ½ **cup** *each* **salad oil and soy sauce**
- 4 **cloves garlic, minced or pressed**
- 3 **to 4 pounds lean boneless beef (sirloin or top round), lamb (shoulder or leg), or chicken (breast or thigh), or a mixture**
  Peanut Sauce (recipe follows)

In a small bowl, stir together curry powder, sugar, oil, soy, and garlic. Cut meat into ¾-inch cubes and place in a plastic bag (if using more than one kind of meat, place each in a separate plastic bag). Pour marinade over meat, seal bag, and refrigerate, turning occasionally, for at least 4 hours or up to 2 days.

Prepare Peanut Sauce and set aside. Thread meat on long, sturdy bamboo skewers (use only one kind of meat on each skewer). Place on a grill about 2 inches above a solid bed of glowing coals. Cook, turning often, for 8 to 10 minutes or until meat is browned and done to your liking. Serve with sauce for dipping. Makes 6 to 8 servings.

PEANUT SAUCE. In a blender or food processor, whirl 1 cup **salted Virginia peanuts** until finely chopped; remove from blender and set aside. Add to blender 1 large **onion,** cut into chunks; 2 cloves **garlic;** and 4 to 5 small **dried whole hot red chiles.** Whirl until smooth.

Heat 2 tablespoons **salad oil** in a wide frying pan over medium heat. Add onion mixture, 2 teaspoons **ground coriander,** and 1 teaspoon **ground cumin;** cook, stirring occasionally, for 5 minutes. Reduce heat to low and add peanuts.

Gradually stir in 1 can (12 oz.) frozen **coconut milk,** thawed; 3 tablespoons firmly packed **brown sugar;** and 2 tablespoons *each* **lemon juice** and **soy sauce.** Cook, uncovered, just below simmering (do not boil), stirring occasionally, until sauce thickens (about 15 minutes).

Pour into 2 or 3 wide shallow rimmed dishes and serve warm or at room temperature. Makes 2½ cups.

Spinach-swirled Meat Loaf

It's meat loaf with a touch of artistry—each juicy slice shows off a swirl of flavorful spinach-cheese filling. Serve it hot for supper, then slice it cold for sandwiches the next day.

- **About 1 slice white or wheat bread**
- 2 **pounds lean ground beef**
- 1 **small onion, finely chopped**
- 2 **eggs, lightly beaten**
- 1 **can (8 oz.) tomato sauce**
- 1 **teaspoon prepared mustard**
- ¾ **teaspoon oregano leaves**
- ½ **teaspoon salt**
- ¼ **teaspoon pepper**
- 1 **package (10 oz.) frozen chopped spinach, thawed**
- 1 **teaspoon garlic salt**
- 1½ **cups (6 oz.) shredded sharp Cheddar cheese**

(Continued on next page)

In a blender or food processor, whirl bread to make crumbs (you should have ¾ cup). In a large bowl, combine bread crumbs with beef, onion, eggs, ½ cup of the tomato sauce, mustard, oregano, salt, and pepper. On a large sheet of wax paper, pat meat mixture into a 10 by 12-inch rectangle.

Squeeze out as much moisture from spinach as possible; distribute over meat to within ½ inch of edges. Sprinkle with garlic salt, then distribute 1 cup of the cheese over spinach to within 1 inch of edges.

Using wax paper to help roll meat, roll up jelly roll style. Pinch seam and ends closed to seal in filling. Carefully place meat roll, seam side down, in a 9 by 13-inch baking dish.

Bake, uncovered, in a 350° oven for 1¼ hours. Remove from oven; spoon out and discard drippings. Pour remaining tomato sauce over meat loaf, return to oven, and continue baking for 15 more minutes.

Remove from oven and sprinkle with remaining ½ cup cheese; return to oven and continue baking for 5 more minutes or until cheese is melted. With wide spatulas, carefully transfer meat loaf to a serving platter. Makes 4 to 6 servings.

Beef Roll Wellington

Treated like a pastry-wrapped fillet of beef, meat loaf can be an elegant dinner party entrée. Ground beef is seasoned with herbs and cheese, then encased in a biscuit overcoat.

- 2 pounds lean ground beef
- 1 egg, lightly beaten
- 1 teaspoon *each* salt and dry basil
- 2 teaspoons dry mustard
- ½ teaspoon oregano leaves
- ¼ teaspoon pepper
- ¼ cup catsup
- 1½ cups soft bread crumbs
- ½ cup *each* chopped onion and celery
- 1 cup (4 oz.) shredded sharp Cheddar cheese
- 1 teaspoon beef-flavored stock base
- 2 cloves garlic, minced or pressed
- 2 packages (4 oz. *each*) sliced boiled ham
- 1½ cups (6 oz.) shredded mozzarella cheese
- 3 tablespoons grated Parmesan cheese
- 1 teaspoon crushed fennel seeds
  Biscuit Crust (recipe follows)
- 1 egg beaten with 1 tablespoon water
- 1 tablespoon sesame seeds

In a large bowl, combine ground beef, the lightly beaten egg, salt, basil, mustard, oregano, pepper, catsup, bread crumbs, onion, celery, Cheddar cheese, stock base, and garlic. Mix well.

On a large sheet of foil, pat meat mixture into a 10 by 12-inch rectangle. With shorter side nearest you, start at opposite end and overlap ham slices, leaving a 1-inch border of ground meat exposed. Sprinkle mozzarella cheese over ham, then Parmesan cheese and fennel seeds. Using foil to help roll meat, start at end nearest you and carefully roll up jelly roll style. Pinch long seam and ends closed to seal in filling.

Place meat roll, seam side down, on a greased rimmed baking sheet. Bake, uncovered, in a 350° oven for 1 hour. Let stand for up to 3 hours. Or cool, cover, and refrigerate until next day; bring to room temperature before continuing.

Prepare Biscuit Crust; on a lightly floured sheet of wax paper, roll dough into a rectangle about 13 by 16 inches.

Place meat roll across dough. Using wax paper to help lift dough, fold dough over meat, overlapping edges. Brush edges with egg mixture and pinch to seal. Fold in ends, enclosing meat, brush with egg mixture, and seal.

Place on a well-greased rimmed baking sheet. With a fork, prick dough all over. Brush with remaining egg mixture and sprinkle with sesame seeds.

Bake, uncovered, in a 375° oven for 40 minutes or until richly browned. Let stand for 10 to 15 minutes before slicing. Makes 6 to 8 servings.

BISCUIT CRUST. In a large bowl, combine 4 cups **baking mix** (biscuit mix), ¼ teaspoon **ground red pepper** (cayenne), and 2 tablespoons chopped **green onion** (including top). Stir in 1⅓ cups **milk.** Turn dough out onto a floured board and knead 8 to 10 times.

Charlie's Cabbage Rolls

Cabbage leaves make perfect blankets for a tempting filling of beef and rice. The little bundles simmer with kielbasa on a bed of tangy sauerkraut.

- 1½ pounds lean ground beef
- 1 medium-size onion, finely chopped
- 1 cup cooked rice
- ½ teaspoon salt
- ¼ teaspoon *each* pepper and paprika
- ¼ cup catsup
- 1 clove garlic, minced or pressed
- ⅛ teaspoon liquid hot pepper seasoning
- 1 large head cabbage
  Boiling salted water
- 1 quart sauerkraut, drained well
- 1 pound kielbasa sausages, cut into 1-inch pieces
- 1 can (8 oz.) tomato sauce

Crumble beef into a wide frying pan over medium heat; cook, stirring to break up, until browned. Spoon off and discard fat. Add onion and cook until soft. Stir in rice, salt, pepper, paprika, catsup, garlic, and hot pepper seasoning; remove from heat and set aside.

Core cabbage, separate leaves, and cut off and discard thickest portion of central rib from 16 large leaves (reserve remaining cabbage for other uses). In a 6 to 8-quart kettle over high heat, cook leaves in boiling salted water to cover just until soft (about 1 minute). Drain well and let cool.

Spread half the sauerkraut in a shallow 4-quart casserole or baking dish. Spoon about ¼ cup of the meat mixture onto base of each cabbage leaf, then fold sides over meat and roll up. Place rolls in a single layer, seam side down, on sauerkraut.

Spoon any remaining meat mixture over rolls, then add sausages, tomato sauce, and remaining sauerkraut. Bake, covered, in a 350° oven for 1½ hours or until heated through. Makes 8 servings.

Giant Flour Tortilla Tacos

(Pictured on page 42)

Crisply fried and shaped like a half-open shell, plate-size flour tortillas are a dramatic container for this Mexican favorite. You can prepare the tortillas beforehand.

    Salad oil
6 to 8 large flour tortillas (10 to 12 inches in diameter)
    Beef Filling (recipe follows)
6 to 8 cups shredded iceberg lettuce
1 or 2 avocados
2 or 3 small tomatoes, thinly sliced
    Pitted ripe olives
    Radishes
    Sour cream
    Fresh coriander (cilantro) sprigs

Pour oil into a wide frying pan to a depth of ½ inch. Heat oil to 375° on a deep-frying thermometer. Add tortillas, one at a time, and cook, turning quickly and carefully with 2 wide spatulas, until bubbly and just golden, but still soft and flexible (about 30 seconds total).

Using spatulas, lift out each tortilla and immediately bend in center so one half is perpendicular to the other. Let drain on paper towels, propped against a can or other sturdy object so it holds its shape as it cools. Repeat until all are fried.

If made ahead, carefully package in large plastic bags and store at room temperature for up to a day. To recrisp, place tortillas, a few at a time, on a baking sheet and heat in a 350° oven for about 5 minutes; let cool on wire racks.

Meanwhile, prepare Beef Filling. To assemble each taco, place a fried tortilla on a plate and sprinkle with about 1 cup of lettuce. Spoon on about 1 cup of the meat filling. Peel, pit, and slice avocados. Garnish each tortilla with some of the avocado, tomato, olives, radishes (cut decoratively, if desired), a dollop of sour cream, and cilantro.

Serve with knife and fork. Makes 6 to 8 tacos.

BEEF FILLING. Crumble 3 pounds lean **ground beef** into a wide frying pan over medium heat; cook, stirring to break up, until browned. Spoon off and discard fat. Add 2 large **onions,** chopped, and cook, stirring, until soft.

Stir in 4 teaspoons **chili powder,** 1½ teaspoons *each* **oregano leaves** and **paprika,** ¾ teaspoon *each* **ground cumin** and **pepper,** 1 tablespoon **Worcestershire,** and 1 large can (15 oz.) **tomato sauce.** Reduce heat and simmer, uncovered, stirring often, until heated through. Season with **garlic salt** to taste.

Not-just-any-chili Chili

It's a far cry from any chili you've ever tasted. Along with the traditional ingredients in this recipe, you'll find such palate-surprisers as beer and aromatic bitters. In fact, of the 18 ingredients in the chili, 12 are there just for flavor. The result is an unforgettable meal-in-a-bowl. A favorite of many, it's bound to become your favorite chili, too.

2 pounds lean ground beef
1 large onion, coarsely chopped
1 large can (1 lb. 12 oz.) tomatoes
1 can (15 oz.) tomato purée
2 cans (15½ oz. *each*) kidney beans, drained
3 tablespoons *each* Worcestershire and aromatic bitters
1 can (12 oz.) beer *or* 1½ cups water
3 cloves garlic, minced or pressed
1 beef bouillon cube
1 teaspoon crushed red pepper
2 bay leaves
1 tablespoon chili powder
1 teaspoon *each* ground coriander and ground cumin; thyme leaves and oregano leaves; and dry basil
    Shredded Cheddar cheese
    Sour cream
    Sliced green onions (including tops)

Crumble beef into a 5 to 6-quart kettle over medium heat; cook, stirring to break up, until browned. Add onion and cook until soft. Stir in tomatoes (break up with a spoon) and their liquid, tomato purée, beans, Worcestershire, bitters, beer, garlic, bouillon cube, red pepper, bay, chili powder, coriander, cumin, thyme, oregano, and basil.

Bring to a boil; reduce heat and simmer, uncovered, stirring occasionally, until chili is thick and flavors are well blended (about 2 hours). Skim and discard fat, and remove bay leaves.

Pour into bowls and pass cheese, sour cream, and onions to spoon over individual servings. Makes 6 to 8 servings.

Most Requested Liver

An Oregon restaurant chef shared this popular menu item with *Sunset*. It's become very popular with many of our readers, as well.

> 6 strips bacon
> 1½ pounds baby beef liver, cut into serving-size pieces
>   All-purpose flour
> 1 large onion, sliced
> 1 medium-size green pepper, seeded and sliced
> 1 envelope dry onion soup mix (amount for 4 servings)
> 1 can (1 lb.) stewed tomatoes
>   Seasoned salt and pepper
>   Hot cooked noodles (optional)

In a wide frying pan over medium heat, cook bacon until crisp. Remove bacon from pan, drain, and set aside. Pour off and reserve drippings; return 2 tablespoons of the drippings to pan.

Dust liver with flour, shaking off excess. Add liver to pan and cook, turning once, until lightly browned on both sides; add drippings to pan as needed. Arrange liver in a 9 by 13-inch baking dish.

Add onion and green pepper to pan and cook until onion is soft. Spoon vegetables evenly over liver, sprinkle with onion soup mix, and pour tomatoes over all. Season to taste with seasoned salt and pepper, and top with bacon.

Bake, covered, in a 350° oven for 25 minutes or until heated through. Serve with noodles, if desired. Makes 6 servings.

Prosciutto & Cheese-topped Veal

For a simple adaptation of the Italian classic, *saltimbocca*, top sautéed veal slices with thin slices of prosciutto and provolone cheese. Then pop the veal under the broiler just until the cheese is melted.

> 1 egg or 1 egg white
> 1½ tablespoons milk
> ⅛ teaspoon garlic powder
> 2 tablespoons *each* fine dry bread crumbs, all-purpose flour, and grated Parmesan cheese
> ¼ teaspoon *each* dry basil and oregano leaves
> ½ pound boneless veal, cut ¼ inch thick
>   About 1½ tablespoons butter or margarine
>   About 1½ tablespoons salad oil
> 2 ounces thinly sliced prosciutto *or* 3 ounces thinly sliced ham
>   About 5 ounces thinly sliced provolone cheese

In a pie pan, beat egg, milk, and garlic powder until blended. In another pie pan, combine bread crumbs, flour, Parmesan cheese, basil, and oregano. Dip veal in egg mixture, then in crumb mixture to coat; set aside.

Heat butter and oil in a wide frying pan over medium-high heat. Add veal and cook, turning once, until lightly browned on both sides (about 1½ minutes on each side). Place veal on a rack in a broiler pan and top each piece with 1 or 2 slices of the prosciutto, cut to fit, then with a slice of the provolone cheese, also cut to fit. Broil about 4 inches from heat just until cheese is melted. Makes 2 servings.

Veal Wellington

Thanks to frozen patty shells, you can assemble these individual Wellingtons quickly and prepare them well before the guests arrive.

> 1½ pounds veal rib chops, lamb shoulder chops, or smoked pork chops, cut 1 inch thick
> 2 tablespoons butter or margarine
> ½ pound mushrooms, sliced
> 2 green onions (including tops), thinly sliced
> 1 package (10 oz.) frozen patty shells, thawed
>   Mustard Cream Sauce or Caper Cream Sauce (recipes follow)

Bone chops and trim and discard fat. If pieces of meat are larger than 3 inches square, cut into smaller pieces (combine 2 small pieces for 1 serving).

In a wide frying pan over medium-high heat, melt 1 tablespoon of the butter. Add meat and cook, turning, until browned on both sides (about 1 minute on each side). Remove from pan and set aside.

Reduce heat to medium and melt remaining 1 tablespoon butter in pan. Add mushrooms and onions and cook, stirring, until liquid has evaporated (5 to 10 minutes). Set aside; let cool.

On a lightly floured board, roll each patty shell into an 8-inch circle. Spoon 1 tablespoon of the mushroom mixture in center of each pastry circle and set a piece of meat on top. Bring edges of pastry over meat, overlapping to enclose filling. Place, seam side down, on a rimmed baking sheet. (At this point, you may cover and refrigerate until next day.)

Bake, uncovered, on lowest rack of a 425° oven for 10 minutes; then move pan to highest rack and continue baking for 8 to 10 more minutes or until pastry is golden brown.

Meanwhile, prepare sauce of your choice. Serve meat immediately; offer sauce to spoon over each serving. Makes 6 servings.

MUSTARD CREAM SAUCE. Pour ¼ cup **dry sherry** into a small frying pan over high heat; add ¼ cup minced **shallots** or green onions (including tops) and cook until soft. Stir in 2 tablespoons **Dijon mustard** and ½ pint (1 cup) **whipping cream**. Bring to a boil, stirring, and cook

until sauce thickens and shiny bubbles form (3 to 4 minutes).

CAPER CREAM SAUCE. Follow recipe for Mustard Cream Sauce (preceding), omitting dry sherry; instead, use ¼ cup **dry vermouth.** Reduce mustard to 1 tablespoon and add 2 tablespoons drained **capers** and ¼ teaspoon **dry tarragon** with cream.

Veal Strips with Artichokes

Sautéed strips of veal taste sublime in a sauce made from sour cream and the liquid from marinated artichoke hearts. The artichokes arrive later for an attractive garnish. Serve over hot cooked spinach noodles.

1½ pounds boneless veal, cut ¼ inch thick
¼ cup all-purpose flour
½ teaspoon salt
¼ teaspoon *each* pepper and paprika
2 jars (6 oz. *each*) marinated artichoke hearts
2 medium-size onions, sliced
½ cup regular-strength chicken broth
2 tablespoons lemon juice
½ pint (1 cup) sour cream
¼ cup grated Parmesan cheese
Hot cooked spinach noodles

Trim and discard membrane from veal; place veal between 2 sheets of wax paper on a cutting board. With a mallet, pound veal until each piece is about ⅛ inch thick. Cut into ¾-inch-wide strips.

In a pie pan, combine flour, salt, pepper, and paprika. Dredge veal in flour mixture, shaking off excess; set aside.

Drain artichokes, reserving marinade. Set artichokes aside. Pour about half the marinade into a wide frying pan; cook over medium heat until bubbly. Add veal strips, a few at a time, and cook until well browned (3 to 5 minutes); lift out and set aside.

Add onions to pan and more marinade if needed; cook for 5 minutes. Add broth and stir, scraping browned particles free from pan. Stir in lemon juice, sour cream, cheese, and veal strips; cook until heated through. Serve over noodles and garnish with artichoke hearts. Makes 4 servings.

Veal Stroganoff

Italian sausages accent this veal and vegetable combination. A subtly seasoned dish, the stroganoff is delicious served with rice or hot cooked noodles.

2 tablespoons salad oil
1½ pounds boneless veal stew meat, cut into 1½-inch cubes
3 mild Italian sausages, cut into 1-inch slices
1 medium-size onion, chopped
½ pound mushrooms, quartered
1 cup regular-strength beef broth
1 medium-size red bell pepper, seeded and chopped
½ cup dry sherry or additional beef broth
½ pint (1 cup) sour cream
2 tablespoons all-purpose flour
Ground nutmeg, salt, and pepper

Heat oil in a wide frying pan over medium-high heat; add veal and sausages and cook, stirring, until well browned on all sides. Stir in onion and mushrooms and cook until onion is soft.

Add broth, bell pepper, and sherry. Bring to a boil; cover, reduce heat, and simmer until meat is tender when pierced (about 1 hour). Increase heat to high and cook, uncovered, until liquid is reduced to about 1 cup. Reduce heat to medium.

In a small bowl, stir together sour cream and flour until well blended, then stir into veal mixture; season to taste with nutmeg, salt, and pepper. Cook, stirring, until bubbly. Makes 4 to 6 servings.

Pork Tenderloin Dinner with Onion-Apple Cream

A sherried cream sauce, seasoned with mustard and horseradish, bastes this savory pork roast as it bakes. Afterwards, the same sauce flavors cooked onion and apple slices for serving at the table.

6 tablespoons whipping cream
2 tablespoons cream sherry
1 teaspoon Dijon mustard
½ teaspoon *each* salt and prepared horseradish
1 whole pork tenderloin (about 12 oz.)
1 large onion
1 small Golden Delicious apple
2 tablespoons butter or margarine
½ pound green beans, ends removed
Parsley sprigs

In a small bowl, stir together cream, sherry, mustard, salt, and horseradish; set aside.

Place pork on a rack in a baking pan. Bake, uncovered, in a 425° oven, brushing often with cream mixture, for 25 to 30 minutes or until meat thermometer inserted in thickest part registers 170°.

Meanwhile, thinly slice onion and apple. In a wide frying pan over medium heat, melt butter. Add onion and apple slices and cook, stirring, until soft and golden (about 20 minutes). Add remaining cream mixture and bring to a boil; then pour into a small bowl and keep warm.

About 5 minutes before pork is done, pour water into a 3-quart pan to a depth of 1 inch. Bring to a boil over high heat. Place beans on a rack above water. Cover, reduce heat to medium, and cook until just crisp-tender (about 5 minutes); drain.

Arrange pork and beans on a platter; garnish with parsley and pass onion-apple cream sauce to spoon over individual servings. Makes 2 servings.

Prune-glazed Oven Pork

The shoulder of today's leaner pork is flavorful and tender, and it makes delicious soups and stews. This casserole stew combines pork with the sweetness of prunes; you'll taste cinnamon, ginger, and rosemary in it, too. The rich pan juices taste wonderful when served on rice or baked sweet potatoes.

1 tablespoon salad oil
2 pounds lean boneless pork butt, cut into 1¼ to 1½-inch cubes
12 to 16 small boiling onions, peeled
1 teaspoon cornstarch
¾ cup prune juice
1 tablespoon lemon juice
¾ teaspoon salt
½ teaspoon dry rosemary
¼ teaspoon *each* ground cinnamon, ground ginger, and pepper
10 pitted prunes

Pour oil into a 9 by 13-inch baking dish; heat in a 500° oven. When oil is hot, add meat and onions and bake, uncovered, for 15 to 20 minutes, stirring often, or until meat is browned.

Meanwhile, place cornstarch in a small bowl and gradually blend in prune juice until smooth. Stir in lemon juice, salt, rosemary, cinnamon, ginger, and pepper.

Remove dish from oven and add prunes; then pour over

ITALIAN-STYLE GRAVY: DELICIOUS & VERSATILE

Endlessly useful and surprisingly easy to make, this rich tomato sauce is used in Italy as the cooking liquid for various meats. The bonus is that no matter what you cook it with, you're likely to have some left over to simmer with another meat or to use as a topping for hot cooked pasta. And it just keeps getting better and better.

Neapolitan Gravy

2 large cans (1 lb. 12 oz. *each*) tomato purée
2 cloves garlic, minced or pressed
½ cup chopped parsley
½ pound mushrooms, sliced
¾ cup dry red wine
2 tablespoons dry basil
1 tablespoon oregano leaves
2 teaspoons salt
1 teaspoon sugar
½ teaspoon pepper
1½ cups water

In a large bowl, combine tomato purée, garlic, parsley, mushrooms, wine, basil, oregano, salt, sugar, pepper, and water. Stir until well blended. Makes about 2½ quarts.

Simmered Italian Sausages. In a 5-quart kettle over medium heat, cook 2 to 2½ pounds **Italian sausages** until browned. Pour in **Neapolitan Gravy**; bring to a boil. Cover,

reduce heat, and simmer, stirring occasionally, until flavors are well blended (about 45 minutes).

Lift out sausages and arrange on a serving platter. Skim and discard fat from gravy. Pour into a bowl and pass at the table to spoon over individual servings. Makes about 6 servings.

Simmered Country-style Spareribs. In a 6 to 8-quart kettle over medium heat, cook 3½ to 4 pounds **country-style spareribs** (cut into serving-size pieces) until browned. Pour in **Neapolitan Gravy**; bring to a boil. Cover, reduce heat, and simmer, stirring occasionally, until meat is tender when pierced (about 3 hours).

Lift out ribs and arrange on a serving platter. Skim and discard fat from gravy. Pour into a bowl and pass at the table to spoon over individual servings. Makes about 6 servings.

Italian Meatballs in Gravy. In a large bowl, combine 2 pounds lean **ground beef**; ½ cup *each* **fine dry bread crumbs** and **milk**; 1 small **onion**, finely chopped; 2 **eggs**; 1 teaspoon **seasoned salt**; and ½ teaspoon *each* **pepper, oregano leaves,** and **garlic salt.** Mix until well blended and shape into 2-inch balls.

In an 8-quart kettle over medium heat, cook meatballs, a few at a time, until browned; add **olive oil** or salad oil if needed. Pour in **Neapolitan Gravy**; bring to a boil. Cover, reduce heat, and simmer, stirring occasionally, until flavors are well blended (about 1 hour). Skim and discard fat from gravy. Serve over hot cooked **spaghetti,** if desired. Makes 6 to 8 servings.

prune juice mixture. Reduce heat to 350° and return dish to oven; continue baking, covered, for 30 more minutes or until meat is tender when pierced. Makes 6 servings.

Pork with Celery, Avgolemono

Eggs and lemon juice flavor a sauce the Greeks call *avgolemono*. The sauce, in turn, flavors this distinctive pork stew. Celery root gives the stew another out-of-the-ordinary touch.

> About 4 tablespoons butter or margarine
> 2 pounds lean boneless pork shoulder or butt, cut into 1½-inch cubes
> 1 medium-size onion, sliced
> 2 medium-size carrots, sliced
> 3 cups water
> 3 chicken bouillon cubes
> 2 to 3 pounds celery root or 1 medium-size bunch celery
> 2 tablespoons all-purpose flour
> 2 eggs
> ¼ cup lemon juice
> Salt and pepper
> Hot cooked noodles (optional)
> Parsley

In a 5-quart kettle over medium heat, melt 1 tablespoon of the butter; add meat, about half at a time, and cook, turning, until browned on all sides. Remove with a slotted spoon and set aside.

Add more butter if needed to make about 2 tablespoons drippings. Add onion and carrots; cook until onion is soft. Return meat to pan, then add water and bouillon cubes. Bring to a boil; cover, reduce heat, and simmer until meat is tender when pierced (1 to 1½ hours).

Cut celery root into quarters and slice about ⅓ inch thick to make 1 quart (or cut large celery stalks lengthwise, then cut into 1½-inch pieces). Add to pan; cook, covered, until vegetables are tender (about 15 minutes).

Pour off and reserve 2 cups of the cooking liquid; skim and discard any excess fat. Keep meat warm.

In a small pan over medium heat, melt 2 tablespoons of the remaining butter. Blend in flour and cook, stirring, until bubbly. Gradually stir in reserved 2 cups cooking liquid and continue cooking and stirring until sauce boils and thickens.

In a small bowl, beat eggs well, then beat in lemon juice. Beating constantly, gradually add hot sauce to egg mixture. Then gradually stir egg sauce into warm (not simmering) stew. Season with salt and pepper to taste.

Serve with noodles, if desired, and garnish with parsley. Makes about 6 servings.

Pork Chops with Crispy Potatoes

Thinly sliced *cornichons*—tiny sour French pickles—are sprinkled over browned chops in this French-inspired dish. Serve the chops on a platter with oven-fried potatoes and shredded lettuce.

> Salad oil
> 6 small thin-skinned potatoes (about 1½ lbs. *total*)
> 4 to 6 pork shoulder chops or steaks, cut ½ inch thick
> Salt and pepper
> ⅔ cup dry white wine
> About ¼ cup thinly sliced cornichons or small dill pickles
> Shredded romaine or iceberg lettuce
> Dijon mustard

Pour oil into a 7 by 11-inch baking dish to a depth of ¼ inch and heat in a 400° oven. Peel potatoes and cut lengthwise into sixths; add to hot oil. Bake, uncovered, for 40 minutes, stirring several times, or until potatoes are golden and tender when pierced.

Meanwhile, sprinkle chops lightly with salt and pepper. Heat 3 or 4 tablespoons oil in a wide frying pan over medium-high heat. Cook chops, 2 or 3 at a time, turning once, until chops are well browned on both sides and meat near bone is no longer pink when slashed (5 to 7 minutes on each side). Transfer chops to a serving platter and keep warm.

Pour off and discard oil from pan. Add wine and cook, scraping browned particles free from pan, until liquid is reduced to about ⅓ cup. Pour over chops and sprinkle with cornichons. Mound potatoes at one end of platter, lettuce at the other. Serve with mustard. Makes 4 to 6 servings.

Stuffed Smoked Pork Chop Roast

Smoked pork chops, layered with a seasoned bread stuffing and skewered together to resemble a roast, are a wise choice for a busy cook, since the smoked chops are already cooked when you buy them. You can assemble this impressive entrée a day ahead and have it on the table in 45 minutes.

> 4 tablespoons butter or margarine
> 6 smoked pork chops, cut ¾ inch thick
> 1 stalk celery, sliced
> 1 small onion, chopped
> ¼ pound mushrooms, sliced
> ½ teaspoon thyme leaves
> ¼ teaspoon oregano leaves
> ⅛ teaspoon ground sage
> 3 tablespoons dry white wine
> 2 cups seasoned stuffing cubes
> Cranberry sauce (optional)

In a wide frying pan over medium heat, melt 2 tablespoons of the butter. Add chops and cook until browned on both sides; remove from pan and set aside.

Melt remaining 2 tablespoons butter in pan; add celery, onion, and mushrooms and cook until mushrooms are soft (about 5 minutes). Stir in thyme, oregano, sage, and wine; remove from heat. Stir in stuffing cubes, blending well.

To assemble, mound about 3 tablespoons of the stuffing mixture on a chop. Top with a second chop (bone in same position), more stuffing, then a third chop. Run 2 wooden skewers, each about 10 inches long, through chops and stuffing to secure. Then continue stacking remaining stuffing and chops.

Lay stack of chops in a 7 by 11-inch baking dish, with rib bones standing on end. Spoon any remaining stuffing around pan. (At this point, you may cover and refrigerate until next day.)

Bake, covered, in a 350° oven for about 30 minutes (45 minutes, if refrigerated) or until heated through. To serve, remove skewers and serve each chop with some of the stuffing. Accompany with cranberry sauce, if desired. Makes 4 to 6 servings.

Stick-to-your-ribs Ribs

It's the sauce that makes ribs such a popular and memorable meal. These ribs cook for an hour with a sauce of molasses, catsup, chopped onions, and spices.

4 **pounds spareribs, cut into pieces**
1 **cup water**
1 **tablespoon butter or margarine**
1 **cup** *each* **finely chopped onions and catsup**
2 **tablespoons Worcestershire**
¼ **teaspoon** *each* **salt and liquid hot pepper seasoning**
½ **cup vinegar**
3 **tablespoons molasses**
½ **teaspoon ground ginger**
¼ **teaspoon thyme leaves**
2 **teaspoons dry mustard**
1 **teaspoon paprika**

Place ribs in a single layer in 2 large baking pans. Pour ½ cup of the water into each pan. Bake, covered, in a 350° oven for 1 hour.

Meanwhile, in a wide frying pan over medium heat, melt butter. Add onions and cook until soft. Stir in catsup, Worcestershire, salt, hot pepper seasoning, vinegar, molasses, ginger, thyme, mustard, and paprika; blend well. Bring to a boil; reduce heat and simmer, uncovered, for 10 minutes.

Remove ribs from oven and pour off and discard water and fat; combine ribs in one pan and pour sauce over meat. Return to oven and bake, uncovered, for 1 more hour or until meat is tender when pierced; baste occasionally. Makes about 4 servings.

Sausages with Cabbage & Apples

(Pictured on page 47)

This lavish assortment of sausages, tender-crisp cabbage, and cooked apple slices is delicious with spicy mustard or horseradish.

6 **to 8 pork sausage links**
3 **large Golden Delicious apples, peeled, cored, and each cut into 6 or 8 wedges**
3 **or 4 kielbasa sausages (about 1 lb.** *total***)**
1 **package (5 oz.) miniature smoke-flavored sausage links**
3 **or 4 knackwurst sausages (about ½ lb.** *total***)**
1 **head cabbage (2 to 3 lbs.), cut into 6 or 8 wedges**
   Prepared mustard and horseradish

Pour water into a wide frying pan to a depth of about ¼ inch. Bring to a boil over high heat. Add pork sausage links; cover, reduce heat, and simmer for 10 minutes. Drain and discard liquid. Continue cooking sausages, uncovered, over medium-low heat until partially browned. Add apple wedges and cook until fruit is browned and fork-tender (about 5 minutes). Remove from heat and keep warm.

Fill a 6 to 8-quart kettle half full with water. Bring to a boil over high heat. Add kielbasa, smoke-flavored sausages, and knackwurst; cover and return to a boil. Add cabbage wedges, pushing down into liquid. Bring to a boil again and cook, uncovered, for 2 to 3 minutes. Lift out cabbage and sausages and drain well.

Arrange cabbage, all sausages, and apples in a serving container. Accompany with mustard and horseradish. Makes 6 to 8 servings.

Jam-glazed Baked Ham

Here's a beautiful centerpiece for a party or holiday meal.

1 **cooked butt or shank half ham (6 to 7 lbs.) or 1 canned ham (5 lbs.)**
1 **egg yolk**
¾ **cup apricot-pineapple jam**
   About ¼ cup pecan halves
   Canned pineapple slices
   Canned apricot halves

Place ham, fat side up, in a baking pan and bake, uncovered, in a 325° oven for 45 minutes.

Remove from oven; diagonally slash outer layer of fat. In a small bowl, mix egg yolk and jam. Brush over ham, then stud with nuts.

Return to oven and bake for 45 to 60 more minutes or until glaze is browned. Transfer ham to a serving platter and garnish with pineapple and apricots. Makes 10 to 12 servings.

Chile & Ham Strata Ramekins

Here's a good way to use leftover cooked ham—make it into a dish that's something like a sandwich, something like French toast, and something like a miniature soufflé. The puffy little ramekins are easy to assemble and can be prepared ahead. With a fruit salad, they're just right for brunch, lunch, or a light supper.

- 1 can (4 oz.) whole green chiles
- 1 cup (about 4 oz.) finely chopped cooked ham
- 2 cups (8 oz.) shredded jack or sharp Cheddar cheese
- 8 slices day-old firm white bread
- 6 eggs
- 2 cups milk
- ½ teaspoon *each* chili powder and dry mustard

Remove seeds from chiles, if desired, and finely chop. In a bowl, mix chiles with ham and 1 cup of the cheese. Divide chile mixture evenly into 4 portions and spread over 4 of the bread slices. Top with remaining 4 bread slices. Place each sandwich in a well-greased shallow ramekin (1½ to 2-cup size).

In a large bowl, beat eggs lightly; then beat in milk, chili

SALAMI FROM SCRATCH

For summer picnics, for snacks with crackers and cheese, or as a year-round sandwich meat, you can't beat this delicious homemade salami. It's so popular with *Sunset* readers that many have written us to share their enthusiasm. One reader serves it instead of bacon or sausage for breakfast; another substitutes deer and elk meat for the beef in the recipe.

We offer three variations to choose from: a smoky-tasting version, an herb-flavored one, and a zingy red pepper variation. The only special ingredient you'll need to make the salami is prepared curing salt—a mixture of salt, sugar, spices, and preservatives. You can buy curing salt from some butchers' equipment and supply companies, and from many feed stores.

The nylon net you'll need is sold by the yard in most fabric stores; purchase inexpensive white net with large holes.

Smoky Beef Salami

- 4 pounds ground beef (maximum fat content 25 percent)
- ¼ cup curing salt
- 2 tablespoons liquid smoke
- 1½ teaspoons garlic powder
- 1½ teaspoons pepper or 2 teaspoons whole black peppercorns

In a large bowl, combine beef, curing salt, liquid smoke, garlic powder, and pepper. Mix *thoroughly.* Cover and refrigerate until next day.

Divide mixture into 4 equal portions. Shape each portion into a compact 8-inch-long log and place each on a 12 by 18-inch piece of nylon net. Roll up tightly in net and tie ends with string. Place logs, slightly apart, on a rack in a broiler pan. Bake, uncovered, in a 225° oven for 4 hours.

Remove net and pat rolls well with paper towels. Let cool slightly, then wrap in foil. Refrigerate for up to 3 weeks; for longer storage, freeze for up to 2 months. Makes about 3 pounds salami.

Herb Beef Salami. Follow recipe for Smoky Beef Salami (preceding), omitting liquid smoke; instead use 3 tablespoons **dry red wine.** Reduce garlic powder to 1 teaspoon and omit pepper. Instead, add 2 tablespoons **mustard seeds,** 1 tablespoon *each* **dry basil** and **oregano leaves,** 1 teaspoon **onion powder,** and ⅔ cup grated **Parmesan cheese.**

Spicy Beef Salami. Follow recipe for Smoky Beef Salami (preceding), omitting liquid smoke; instead, use 3 tablespoons **dry white wine.** Reduce garlic powder to 1 teaspoon and omit pepper. Instead, add 2 tablespoons **chili powder,** 2 teaspoons **crushed red pepper,** and 1 teaspoon **ground cumin.**

powder, and mustard. Pour egg mixture evenly over sandwiches. Cover and refrigerate for at least 2 hours or until next day.

Uncover sandwiches and sprinkle with remaining 1 cup cheese. Place ramekins on a baking sheet and bake, uncovered, in a 350° oven for 40 to 45 minutes or until egg mixture is set and sandwiches are puffed in center. Let stand for about 5 minutes before serving. Makes 4 servings.

Leg of Lamb, Rosemary

Distinguished by a rich brown gravy, this succulent leg of lamb is roasted with an unpeeled onion adorned with a sprig of fragrant rosemary.

1 clove garlic, minced or pressed
½ teaspoon ground ginger
¼ teaspoon *each* salt and pepper
1 leg of lamb (about 5 lbs.)
1 large onion, unpeeled
1 sprig (about 6 inches long) rosemary or ¾ teaspoon dry rosemary
1 can (14 oz.) regular-strength beef broth
1 tablespoon *each* cornstarch and water
2 tablespoons *each* catsup and soy sauce
½ teaspoon grated lemon peel

In a small bowl, combine garlic, ginger, salt, and pepper; rub over lamb. Place meat on a rack in a roasting pan. Pierce a hole through onion; pull rosemary through hole (or poke in dry rosemary) and put in pan.

Bake, uncovered, in a 350° oven, basting generously with broth, for 1½ to 2 hours or until a meat thermometer inserted in thickest portion of meat (without touching bone) registers 155° for medium. Transfer to a serving platter and keep warm.

Skim and discard fat from pan juices; pour juices through a wire strainer into a small pan, pressing onion hard. Discard on-

ion. In a small bowl, combine cornstarch and water, and stir into juices with catsup, soy, and lemon peel. Cook, stirring, over medium heat until gravy boils and thickens. Pour into a bowl and pass at the table to spoon over individual servings. Makes 6 to 8 servings.

Fruit & Lamb Curry

Juicy nectarine slices provide a nice contrast in this spicy curry, simmered in apple juice. Serve with condiments and hot cooked rice or bulgur wheat.

2 pounds lean boneless lamb or pork, cut into 1-inch cubes
 Salt and pepper
1 tablespoon salad oil
1 large onion, chopped
2 cloves garlic, minced or pressed
4 teaspoons curry powder
¼ teaspoon ground ginger
2 cups apple juice
1 tablespoon *each* cornstarch and water
4 nectarines, sliced
 Hot cooked rice or bulgur wheat
 Condiments (suggestions follow)

Sprinkle meat with salt and pepper. Heat oil in a 4-quart pan over medium heat; add meat, a portion at a time, and cook until well browned on all sides. Lift out meat and set aside.

Add onion, garlic, curry powder, and ginger to pan; cook until onion is soft. Stir in apple juice, scraping browned particles free from pan.

Return meat to pan. Bring to a boil; cover, reduce heat, and simmer until meat is tender when pierced (about 1 hour). Skim and discard fat. In a small bowl, combine cornstarch and water; add to pan and cook over medium heat, stirring, until sauce thickens. Add nectarines and cook until heated through.

Serve with rice; pass condiments. Makes 6 to 8 servings.

CONDIMENTS. Offer bowls of **coconut chips, Major Grey chutney, salted nuts,** and chopped hard-cooked **eggs.**

Lemon-Mint Lamb Meatballs

Poaching makes these mint-flavored lamb meatballs moist and tender. The pan juices are thickened to make a savory sauce; pour it over the meatballs before serving.

 Meatball Mixture (recipe follows)
2 tablespoons salad oil
⅓ cup finely chopped parsley
1½ cups thinly sliced green onions (including tops)
1 can (14 oz.) regular-strength chicken broth
⅓ cup lemon juice
1 tablespoon *each* cornstarch and water

Prepare Meatball Mixture and shape into 1-inch balls; set aside.

Heat oil in a wide frying pan over medium heat. Add parsley and onions and cook until soft. Pour in broth and lemon juice; bring to a boil. Drop meatballs gently into broth mixture; reduce heat and simmer, uncovered, until meatballs are no longer pink when slashed (about 15 minutes).

With a slotted spoon, transfer meatballs to a serving platter. Skim and discard fat from pan juices. In a small bowl, combine cornstarch and water; add to juices and cook over medium heat, stirring, until sauce thickens. Pour over meat. Makes 6 servings.

MEATBALL MIXTURE. In a large bowl, combine 2 pounds lean **ground lamb, 2 eggs,** ¼ cup **all-purpose flour,** 1 tablespoon crumbled **dry mint,** 1½ teaspoons **salt,** and 1 teaspoon **pepper.** Mix until well blended.

POULTRY

Chicken, turkey, duck & game hens

Chicken & Artichoke Casserole

What could be better than tender poached chicken breasts and artichoke hearts, bathed in a velvety sauce that's accented with sherry and rosemary? Top it all with buttery sautéed mushrooms.

1   **can (about 14 oz.) regular-strength chicken broth**

4   **whole chicken breasts (about 4 lbs. *total*)**

1   **can (14 oz.) artichoke hearts, drained**

6   **tablespoons butter or margarine**

¼   **cup all-purpose flour**

¼   **teaspoon salt**

⅛   **teaspoon pepper**

¾   **cup half-and-half (light cream)**

½   **cup grated Parmesan cheese**

2   **tablespoons dry sherry (optional)**

½   **teaspoon dry rosemary**

¼   **pound mushrooms, sliced**

In a frying pan or Dutch oven, bring chicken broth to a simmer over medium heat. Place chicken breasts in broth in a single layer, cover, and poach until tender when pierced with a fork (about 15 minutes). Lift chicken from broth and let cool.

Reserve ¾ cup of the broth for sauce (save remainder for other uses). When cool enough to handle, remove skin and bones from chicken. Arrange chicken breasts in a shallow 8 by 12-inch baking dish, overlapping them slightly. Distribute artichoke hearts on top of chicken and set aside.

In a pan over medium heat, melt 4 tablespoons of the butter. Blend in flour, salt, and pepper and cook, stirring, until bubbly. Gradually stir in reserved chicken broth and half-and-half. Cook, stirring, until mixture boils and thickens. Add cheese,

sherry, and rosemary; stir until cheese is melted and sauce is smooth. Pour sauce over chicken.

In a frying pan over medium heat, melt remaining 2 tablespoons butter. Add mushrooms and cook until golden; arrange mushrooms down center of casserole. (At this point, you may cool, cover, and refrigerate until next day.)

Bake, uncovered, in a 325° oven for 30 minutes or until heated through. Makes 6 to 8 servings.

Creamy Baked Chicken Breasts

Saving you time, effort, and money—without the least sacrifice of elegance or flavor—this one-step baked chicken deserves all the acclaim it has received.

4 whole chicken breasts (about 4 lbs. *total*), split and skinned
8 slices (about 1 oz. *each*) Swiss cheese
1 can (10¾ oz.) condensed cream of chicken soup
¼ cup dry white wine or water
2 cups seasoned stuffing mix
⅓ cup butter or margarine, melted

Bone chicken breasts, if desired. Arrange chicken in a shallow 7 by 11 or 9 by 13-inch baking dish. Top each piece with a slice of cheese.

In a small bowl, stir together soup and wine; spoon evenly over chicken. Coarsely crush stuffing mix and sprinkle over chicken. Drizzle evenly with melted butter.

Bake, uncovered, in a 350° oven for 50 to 55 minutes or until meat in thickest portion is no longer pink when slashed. Makes 6 to 8 servings.

Chicken & Barley Casserole

This rib-sticking casserole of chicken breasts and barley is perfect for a cold-weather supper. "It's a real family favorite," said several members of the *Sunset* fan club.

4 whole chicken breasts (about 4 lbs. *total*), split, skinned, and boned
Salt, pepper, and paprika
4 or 5 tablespoons butter or margarine
¼ pound mushrooms, sliced
1 cup pearl barley
1 medium-size onion, chopped
1 teaspoon dry basil
2 cans (14 oz. *each*) regular-strength chicken broth
¼ cup dry sherry
1 package (9 oz.) frozen artichoke hearts, thawed
Chopped parsley

Sprinkle chicken with salt, pepper, and paprika. In a wide frying pan over medium heat, melt 2 tablespoons of the butter. Add chicken breasts, a few pieces at a time, and cook until well browned on both sides. Add 1 more tablespoon of the butter if needed. Remove chicken from pan and set aside.

In same pan, melt remaining 2 tablespoons butter. Add mushrooms and cook until soft. Remove mushrooms from pan and set aside. Add barley and onion to pan juices. Cook, stirring, until onion is soft. Add basil and 1 can of the broth. Cover, reduce heat, and simmer, stirring occasionally, for about 30 minutes.

Stir in mushrooms (reserve a few for garnish). Arrange chicken breasts over barley mixture. Pour remaining chicken broth and sherry over all. Cover and simmer gently for 20 minutes. Gently mix in artichoke hearts and continue to simmer until barley is tender (about 10 more minutes).

To serve, skim off and discard any excess fat from top of dish. Sprinkle with parsley and garnish with reserved mushrooms. Makes 6 to 8 servings.

Yogurt Chicken with Oranges

Oranges and yogurt blend their flavors eloquently in this marvelous chicken entrée. Serve it with hot fluffy rice or buttered noodles and a tossed green salad.

4 large oranges
2 tablespoons butter or margarine
2 tablespoons salad oil
4 whole chicken breasts (about 4 lbs. *total*), split, skinned, and boned
1 large onion, chopped
2 cloves garlic, minced or pressed
½ teaspoon *each* ground coriander and ground cumin
1 tablespoon sugar
1 tablespoon cornstarch
½ pint (1 cup) plain yogurt, homemade (page 85) or purchased
Salt and pepper

Remove peel and white membrane from 2 of the oranges. Cut fruit crosswise into thin slices; cover and set aside. Grate 1 of the remaining oranges to make 1 teaspoon peel; ream its juice and that of remaining orange to make ¾ cup juice; set aside.

Heat butter and oil in a wide frying pan over medium heat. Add chicken pieces and cook, turning, until browned on all sides; remove from pan. Add onion and garlic to pan and cook until soft.

Return chicken to pan along with orange juice, orange peel, coriander, cumin, and sugar. Cover and simmer until meat in thickest portion is no longer pink when slashed (about 15 minutes).

Transfer chicken pieces to a serving platter. Mix cornstarch with yogurt and stir into pan juices; cook just until thickened. Season with salt and pepper to taste. Pour sauce over chicken. Garnish with orange slices. Makes 6 to 8 servings.

Chutney Chicken

For an aura of India, bake tender chicken breasts in a fruit-laden sauce. If you like, serve this exuberant entrée on a bed of steamed white rice.

3 whole chicken breasts (about 3 lbs. *total*), split, skinned, and boned, *or* 6 chicken legs with thighs attached
Salt, pepper, and paprika
3 tablespoons butter or margarine
1 medium-size apple, cored and diced
1 teaspoon curry powder
½ teaspoon ground cinnamon
¼ teaspoon *each* thyme leaves and ground ginger
¼ cup Major Grey chutney, chopped
1 can (11 oz.) mandarin oranges
¾ cup seedless grapes

Sprinkle chicken with salt, pepper, and paprika, arrange in a 9 by 13-inch baking dish and dot with half the butter. Broil about 6 inches from heat until browned (10 to 12 minutes).

In a wide frying pan over medium heat, melt remaining butter. Add apple, curry, cinnamon, thyme, ginger, and chutney. Drain liquid from oranges into pan (reserving fruit) and cook until slightly reduced. Pour apple mixture over chicken.

Bake, uncovered, in a 350° oven for 15 minutes. Top with oranges and grapes. Return to oven and bake for 5 to 10 more minutes (15 to 20 more minutes, if using legs) or until juices run clear when meat is slashed. Makes 6 servings.

Baked Chicken Breasts, Mexican-style

Festive vegetable garnishes and a bed of shredded lettuce set a perfect stage for baked chicken with a Mexican accent. Just add warm tortillas with butter, or perhaps some corn muffins, and you have a sensational summer meal.

- 2 eggs
  Green chile salsa *or* taco sauce
- ¼ teaspoon salt
- 1 cup fine dry bread crumbs
- 1 teaspoon *each* chili powder and ground cumin
- ¾ teaspoon garlic salt
- ¼ teaspoon oregano leaves
- 3 whole chicken breasts (about 3 lbs. *total*), split, skinned, and boned
- 4 tablespoons butter or margarine
- 4 to 6 cups shredded iceberg lettuce
  About ½ pint (1 cup) sour cream
- 4 green onions (including tops), thinly sliced
- 12 to 18 cherry tomatoes
- 1 or 2 limes, cut into wedges
- 1 ripe avocado, peeled, pitted, sliced, and sprinkled with lemon juice

In a shallow bowl, beat together eggs, 3 tablespoons of the salsa, and salt.

In another shallow bowl, combine bread crumbs, chili powder, cumin, garlic salt, and oregano. Dip each chicken piece in egg mixture and roll in crumb mixture; then dip in egg mixture and roll in crumb mixture again. Set aside.

Place butter in a shallow baking pan (large enough to hold chicken pieces in a single layer); set pan in an oven while it's preheating to 375°.

When butter has melted, remove pan from oven and add chicken pieces, turning to coat with butter. Place chicken, boned side down, in pan.

Bake, uncovered, in a 375° oven for 35 minutes, or until meat in thickest portion is no longer pink when slashed.

To serve, arrange chicken on a bed of lettuce; garnish with sour cream, onions, tomatoes, lime wedges, and avocado. At the table, pass additional sour cream and salsa. Makes 4 to 6 servings.

Chicken Breasts in Mushroom Sauce

With some advance preparation, you can cook this party-perfect entrée at the table while your guests keep you company. Simply sauté chicken breasts in an electric frying pan with mushrooms and shallots, then simmer very briefly in a sherry-flavored sauce.

- 1 egg
- 2 tablespoons milk
- ⅓ cup all-purpose flour
- 1 teaspoon salt
- ¼ teaspoon *each* paprika and pepper
- 3 whole chicken breasts (about 3 lbs. *total*), split, skinned, and boned
- ½ pound mushrooms, halved
- ¼ cup minced shallots or green onions (white parts only)
- ½ cup dry sherry or dry white wine
- 2 tablespoons lemon juice
- 1 cup regular-strength chicken broth
- 1 tablespoon cornstarch
- 4 tablespoons butter or margarine
  Chopped parsley
  Hot cooked rice or noodles

In a bowl, beat egg lightly with milk. In a bag, combine flour with salt, paprika, and pepper. Dip each chicken piece into egg mixture; drain briefly, then place in bag and shake to coat completely. Arrange chicken on a rack; let stand for about 30 minutes, or loosely cover and refrigerate for up to 6 hours.

In a small bowl, combine mushrooms and shallots; in another bowl, stir together sherry, lemon juice, broth, and cornstarch. (At this point, you may cover and let stand for up to 6 hours.)

To cook at the table, heat an electric frying pan to 325°. Or heat a heavy 10 or 12-inch frying pan over medium-low heat. Add butter and heat until bubbly. Add chicken and cook, turning, until brown (3 to 4 minutes on each side).

Push chicken to edges of pan and add mushrooms and shallots. Cook, stirring, until soft (about 3 minutes). Stir through broth mixture; pour into pan and cook, stirring, until mixture boils and thickens.

Reduce heat to 250° or to low; cover pan and cook until meat in thickest portion is no longer pink when slashed (about 3 minutes). Sprinkle with parsley and serve over rice. Makes 4 to 6 servings.

Chicken Breasts Veronique

(Pictured on page 71)

In French cookery, *veronique* means cooked with grapes, as in this handsome and sophisticated presentation of boned chicken breasts in a tarragon-scented sauce. The combination deserves candlelight and a chilled bottle of wine.

- 4 whole chicken breasts (about 4 lbs. *total*), split, skinned, and boned
  Salt
- 4 tablespoons butter or margarine
- 2 tablespoons orange marmalade
- ½ teaspoon dry tarragon
- 1 cup dry white wine
- 16 medium-size mushrooms, fluted
- ½ pint (1 cup) whipping cream
- 1 teaspoon cornstarch
- 4 teaspoons water
- 1½ cups seedless grapes
  Parsley sprigs

Sprinkle chicken lightly with salt. In a wide frying pan over medium heat, melt 2 tablespoons of the butter. Add chicken breasts and cook, turning, until golden on each side.

Stir in marmalade, tarragon and wine. Cover, reduce heat, and simmer until meat in thickest portion is no longer pink when slashed (about 15 minutes). Transfer chicken to a warm serving dish, reserving juices.

Meanwhile, in a pan over medium heat, melt remaining 2 tablespoons butter. Add mushrooms and cook, stirring, until liquid has evaporated. Set aside.

Add cream to pan juices. Quickly bring to a full rolling boil over medium-high heat. Mix cornstarch and water; stir into sauce. Return sauce to a boil, stirring. Add grapes, return sauce to a boil again, and pour over chicken. Garnish with mushrooms and parsley. Makes 4 to 8 servings.

Chicken Saltimbocca

The Italians know how to say it: chicken "jump-in-the-mouth" (*saltare* for jump and *bocca* for mouth). In its bubbly coating of melted cheese, this entrée will practically leap from the plate straight into your mouth—and melt there once it arrives.

- 2 whole chicken breasts (about 2 lbs. *total*), split, skinned, and boned
  Olive oil or salad oil
- 3 tablespoons butter or margarine
- ¼ cup dry sherry or chicken broth
- ¼ teaspoon sage leaves, crumbled
- 2 thin slices (about 1 oz. *each*) cooked ham
- 4 slices (about 1 oz. *each*) process Swiss cheese
- ½ cup grated Parmesan cheese

Place chicken breasts between 2 sheets of plastic wrap on a cutting board. With a mallet, pound breasts until each is 2½ to 3 times its original size.

Pour just enough oil into a wide frying pan to coat bottom; place over high heat. When oil is hot, ease chicken pieces, without crowding, into pan; cook until edges become white (1 to 1½ minutes). Turn pieces over and cook until meat turns white on both sides and begins browning on second side (1 to 1½ minutes); add small amounts of oil, as needed, to prevent sticking.

Arrange chicken pieces, slightly overlapping, in a shallow 8 by 12-inch baking dish.

Reduce heat to medium-high and add butter to pan; when butter has melted, add sherry and sage, scraping browned bits free. Pour evenly over chicken. (At this point, you may let stand for up to an hour.)

Cut ham and cheese slices into strips; distribute evenly over chicken. Sprinkle with Parmesan cheese. Bake, uncovered, in a 475° oven for about 6 minutes or until cheese is melted and bubbly. Makes 4 servings.

Italian-style Chicken Scallops

Because you first pound the meat to very thin scallops, this crumb-coated chicken crowned with melted mozzarella cheese takes only minutes to cook.

- ½ cup *each* cornflake crumbs, all-purpose flour, and grated Parmesan cheese
- 1 teaspoon Italian herb seasoning *or* ¼ teaspoon *each* dry basil and oregano, thyme, and marjoram leaves
- ¼ teaspoon *each* pepper and ground coriander
- 3 whole chicken breasts (about 3 lbs. *total*), split, skinned, and boned
- 1 egg
- 3 tablespoons milk
- ¼ cup chopped onion
- 2 cloves garlic, minced or pressed
- 3 tablespoons salad oil
- 3 tablespoons butter or margarine
- 6 slices (about 1 oz. *each*) mozzarella cheese

In a pie pan, combine cornflake crumbs, flour, Parmesan cheese, Italian seasoning, pepper, and coriander; set aside.

Place chicken breasts between 2 sheets of plastic wrap on a cutting board. With a mallet, pound breasts until each is about ⅜ inch thick.

In a blender or food processor, whirl egg, milk, onion, and garlic, and pour mixture into a bowl. Dip each chicken piece into egg mixture, then into crumb mixture to coat evenly.

Heat oil and butter in a wide frying pan over medium-high heat. Add 3 pieces of chicken and cook until no longer pink when slashed (about 1½ minutes on each side). As breasts are cooked, drain briefly and arrange on a baking sheet; repeat with remaining chicken.

Top each chicken scallop with a slice of cheese. Broil 6 inches from heat until cheese is melted. Makes 4 to 6 servings.

PLUMP TAMALES:
A SOUTH-OF-THE-BORDER TREAT

Making tamales looks complicated, but it's really not difficult, once you've tried your hand at one or two. Here we show you how tamales go together; the delicious result has prompted much fan mail.

To make this Mexican specialty, you spread a layer of masa dough on dried corn husks, then wrap the husks around a savory filling and steam them. The masa dough is made from masa harina (also called dehydrated masa flour), a coarse flour derived from specially prepared corn. Fillings vary—beef, pork, and chicken are commonly used ingredients. Our tamales are generously filled with chunks of mildly seasoned chicken and topped with a green-taco-sauce-flavored gravy, which you make as mild or as hot as you wish.

Look for dried corn husks in grocery stores that carry Mexican foods; the husks keep indefinitely. Or you can dry your own husks by leaving green ones in a warm, sunny spot until they turn yellow (this can take from 3 to 8 days); then store them in a dry place. You can use fresh corn husks, too, but they're not as pliable and easy to handle as soaked dried husks. Also, since American ears of corn are smaller than Mexican varieties, you'll need to "patch" several together with masa dough to make each tamale.

Serve the tamales with a green salad, sliced tomatoes, and avocado slices or guacamole. Add Chilled Citrus Sangría (page 9) and a fruity dessert, and you'll have a festive Mexican meal.

Chicken Tamales

Soaked dried corn husks (directions follow)
Chicken Filling & Chicken Broth (recipe follows)
Tamale Masa Dough (recipe follows)
1 tablespoon cornstarch blended with 1 tablespoon water
2 or 3 tablespoons bottled green taco sauce
Sour cream

Ahead of time, soak dried corn husks. Prepare Chicken Filling & Chicken Broth and Tamale Masa Dough.

For each of the 12 tamales, select 2 wide (or 3 smaller) soaked dried corn husks. Placing husks side by side, arrange in a rectangle at least 10 inches wide, with tip of one positioned by base of next. Where husks overlap, spread a little masa to seal (step 1); also use masa to mend tears.

Place ⅓ cup of the masa in center of husks and spread to make a 5 by 7-inch rectangle; make one edge of masa flush with one edge of husks (step 2).

Divide chicken filling into 12 equal portions and spoon a portion in center of each masa rectangle. Enclose filling in masa-coated section, matching masa at edges; then continue wrapping uncoated portion of husk around outside of tamale (step 3).

Tear another husk into thin strips and use strips to tie ends of tamale securely (step 4). Repeat to make each tamale.

Arrange tamales loosely in a steamer or on a rack in a large pan over at least 1 inch of water, stacking at right angles so steam can circulate. Cover and cook over boiling water (adding hot water as needed) until masa is firm and peels readily from corn husks (about 1 hour and 20 minutes).

Meanwhile, stir through cornstarch mixture and pour into a small pan. Add remaining 1¼ cups chicken broth (reserved from chicken filling). Bring to a boil over high heat, stirring. Add green taco sauce to taste.

Serve tamales hot; peel back husk and spoon some of the taco sauce gravy onto each tamale. Accompany with sour cream. Makes 6 servings.

Soaked dried corn husks. You'll need about 3 ounces **dried corn husks** (you may have to purchase in a larger quantity; seal remaining husks in a plastic bag). Gently separate husks, discarding silks and any other particles. Place husks in a large pan or bowl and cover with warm **water.** Let soak for at least 2 hours or until next day; keep damp until used, then pat each husk with a towel to dry slightly.

Chicken Filling & Chicken Broth. Use 2 broiler-fryer **chickens** (about 3 lbs. *each*), cut into pieces (reserve giblets for other uses). *Or* use 6 chicken legs with thighs attached and 2 whole large chicken breasts (about 4 lbs. chicken *total*). Place all chicken but breasts in a kettle. Add 1 large **onion,** sliced, 3 whole cloves **garlic,** and 1 can (about 14 oz.) regular-strength **chicken broth.** Bring to a boil over high heat; cover, reduce heat, and simmer for 25 minutes. Cut each breast in half and add to pan; continue to simmer, covered, until breasts are no longer pink in thickest portion (about 20 more minutes).

Lift out chicken (reserving broth) and let cool slightly, then remove and discard skin and bones. Cut each breast section into 3 pieces; cut any other large pieces of chicken into portions about the size of breast meat. If made ahead, cover and refrigerate.

Pour chicken broth through a strainer and reserve; discard vegetables. Measure broth; add **water** to make 3 cups (or boil to reduce to this amount). Cover and refrigerate.

Heat 2 tablespoons **salad oil** in a wide frying pan over medium heat. Add 1 large **onion,** finely chopped, and cook until soft. Add 1 large **green pepper,** seeded and slivered, and 1 tablespoon **chili powder.** Cook, stirring, just until pepper is slightly limp. Remove from heat and stir in chicken; season to taste with **salt** and **pepper.**

Tamale Masa Dough. In large bowl of an electric mixer, beat 1 cup (½ lb.) **butter** or margarine, softened, until fluffy; blend in 3 cups **masa harina** (dehydrated masa flour), 1 teaspoon **salt,** and 1¾ cups of the **chicken broth** (reserved from chicken filling). Beat until dough holds together well. If made ahead, cover and refrigerate; bring to room temperature before using. Makes about 4½ cups.

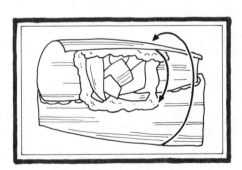

1   Place 2 wide husks side by side, with tip of one positioned by base of next; use masa dough to seal.

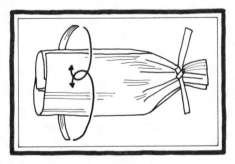

2   Spread a 5 by 7-inch rectangle of masa dough in center of husks, making dough flush with one edge.

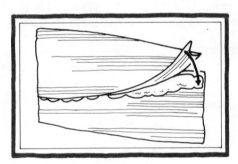

3   Bring edges of masa dough together over filling; then wrap uncoated portion of husk around tamale.

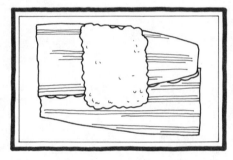

4   Tear another husk into thin strips; use strips to close ends of tamale, tying securely.

Mexican-style Chicken Kiev

Cumin, chili powder, and spicy green chiles lend a south-of-the-border flavor to this make-ahead variation of Chicken Kiev. Make the zesty tomato sauce as mild or as potent as you like.

½ cup fine dry bread crumbs

¼ cup grated Parmesan cheese

1 teaspoon chili powder

½ teaspoon garlic salt

¼ teaspoon *each* ground cumin and pepper

4 whole chicken breasts (about 4 lbs. *total*), split, skinned, and boned

1 large can (7 oz.) whole green chiles, slit lengthwise, seeded, and cut into a total of 8 equal pieces

4 ounces jack cheese, cut into 8 strips, *each* ½ inch thick and 1½ inches long

6 tablespoons butter or margarine, melted

Spicy Tomato Sauce (recipe follows)

In a pie pan, combine bread crumbs, Parmesan cheese, chili powder, garlic salt, cumin, and pepper; set aside.

Place chicken breasts between 2 sheets of plastic wrap on a cutting board. With a mallet, pound breasts until each is about ¼ inch thick.

Lay a piece of chile and a strip of jack cheese across width of each breast. Fold in sides so they overlap and seal in filling; fold ends over top. Dip each chicken bundle in melted butter and drain briefly; then roll in crumb mixture to coat evenly.

Place bundles seam side down, without touching, in a 9 by 13-inch baking dish. Drizzle with any remaining butter. Cover and refrigerate for at least 4 hours or until next day.

Bake, uncovered, in a 400° oven for 20 minutes or until chicken is no longer pink when gently slashed (so filling doesn't ooze out).

Meanwhile, prepare Spicy Tomato Sauce and pour into a serving bowl.

To serve, transfer chicken to a serving plate; pass sauce at the table to spoon over individual portions. Makes 6 to 8 servings.

SPICY TOMATO SAUCE. In a small pan, heat 1 can (15 oz.) **tomato sauce,** ½ teaspoon **ground cumin,** and ⅓ cup sliced **green onions** (including some tops) until hot. Season to taste with **salt, pepper,** and **liquid hot pepper seasoning.**

Easy Baked Chicken Kiev

This baked chicken Kiev is lower in calories and easier to prepare than the deep-fried version. An added advantage: since it must be chilled for several hours before baking, it can be assembled ahead of time and just popped into the oven 20 minutes before serving.

½ cup *each* fine dry bread crumbs and grated Parmesan cheese

1½ teaspoons oregano leaves

½ teaspoon garlic salt

¼ teaspoon pepper

4 tablespoons butter or margarine, softened

1 tablespoon chopped parsley

4 whole chicken breasts (about 4 lbs. *total*), split, skinned, and boned

4 ounces jack cheese, cut into 8 strips, *each* ½ inch thick and 1½ inches long

5 tablespoons butter or margarine, melted

In a pie pan, combine bread crumbs, Parmesan cheese, 1 teaspoon of the oregano, garlic salt, and pepper; set aside.

In a small bowl, stir together the softened butter, parsley, and remaining ½ teaspoon oregano; set aside.

Place chicken breasts between 2 sheets of plastic wrap on a cutting board. With a mallet,

pound breasts until each is about ¼ inch thick.

Spread each chicken piece with herb-butter mixture, and lay a strip of jack cheese across the width of each breast. Fold in sides so they overlap and seal in filling; fold ends over top. Dip each chicken bundle in melted butter and drain briefly; then roll in crumb mixture to coat evenly.

Place bundles seam side down, without touching, in a 9 by 13-inch baking dish. Drizzle with any remaining butter. Cover and refrigerate for at least 4 hours or until next day.

Bake, uncovered, in a 400° oven for 20 minutes or until chicken is no longer pink when gently slashed (so filling doesn't ooze out). Makes 6 to 8 servings.

Crab-stuffed Chicken Breasts

What does the crusty crab have in common with the feisty and fat little hen? Both provide us with succulent supper meat—light, white, and tender. Here they appear in combination.

4 whole chicken breasts (about 4 lbs. *total*), split, skinned, and boned

4 tablespoons butter or margarine

½ cup thinly sliced green onions (including tops)

¼ pound mushrooms, thinly sliced

3 tablespoons all-purpose flour

¼ teaspoon thyme leaves

½ cup *each* regular-strength chicken broth, milk, and dry white wine
Salt and pepper

½ pound cooked fresh or canned crabmeat

⅓ cup *each* finely chopped parsley and fine dry bread crumbs

1 cup (4 oz.) shredded Swiss cheese

Place chicken breasts between 2 sheets of plastic wrap on a cutting board. With a mallet, pound breasts until each is about ¼ inch thick; set aside.

In a wide frying pan over medium heat, melt butter. Add onions and mushrooms and cook until soft. Mix in flour and thyme and cook, stirring, until bubbly. Gradually pour in broth, milk, and wine and continue cooking and stirring until sauce boils and thickens. Season to taste with salt and pepper.

In a small bowl, stir together crab, parsley, bread crumbs, and ¼ cup of the sauce. Divide mixture and spoon down center of each chicken breast. Fold in sides so they overlap and seal in filling; fold ends over top.

Place bundles, seam side down, in a lightly greased 9 by 13-inch baking dish. Spoon remaining sauce over chicken and sprinkle with cheese. (At this point, you may cool, cover, and refrigerate until next day.)

Bake, covered, in a 400° oven for about 40 minutes (50 minutes, if refrigerated) or until chicken is no longer pink when slashed. Makes 6 to 8 servings.

Chicken in Lemon Cream

The lemon essence doesn't hit you hard in the taste buds. Instead, it contributes subtly and delectably to the cream sauce that cloaks this favorite rendition of chicken breasts. Buttered carrots make a colorful side dish.

- 3 **whole chicken breasts (about 3 lbs. *total*), split, skinned, and boned**
  Salt and pepper
  All-purpose flour
- 2 **tablespoons salad oil**
- 2 **tablespoons butter or margarine**
- 1 **clove garlic, minced or pressed**
- 1½ **tablespoons thinly sliced green onion (including top)**
- 1½ **tablespoons lemon juice**
- ½ **cup dry white wine**
- 1½ **teaspoons all-purpose flour**
- 2 **teaspoons sugar**
- ¼ **teaspoon dry tarragon**
- ½ **cup sour cream**

Place chicken breasts between 2 sheets of plastic wrap on a cutting board. With a mallet, pound breasts until each is ¼ inch thick. Sprinkle with salt and pepper and dust with flour, shaking off excess.

Heat oil and butter in a wide frying pan over medium-high heat. Add 3 pieces of chicken; cook, turning, until chicken is no longer pink when slashed (about 3 minutes on each side). Remove from pan and keep warm on a serving platter. Repeat with remaining pieces.

To pan juices, add garlic, onion, lemon juice, and wine. Cook, scraping browned bits free, until mixture boils; remove from heat. Combine the 1½ teaspoons flour, sugar, and tarragon with sour cream; stir into wine mixture. Cook, stirring, until sauce boils gently. Pour over chicken. Makes 4 to 6 servings.

Slivered Chicken with Walnuts

If you don't have walnuts, use cashews or peanuts instead. Any one of the three will taste rich and blend elegantly with the chicken in this wonderful stir-fry dish for two.

- **Cooking Sauce (recipe follows)**
- 1 **whole chicken breast (about 1 lb.), split, skinned, and boned**
- 1 **tablespoon soy sauce**
- 1 **teaspoon cornstarch**
- 3 **tablespoons salad oil**
- ½ **cup walnut halves**
- 1 **medium-size green pepper, seeded and cut into 1-inch squares**
- ½ **teaspoon finely minced fresh ginger**

Prepare Cooking Sauce and set aside.

Cut chicken into matchstick pieces and mix with soy and cornstarch; set aside.

Heat a wok or wide frying pan over medium-high heat. When wok is hot, add oil; when oil is hot, add walnuts and stir-fry until browned (about 1 minute). Remove with a slotted spoon and set aside. Add chicken to oil and stir-fry until chicken is opaque (about 3 minutes); remove from wok and set aside.

Add green pepper and ginger to wok; stir-fry until pepper is tender-crisp (about 1 minute). Return chicken to pan. Stir Cooking Sauce; add to wok and cook, stirring, until sauce bubbles and thickens. Stir in walnuts. Makes 2 servings.

COOKING SAUCE. In a small bowl, stir together ½ teaspoon **cornstarch**, a dash of **liquid hot pepper seasoning**, ¾ teaspoon *each* **sugar** and **wine vinegar**, 1 teaspoon **dry sherry** or water, and 1 tablespoon **soy sauce**.

Chicken with Basil

Though most familiar to us in Italian cooking, basil is also widely used in the cuisine of Thailand. For *gai koprow* (chicken with basil), Thai cooks combine the herb with mint and hot chiles.

- 3 **to 4 tablespoons finely chopped canned green chiles, seeded**
- 2 **tablespoons soy sauce**
- 1 **teaspoon *each* sugar and vinegar**
- ½ **cup chopped fresh basil leaves or 2 tablespoons dry basil**
- 1 **teaspoon chopped fresh mint leaves or ¼ teaspoon dry mint**
- ½ **teaspoon cornstarch**
- 3 **tablespoons salad oil**
- 2 **whole chicken breasts (about 2 lbs. *total*), split, skinned, boned, and cut into strips ¼ inch thick and 2 inches long**
- 1 **clove garlic, minced or pressed**
- 1 **large onion, halved and cut into ¼-inch slices**

(Continued on next page)

In a small bowl, mix chiles, soy, sugar, vinegar, basil, mint, and cornstarch; set aside.

Heat a wok or wide frying pan over high heat. When wok is hot, add 2 tablespoons of the oil. When oil is hot, add chicken and garlic; cook, stirring constantly, until meat is opaque (about 3 minutes); remove from wok and set aside.

Heat remaining 1 tablespoon oil in wok, add onion and cook, stirring, for 1 minute. Stir chile mixture and pour over onion. Return chicken and juices to wok; cook, stirring, until sauce thickens slightly. Makes 3 or 4 servings.

Chinese Chicken & Egg Buns

One of the more delectable delicacies in San Francisco's Chinatown is chicken-and-egg-filled buns known as *guy bow*. They're big and hearty—one or two will be ample for lunch.

One reader says, ''These little gems are worth all the time they take to make.''

2 **loaves (1 lb. *each*) frozen bread dough**
   Salad oil
6 **small dried Oriental mushrooms (about ½ oz. *total*)**
   Cooking Sauce (recipe follows)
2 **whole chicken breasts (about 2 lbs. *total*), split, skinned, boned, and cut into bite-size pieces**
2 **tablespoons soy sauce**
2 **cloves garlic, minced or pressed**
2 **teaspoons minced fresh ginger**
2 **tablespoons salad oil**
2 **stalks celery, thinly sliced**
3 **green onions (including tops), sliced into 2-inch lengths**
1 **can (about 8½ oz.) sliced bamboo shoots, drained**
4 **hard-cooked eggs, quartered**
   Melted butter

Rub surfaces of frozen dough with salad oil and cover with plastic wrap; thaw just until pliable (1 to 2 hours at room temperature).

Rinse mushrooms and soak in hot water to cover until soft and pliable (about 20 minutes). Cut off and discard tough stems; then cut mushrooms into thin strips and set aside.

Prepare Cooking Sauce and set aside. Combine chicken, soy, garlic, and ginger.

Heat a wok or wide frying pan over medium-high heat. When wok is hot, add the 2 tablespoons oil. When oil is hot, add chicken and stir-fry until chicken is opaque (about 3 minutes).

Add celery and stir-fry for 1 minute. Stir in mushroom strips, onions, and bamboo shoots. Stir Cooking Sauce; add to wok and cook, stirring, until sauce bubbles and thickens. Let cool.

With a lightly floured knife, cut each thawed loaf of dough into 4 equal pieces. Roll each piece into a ball. On a lightly floured board, roll each ball into a 7-inch circle. Place 2 egg quarters in center of each dough circle; top with ½ cup of the chicken mixture.

Gather edges of dough up around filling, being careful not to stretch dough. Pleat in excess dough and tightly pinch edges together to seal. Place buns, pinched side down, about 2 inches apart on a lightly greased baking sheet. Cover lightly and let rise in a warm place until puffy (30 to 45 minutes).

Brush tops of buns with melted butter. Bake in a 350° oven for 30 to 35 minutes or until browned. Serve warm. If made ahead, cool buns thoroughly on racks, cover, and refrigerate; or wrap airtight and freeze.

To reheat, bake, uncovered, in a 350° oven until heated through (about 20 minutes, if refrigerated; 35 minutes, if frozen). Makes 8 buns.

COOKING SAUCE. In a small bowl, stir together 1 tablespoon cornstarch, ½ teaspoon **sugar,** ¼ teaspoon **salt,** 2 tablespoons *each* **soy sauce** and **dry sherry,** and ⅓ cup **water.**

Cashew Chicken

Many versions of this Oriental specialty vie for popularity, but this vegetable-laden one is our winner. Serve it with hot fluffy rice and fresh fruit of the season.

1 **teaspoon cornstarch**
½ **cup regular-strength chicken broth**
1 **whole chicken breast (about 1 lb.), split, skinned, and boned**
1 **tablespoon *each* cornstarch and soy sauce**
4 **tablespoons salad oil *or* 3 tablespoons salad oil and 1 tablespoon sesame oil**
1 **stalk celery, thinly sliced**
¼ **pound green beans, sliced diagonally into ½-inch pieces**
1 **large carrot, sliced diagonally into ¼-inch pieces**
1 **small onion, halved and cut into ¼-inch slices**
1 **clove garlic, minced or pressed**
2 **tablespoons water**
⅓ **cup roasted cashews**
   Fresh coriander (cilantro) sprigs (optional)

In a small bowl, combine the 1 teaspoon cornstarch with broth; set aside.

Cut chicken into matchstick pieces and place in another small bowl. Add the 1 tablespoon cornstarch and soy; mix well and set aside.

Heat a wok or wide frying pan over medium-high heat. When wok is hot, add 2 tablespoons of the oil. When oil is hot, add chicken and stir-fry until chicken is opaque (about 3 minutes); remove from wok and set aside.

Add remaining 2 tablespoons oil to pan. When oil is hot, add celery, beans, carrot, onion, and garlic; stir-fry for 1 minute. Add water; cover and cook until vegetables are just tender-crisp (about 3 minutes).

Return chicken to pan. Stir through chicken broth mixture once; add to wok and cook, stirring, until sauce bubbles and thickens. Stir in most of the cashews, reserving some for garnish.

Turn out into a serving dish and garnish with remaining nuts and coriander sprigs, if desired. Makes 2 servings.

Yorkshire Chicken

This unusual chicken dish is blanketed with Yorkshire pudding.

1¼ cups all-purpose flour
⅛ teaspoon pepper
1½ teaspoons salt
4 chicken legs with thighs attached (about 2 lbs. *total*)
2 tablespoons salad oil
2 tablespoons butter or margarine
3 eggs
1½ cups milk
1 teaspoon *each* baking powder and ground sage

In a bag, combine ¼ cup of the flour with pepper and ½ teaspoon of the salt. Place chicken, 2 pieces at a time, in bag and shake to coat completely.

Heat oil and butter in a wide frying pan over medium heat; add chicken and cook, turning, until browned on all sides. Transfer chicken and drippings to a 9 by 13-inch baking dish. Tilt dish to distribute drippings evenly; then place in a 350° oven to heat.

In a blender or food processor, whirl eggs; blend in milk. Add the remaining 1 cup flour, remaining 1 teaspoon salt, baking powder, and sage; whirl until smooth. Remove baking dish from oven and pour egg mixture evenly over chicken. Return to oven and bake, uncovered, for 1 hour or until puffy and browned. Makes 4 servings.

CRUNCHY CRUST FOR OVEN-FRYING

Make your own seasoned coating mix for easy and nutritious oven-frying. The mix is simple to prepare, keeps in the refrigerator for several months, and—unlike commercial mixes—contains no flour or sugar.

Seasoned Coating Mix

⅔ cup yellow cornmeal
½ cup grated Parmesan cheese
⅓ cup *each* sesame seeds and toasted wheat germ
4 teaspoons *each* garlic powder and parsley flakes
1 tablespoon thyme leaves
2 teaspoons sage leaves
1 teaspoon *each* salt and pepper

In a large plastic bag, combine cornmeal, cheese, sesame seeds, wheat germ, garlic powder, parsley, thyme, sage, salt, and pepper. Shake bag to mix ingredients; close tightly and store in the refrigerator. Makes about 2 cups.

Crunchy Chicken. Place 2½ tablespoons **salad oil** and 2½ tablespoons **butter** or margarine in a 10 by 15-inch rimmed baking sheet. Set pan in a 400° oven just until

butter is melted. Measure 1 cup of the coating mixture into a pie pan. In a shallow dish, beat together 2 **eggs** and 1 tablespoon **milk** until blended.

Cut 1 **broiler-fryer chicken** (3 to 3½ lbs.) into pieces; rinse and pat dry. Dip each piece in egg mixture and drain briefly; then dip in coating mix, turning to coat all sides. Arrange chicken on baking sheet and turn to coat with butter mixture.

Bake in a 400° oven, turning pieces once, for 1 hour or until meat near thighbone is no longer pink when slashed. Makes about 4 servings.

Crunchy Fish. Follow recipe for Crunchy Chicken, but instead of chicken, use 1½ pounds **boneless fish fillets** (such as red snapper, sole, halibut, or lingcod), cut into serving-size pieces. Bake in a 500° oven, turning pieces once, for 7 to 10 minutes or until fish flakes readily when prodded in thickest portion with a fork. Makes about 4 servings.

Crunchy Pork Chops. Follow recipe for Crunchy Chicken, but instead of chicken, use 2 pounds **shoulder pork chops** (about ¾ inch thick). Bake in a 400° oven, turning pieces once, for 30 minutes or until meat near bone is no longer pink when slashed. Makes about 4 servings.

Indian Sweet & Sour Chicken

Creamy yogurt served alongside is a refreshing contrast to the spicy sauce in this Indian-style dish. Lemon wedges and sprigs of fresh coriander make a colorful garnish.

- 6 chicken legs with thighs attached (about 3 lbs. *total*)
- ⅓ to ½ cup all-purpose flour
- 4 tablespoons salad oil
- 2 medium-size onions, thinly sliced
- 3 large cloves garlic, minced or pressed
  About 2 tablespoons sugar
- 2 tablespoons finely chopped fresh ginger
- 1 tablespoon *each* paprika and turmeric
- 1 teaspoon ground coriander
- ¼ teaspoon *each* ground cardamom, black pepper, and ground red pepper (cayenne)
- ⅓ cup red wine vinegar
- 1 can (about 14 oz.) regular-strength chicken broth
  Salt
- 2 tablespoons toasted sesame seeds
  Lemon wedges
  Fresh coriander (cilantro) sprigs
  Hot cooked rice
  Plain yogurt, homemade (page 85) or purchased

Dredge chicken pieces in flour. Heat 3 tablespoons of the oil in a wide frying pan over medium-high heat. Add chicken and cook, turning, until golden brown on all sides; remove with a slotted spoon and set aside.

To pan drippings, add remaining 1 tablespoon oil, onions, and garlic; reduce heat to medium and cook, stirring, until onions are golden. Stir in 2 tablespoons of the sugar, ginger, paprika, turmeric, coriander, cardamom, black pepper, and red pepper. Cook, stirring, for 1 minute; stir in vinegar and chicken broth.

Add chicken; cover, reduce heat, and simmer until meat near thighbone is no longer pink when slashed (about 30 minutes).

Remove chicken and arrange on a rimmed serving platter. Skim off and discard fat from sauce. Season sauce with salt to taste and stir in additional sugar, if desired. Pour sauce over chicken and sprinkle with sesame seeds.

Garnish with lemon wedges and coriander sprigs. Accompany with rice and yogurt. Makes 6 servings.

Crusty Oven-baked Chicken

This delicious soy-marinated oven-fried chicken has stirred up a flurry of fan mail. The seasoned crumb and sesame seed coating bakes to a wonderful crispness. Offer golden French fries, beer or white wine, and whole fresh fruit to round out the meal.

- ½ cup soy sauce
- 2 tablespoons salad oil
- 1 clove garlic, minced or pressed
- 1 broiler-fryer chicken (3 to 3½ lbs.), cut into pieces
- ½ cup *each* regular wheat germ and fine dry bread crumbs
- 2 tablespoons *each* sesame seeds and chopped parsley
- ½ teaspoon *each* pepper and paprika
  Parsley sprigs (optional)

In a bowl, combine soy, oil, and garlic. Arrange chicken pieces in a single layer in a shallow dish or pan. Pour soy mixture over chicken and turn to coat all sides. Let stand for about 10 minutes, turning pieces over after 5 minutes.

Meanwhile, combine wheat germ, bread crumbs, sesame seeds, parsley, pepper, and paprika in a pie pan.

Lift chicken pieces from marinade, drain briefly and turn in wheat germ mixture to coat all sides. Shake off excess crumbs.

Arrange chicken pieces on a well-greased rimmed baking sheet.

Bake, uncovered, in a 350° oven for about 1 hour or until meat near thighbone is no longer pink when slashed. Transfer to a serving platter and garnish with parsley, if desired. Makes about 4 servings.

Baked Chicken with Garlic Spaghetti

Herbs, marinara sauce, and a bold boost of garlic lend distinction to this easy chicken-with-pasta entrée. High on the popular poultry poll, this unusual pairing has won the hearts of many.

- 1 broiler-fryer chicken (3 to 3½ lbs.), cut into pieces
  Salt and pepper
- ½ teaspoon *each* dry rosemary and thyme leaves
- 3 cups Fresh Marinara Sauce (page 104) or 3 cans (about 8 oz. *each*) marinara sauce
- 12 ounces spaghetti
- ⅓ cup butter or margarine
- 3 cloves garlic, minced or pressed
- ½ teaspoon *each* oregano leaves and onion powder
  Grated Parmesan cheese

Sprinkle chicken with salt, pepper, rosemary, and thyme. Place pieces, skin side down, in a greased baking pan.

Bake, uncovered, in a 375° oven for about 20 minutes. Baste with some of the marinara sauce and bake for 10 more minutes. Turn pieces over and baste with more sauce. Bake, basting with sauce several times, for about 25 more minutes or until meat near thighbone is no longer pink when slashed.

Meanwhile, cook spaghetti according to package directions; drain well.

In a wide frying pan over medium heat, melt butter. Add garlic and cook, stirring, until light golden. Add oregano, onion powder, and cooked spaghetti; stir well to coat.

Turn spaghetti mixture onto a rimmed serving platter; arrange chicken pieces on top. Heat remaining marinara sauce and pass at the table. Pass Parmesan cheese to spoon over each serving. Makes about 4 servings.

Parmesan Yogurt Chicken

Here's a popular chicken entrée with a flavor all its own. Yogurt and seasonings keep the meat moist and tasty during baking; a sprinkling of Parmesan cheese and a few minutes under the broiler create a tempting golden crust.

- 1 **broiler-fryer chicken (3 to 3½ lbs.), cut into pieces**
- 2 **tablespoons lemon juice**
  Salt and pepper
- ½ **cup plain yogurt, homemade (page 85) or purchased**
- ¼ **cup mayonnaise**
- 1 **tablespoon** *each* **Dijon mustard and Worcestershire**
- ½ **teaspoon ground thyme**
- ¼ **teaspoon ground red pepper (cayenne)**
- ¼ **cup thinly sliced green onions (including tops)**
- ½ **cup grated Parmesan cheese**

Arrange chicken pieces, skin side up, in a greased baking pan. Drizzle with lemon juice and sprinkle with salt and black pepper.

In a small bowl, mix yogurt, mayonnaise, mustard, Worcestershire, thyme, red pepper, and onions. Spread mixture evenly over chicken. Bake, uncovered, in a 350° oven for 50 minutes or until meat near thighbone is no longer pink when slashed.

Drain off pan juices. Sprinkle chicken evenly with cheese. Broil about 6 inches from heat until cheese is lightly browned (about 3 minutes). Makes about 4 servings.

Roast Chicken with Herbs

In France, they call it *poulet rôti aux herbes*—but it's a treat in any language. Serve it hot, or make it ahead and enjoy it cold.

- 1 **broiler-fryer chicken (3 to 3½ lbs.)**
- 3 **cloves garlic**
- 2 **bay leaves**
- 3 **tablespoons butter or margarine, melted**
- ¾ **teaspoon salt**
- ½ **teaspoon pepper**
- ¼ **teaspoon** *each* **thyme, marjoram, and oregano leaves; ground sage; and dry basil**

Remove giblets and reserve for other uses. Rinse chicken and pat dry. Split 1 clove of garlic and rub skin of chicken with cut sides of garlic. Place garlic cloves (including cut clove) and bay leaves inside chicken cavity.

In a small bowl, stir together butter, salt, pepper, thyme, marjoram, oregano, sage, and basil. Put about 1 tablespoon of the mixture into cavity of chicken. Tie legs together. Generously brush chicken with remaining butter mixture.

Place chicken, breast side down, on a rack in a shallow baking pan. Bake, uncovered, in a 425° oven for 45 minutes. Turn chicken over and continue baking, basting occasionally with any remaining butter mixture or pan drippings, for 40 to 45 more minutes or until meat near thighbone is no longer pink when slashed.

If made ahead, cool, cover, and refrigerate until next day. Makes about 4 servings.

Mexican Chicken Lasagne

For a new twist on lasagne, try this version using Mexican seasonings and chicken or turkey. A good choice for feeding a crowd, it can be made ahead and is a great way to use leftover poultry.

- 2 **tablespoons salad oil**
- 1 **large onion, chopped**
- 2 **cloves garlic, minced or pressed**
- 1 **red or green bell pepper, seeded and chopped**
- 2 **cans (10¾ oz.** *each***) condensed tomato soup**
- 1 **can (10 oz.) enchilada sauce (mild to hot, depending on your taste)**
- 1½ **teaspoons salt**
- ½ **teaspoon pepper**
- 2 **tablespoons chili powder**
- 1 **teaspoon ground cumin**
  Cheese Filling (recipe follows)
- 1 **package (10 oz.) lasagne, cooked according to package directions and drained**
- 4 **cups cooked chicken or turkey, cut into bite-size pieces**
- 6 **ounces** *each* **sliced sharp Cheddar cheese and sliced jack cheese**

Heat oil in a wide frying pan over medium heat. Add onion, garlic, and red pepper; cook, stirring, until onion is soft. Stir in soup, enchilada sauce, salt, pepper, chili powder, and cumin. Reduce heat and simmer, uncovered, until thickened (about 10 minutes); stir often.

Prepare Cheese Filling.

Grease a 9 by 13-inch baking dish and spread with a thin layer of sauce. Arrange half the lasagne noodles in an even layer over sauce. Spread half the Cheese Filling over noodles and top with half the remaining sauce. Arrange half the chicken pieces over sauce and top with half the sliced cheeses.

Repeat layering, ending with cheese slices. (At this point, you may cool, cover, and refrigerate until next day.)

(Continued on page 67)

Bake, covered, in a 375° oven for 35 minutes (50 minutes, if refrigerated) or until bubbly. Let stand, uncovered, for about 5 minutes before cutting into squares. Makes 10 to 12 servings.

CHEESE FILLING. In a bowl, stir together 1 pint (2 cups) **small curd cottage cheese,** 2 **eggs,** ⅓ cup chopped **parsley,** and 3 to 4 tablespoons diced canned **green chiles.**

Chicken & Vegetable Crêpes

Mingle chicken, artichokes, and mushrooms in a cream sauce; then nestle the savory filling inside a rolled-up crêpe to make one of the most succulent lunch or supper dishes you'll ever taste.

5   tablespoons butter or margarine
1   small onion, chopped
¼   pound mushrooms, sliced
3   tablespoons all-purpose flour
⅔   cup regular-strength chicken broth
½   cup half-and-half (light cream) or milk
3   cups cooked chicken, turkey, or ham, cut into bite-size pieces
⅓   cup grated Parmesan cheese
½   teaspoon *each* dry rosemary and salt
1   package (9 oz.) frozen artichoke hearts (thawed, drained, and cut into thirds), *or* 1 package (10 oz.) frozen peas (thawed), *or* 12 to 16 cooked asparagus spears
12 to 16 Basic Crêpes (page 117), at room temperature
¾   cup shredded Swiss cheese

In a wide frying pan over medium heat, melt 2 tablespoons of the butter. Add onion and mushrooms and cook until onion is soft. Add remaining 3 tablespoons butter and flour and cook, stirring, until bubbly. Gradually pour in broth and cream and continue cooking and stirring until sauce boils and thickens.

Remove from heat and stir in chicken, Parmesan cheese, rosemary, salt, and artichokes or peas (do not add asparagus at this point); let cool slightly.

Spoon filling down center of each crêpe. If asparagus is used, lay an asparagus spear over filling in each crêpe. Roll to enclose. Arrange crêpes, seam side down, in a shallow casserole. (At this point, you may cool, cover, and refrigerate until next day. To freeze, place crêpes, seam side down, on a greased baking sheet and freeze until firm; then package airtight and return to freezer. Use within 2 weeks.)

Bake, covered, in a 375° oven for 20 minutes (30 minutes, if refrigerated; 35 to 40 minutes, if frozen) or until heated through. Uncover and sprinkle with Swiss cheese. Bake, uncovered, for 5 more minutes or until cheese is melted. Makes 6 to 8 servings.

Chicken-Cream Enchiladas

One of the most delectable and thrifty ways to enjoy chicken is inside the soft baked wrapping of an enchilada.

2   tablespoons butter or margarine
2   large onions, thinly sliced
2   cups diced cooked chicken
½   cup chopped pimentos *or* roasted red bell pepper
2   small packages (3 oz. *each*) cream cheese, diced
    Salt
    Salad oil or solid shortening
12 corn tortillas
⅔   cup whipping cream
2   cups (8 oz.) shredded jack cheese
    Garnishes: radishes, pitted ripe olives, fresh coriander (cilantro)
    Lime wedges

In a wide frying pan over medium heat, melt butter. Add onions and cook, stirring occasionally, until soft and just beginning to brown (about 20 minutes). Remove from heat and add chicken, pimentos, and cream cheese. With 2 forks, mix lightly until blended. Season to taste with salt; set aside.

Heat oil (about ⅛ inch deep) in a small frying pan over medium heat. When oil is hot, dip each tortilla into oil for *a few seconds* just until tortilla begins to blister and becomes limp. *Do not fry until firm or crisp.* Remove with tongs, drain briefly, and stack.

Spoon about ⅓ cup of the chicken filling down center of each tortilla; roll to enclose. Place enchiladas, seam side down, in a 9 by 13-inch baking dish. (At this point, you may cover and refrigerate until next day.)

Spoon whipping cream onto enchiladas; sprinkle evenly with jack cheese. Bake, uncovered, in a 375° oven for 20 minutes or until heated through. (If refrigerated, bake, covered, for 15 minutes; then uncover and bake for 15 more minutes.)

To serve, garnish with radishes, olives, and coriander. Pass lime wedges at the table. Makes 6 servings.

Spinach-stuffed Game Hens

(Pictured on front cover)

Extra stuffing can be heated separately and used either as a side dish or as a decorative bed for these elegant little birds.

2   Rock Cornish game hens (about 24 oz. *each*), thawed if frozen
    Spinach-Rice Stuffing (recipe follows)
    Green Onion Baste (recipe follows)

Remove giblets from game hens and reserve for other uses. Pre-

PEEKING OUT from beneath a flaky pastry crust, holiday leftovers are elegantly transformed in Individual Turkey-Vegetable Casseroles (page 68). Small cooky cutter produced decorative —and appropriate—steam vent.

pare Spinach-Rice Stuffing; put ¾ to 1 cup of the stuffing into body cavity of each hen. Secure openings with metal skewers and tie legs together. Tuck wing tips under, akimbo-style. Prepare Green Onion Baste.

For covered grill cooking, bank about 20 glowing coals on each side of firebed and place a deep metal drip pan in center. Place grill 4 to 6 inches above drip pan; grease grill lightly.

Arrange birds, breast side up, on grill directly over drip pan. Cover barbecue and adjust dampers according to manufacturer's directions. Cook, basting occasionally with onion mixture, for 45 to 60 minutes or until well browned and legs move easily when jiggled.

For oven-roasting, arrange hens, breast side down, on a rack in a roasting pan; brush with onion mixture. Roast, uncovered, in a 425° oven for 30 minutes. Turn hens breast side up, brush again with onion mixture, and continue roasting, basting occasionally, for 20 to 30 more minutes or until well browned and legs move easily when jiggled.

Snip each bird in half with poultry shears or kitchen scissors, if desired. Makes 2 to 4 servings.

SPINACH-RICE STUFFING. In a frying pan, heat 2 tablespoons **salad oil.** Add 1 bunch (about ¾ lb.) **spinach,** cut into ¼-inch strips; 1 can (8 oz.) **water chestnuts,** drained and sliced; and ½ cup *each* minced **green onions** (including tops) and diced **celery.**

Cook, stirring, until spinach wilts (about 1 minute); remove from heat. Add 2 cups cold cooked **rice,** ¼ teaspoon **dry rosemary,** and **salt** and **pepper** to taste.

GREEN ONION BASTE. In a small bowl, beat ½ cup (¼ lb.) **butter** or margarine (softened) until fluffy.

Blend in 1½ tablespoons *each* finely chopped **parsley** and finely minced **green onion** (including top); ½ teaspoon **dry mustard;** ½ teaspoon **fines herbes** (or ⅛ teaspoon *each* parsley flakes, dry tarragon, dry chervil, and freeze-dried chives); ¼ teaspoon **garlic powder;** ⅛ teaspoon *each* **salt** and **liquid hot pepper seasoning;** and a dash of freshly ground **pepper.**

Rock Cornish Game Hens with Mustard Cream & Mushrooms

Tender roasted game hens—bathed in mustard-cream sauce and surrounded by mushrooms—make exquisite company fare.

> 3 Rock Cornish game hens (about 24 oz. *each*), thawed if frozen
>   Salt and pepper
> ½ cup (¼ lb.) butter or margarine, melted
> 1 teaspoon dry mustard
>   About ¾ pound large mushrooms
> 1 cup milk
> ¼ cup all-purpose flour
> 1½ teaspoons Dijon mustard

Remove giblets from hens and reserve for other uses. With poultry shears or kitchen scissors, snip hens in half lengthwise. Sprinkle halves with salt and pepper and place, skin side down, about an inch apart in a shallow roasting pan. In a small bowl, combine butter and dry mustard, stirring until blended.

Bake birds in a 400° oven for 30 minutes, basting with mustard-butter mixture (using all). Turn hen halves skin side up and add mushrooms, turning them in drippings. Return birds to oven and bake for 30 to 40 more minutes or until hen halves are golden brown and meat near thighbone is no longer pink when slashed. Baste hen halves and mushrooms several times with pan drippings.

Arrange hen halves and mushrooms in a serving dish; keep warm. Stir ½ cup of the milk into pan drippings, scraping browned particles free.

In a pan, blend flour with remaining ½ cup milk until smooth; gradually stir in pan drippings. Cook over medium heat, stirring constantly, until mixture boils and thickens; stir in Dijon mustard. Pour sauce into a bowl and pass at the table to spoon over individual servings. Makes 6 servings.

Individual Turkey-Vegetable Casseroles

(Pictured on page 66)

Hidden under a golden crust, tender morsels of turkey, sliced mushrooms, carrots, and peas are deliciously combined in an onion-laden cream sauce.

> 4 tablespoons butter or margarine
> 2 medium-size onions, finely chopped
> ½ pound mushrooms, thinly sliced
> 3 tablespoons all-purpose flour
> 1 teaspoon salt
> ¼ teaspoon *each* dry rosemary and pepper
> 2 chicken bouillon cubes dissolved in 1¼ cups boiling water
> ½ cup whipping cream
> 1 package (10 oz.) frozen peas and carrots
> 2½ to 3 cups cooked turkey or chicken, cut into ¾-inch cubes
> 2 tablespoons dry sherry (optional)
>   Pastry for a double-crust 9-inch pie (page 146)
> 1 egg yolk
> 1 tablespoon water

In a wide frying pan over medium heat, melt butter. Add onions and mushrooms and cook until onions are soft. Stir in flour, salt, rosemary, and pepper; cook until bubbly. Gradually blend in bouillon and cream; cook, stirring, until mixture bubbles and thickens. Stir in peas and carrots, turkey, and sherry, if desired.

Spoon turkey mixture into four 2-cup casserole dishes. (At this point, you may cool, cover, and refrigerate until next day.)

Divide pastry into 4 equal portions. On a lightly floured board, roll each portion into a circle 1½ to 2 inches larger than diameter of individual casseroles. Use a small cooky cutter to cut out a design in center of each circle, if desired. Fit pastry over casseroles, pinch dough to casserole to seal, and crimp edges decoratively. Combine egg yolk with water and brush over pastry.

Bake in a 425° oven for 20 to 25 minutes or until pastry is golden brown and filling is bubbly. (Check casseroles after 10 minutes; if edges are browning too quickly, protect with foil.) Makes 4 servings.

Almond Turkey with Peas

This flavorful medley of cooked turkey and bright green peas (both in the pod and out) may inspire you to roast the large bird even when the calendar doesn't call for it.

¼ cup slivered almonds
4 teaspoons cornstarch
1 tablespoon soy sauce
¾ cup regular-strength chicken broth
2 tablespoons salad oil, butter, or margarine
½ pound mushrooms, sliced
1 package (10 oz.) frozen peas
1 package (6 oz.) frozen pea pods
½ cup sliced canned water chestnuts
3 cups cooked turkey or chicken, cut into bite-size pieces
⅓ cup sliced green onions (including tops)
Hot cooked rice

Spread almonds in a shallow pan; toast, stirring once, in a 350° oven for about 8 minutes or until lightly browned. Set aside.

In a small bowl, combine cornstarch, soy, and ¼ cup of the chicken broth; set aside.

Heat oil in a wide frying pan over medium heat. When oil is hot, add mushrooms and cook until soft. Stir in peas, pea pods, and remaining ½ cup broth. Cover and cook just until peas are thawed (about 3 minutes).

Mix in water chestnuts, turkey, and onions; stir-fry for about 2 minutes. Stir through cornstarch mixture once and add to pan. Cook, stirring, until sauce bubbles and thickens. Serve over rice; garnish with toasted almonds. Makes 4 to 6 servings.

Turkey-Artichoke Pie

With its bubbly mushroom topping and spinach-rice crust, this turkey and artichoke pie provides a full meal in a single slice.

1 package (10 oz.) frozen chopped spinach
2 cups cooked white or brown rice
4 tablespoons butter or margarine, softened
1 package (9 oz.) frozen artichoke hearts, thawed, drained, and cut into thirds
1½ cups diced cooked turkey or chicken
1 cup (4 oz.) shredded jack cheese
¼ pound mushrooms, sliced
2 tablespoons all-purpose flour
½ teaspoon *each* curry powder and garlic powder
1 teaspoon prepared mustard
1 cup milk
Salt and pepper

Cook spinach according to package directions; let cool, then squeeze out as much moisture as possible. In a small bowl, combine spinach, rice, and 2 tablespoons of the butter. Press mixture evenly over bottom and

sides of a well-greased 9-inch pie pan. Cover and refrigerate for at least 30 minutes or for up to an hour.

Arrange artichoke pieces evenly over crust, top with turkey, and sprinkle evenly with cheese; set aside.

In a frying pan over medium heat, melt remaining 2 tablespoons butter. Add mushrooms and cook until soft. Stir in flour, curry powder, garlic powder, and mustard; cook, stirring, until bubbly. Gradually pour in milk and cook, stirring, until sauce boils and thickens. Season to taste with salt and pepper and pour over pie. (At this point, you may cool, cover, and refrigerate until next day.)

Bake, uncovered, in a 350° oven for 45 minutes (1 hour, if refrigerated) or until heated through. Makes 4 to 6 servings.

Turkey-Chili Crêpes

Versatile ground turkey mingles here with Mexican seasonings for an unusual and zesty crêpe filling.

2 tablespoons butter or margarine
1 pound ground turkey
2 cloves garlic, minced or pressed
1 large onion, chopped
1 teaspoon *each* ground cumin, salt, and chili powder
1 can (4 or 7 oz.) diced green chiles
½ cup sour cream
1½ cups (6 oz.) shredded jack cheese
12 to 14 Basic Crêpes (page 117), at room temperature
1 cup (4 oz.) shredded Cheddar cheese

In a wide frying pan over medium heat, melt butter. Add turkey and cook, stirring, until lightly browned and crumbly. Add garlic, onion, cumin, salt, and chili powder; cook until onion is soft. Remove from heat and stir in chiles, sour cream, and jack cheese; mix well.

(Continued on next page)

Place about ⅓ cup of the filling down center of each crêpe. Roll up and place, seam side down, in a single layer in two 9-inch square baking dishes or one 9 by 13-inch baking dish. (At this point, you may cover and refrigerate until next day.)

Bake, covered, in a 375° oven for 20 to 30 minutes or until heated through. Sprinkle evenly with Cheddar cheese and bake, uncovered, for 2 to 3 more minutes or just until cheese is melted. Makes 6 or 7 servings.

Barbecued Duck Halves

Emerging from the grill with crackling-crisp skin, these duckling halves can rival any barbecued meat for juicy goodness.

4½ to 5-pound duckling, thawed
⅓ cup lemon juice
1 clove garlic, minced or pressed
¼ teaspoon *each* dry mustard and rosemary
⅛ teaspoon pepper
2 tablespoons honey

Remove giblets from duckling and reserve for other uses.

To halve and partially bone the duck, place duck breast side down. Insert tip of a sharp knife into neck cavity and cut through wishbone. Then turn breast side up, and cut along breastbone; continue cutting meat from bone, following contour of one side of rib cage; cut through joint where wing is connected.

Continue along side of duck to thigh joint, then twist and pull gently until thighbone is free from socket. Continue until half the duck is free from carcass. Trim off excess skin.

Repeat on other side of duck to make 2 semiboneless halves; wing and leg bones remain. (Reserve rib cage and backbone for soup stock, if desired.) Pierce skin with a fork and place duck halves in a shallow pan.

In a small bowl, combine lemon juice, garlic, mustard, rosemary, and pepper. Pour over duck, cover, and refrigerate for 2 to 4 hours.

Bank about 20 glowing coals on each side of firebed. In center, place a deep metal drip pan. Place grill about 6 inches above drip pan; grease grill lightly.

Lift duck from marinade and drain briefly (reserving marinade). Arrange duck halves, skin side up, on grill directly over drip pan. Cover barbecue, leaving dampers open to maintain a hot fire. Add 5 or 6 briquets on each side every 30 minutes to maintain a constant temperature.

Stir honey into reserved marinade. Cook duck for 2 to 2¼ hours or until thigh meat feels soft when squeezed. Brush duck with honey mixture during last 30 minutes of cooking.

With poultry shears or kitchen scissors, snip each duck half in two. Makes 4 servings.

Peking-style Duck

There's a whole ritual involved in eating Peking-style duck. Each guest slices morsels of crisp skin and succulent meat, and then prepares a "sandwich" using a flour tortilla with Chinese hoisin sauce (available in Oriental markets), coriander, and green onions.

2 ducklings (4½ to 5 lbs. *each*), thawed if frozen
1 teaspoon *each* ground ginger and ground cinnamon
½ teaspoon ground nutmeg
¼ teaspoon *each* ground cloves and pepper
¼ cup soy sauce
About 1 cup hoisin sauce
12 to 18 flour tortillas
About 1½ cups slivered green onions (including some tops)
½ to 1 cup coarsely chopped fresh coriander (cilantro)

Remove giblets and reserve for other uses. With a fork, pierce duck skin well. Trim off excess neck skin; fasten remaining skin to back with a skewer.

In a small bowl, combine ginger, cinnamon, nutmeg, cloves, and pepper. Sprinkle about ½ teaspoon of the spice mixture inside each duck; rub remaining mixture evenly over exterior of birds. Leave body cavity open for more even cooking.

Bank about 20 glowing coals on each side of firebed and place a deep metal drip pan in center. Arrange birds, breast side up, on a well-greased grill 4 to 6 inches above drip pan. Cover barbecue, leaving dampers open to maintain a hot fire. Add 5 or 6 briquets on each side of fire every 30 minutes to maintain a constant temperature.

In a small bowl, combine soy and 2 tablespoons of the hoisin sauce. Cook ducks for about 2 to 2¼ hours or until thigh meat is soft when squeezed. During last 20 minutes of cooking, brush ducks often with soy mixture.

About 30 minutes before serving, lightly dampen tortillas, cut in halves or quarters, stack, and wrap in foil. Heat in a 350° oven for 10 to 15 minutes or until steamy; place in a napkin-lined basket to keep warm. Put remaining hoisin sauce, onions, and coriander in separate serving bowls.

To eat, spread warm tortilla pieces with hoisin; slice small pieces of duck skin and meat (discarding fat) and place on tortilla. Top with a few onion slivers and some coriander, and fold to eat out of hand. Makes 6 to 8 servings.

FOR UNEXPECTED FLAVOR and contrasting texture, surround tender Chicken Breasts Veronique (page 57) with whole grapes and fluted mushrooms. Accompany this delicate offering with parsley-flecked potatoes, buttered broccoli, and chilled white wine.

FISH & SHELLFISH

From the pan, oven, or barbecue

Whole Barbecued Salmon in Foil

If you're lucky enough to have a whole salmon, try cooking it outdoors. Served plain or with dill sauce, a charcoal-broiled salmon makes a festive party entrée.

Dill Sauce (recipe follows), optional
1 whole salmon (5 to 8 lbs.), cleaned and scaled, with head removed
Salt and pepper
1 lemon, sliced
1 small onion, sliced
Parsley sprigs

Prepare Dill Sauce, if desired, and refrigerate.

Sprinkle body cavity of salmon with salt and pepper. Tuck in lemon slices, onion slices, and parsley sprigs.

Cut 2 pieces of foil, exactly to fit each side of fish just to the tail; press smoothly against fish on each side.

Tear off a 24-inch-long piece of heavy-duty foil, 18 inches wide. Center fish on foil, folding back one edge to expose fish tail. Join long edges of foil in center, crease a 1-inch seam, then fold over and over to seal foil tightly against side of fish. Seal foil at head end and press tightly against fish near exposed tail.

Place fish, foil seam up, on a grill 6 inches above a solid bed of glowing coals. Arrange a wad of foil under tail to support it and shield it from heat.

Cook, carefully turning fish over every 10 minutes, for 30 minutes or until fish flakes readily when prodded in thickest portion with a fork; brush tail with water occasionally. If not done after 30 minutes, continue cooking, turning and checking for doneness about every 5 minutes.

To serve, open foil seam, lift off foil piece on top of fish, and remove skin, if desired. Cut directly to bone, slide a wide spatula between meat and bone, and lift off each serving. Top with sauce, if desired. Makes 8 to 12 servings.

DILL SAUCE. In a bowl, mix 1 cup **mayonnaise,** ½ cup finely chopped **dill pickles,** and 2 **green onions** (including tops), thinly sliced. Stir in 1 teaspoon **dill weed,** ¼ teaspoon **celery seeds,** ½ teaspoon **Worcestershire,** and 2 teaspoons **lemon juice.** Cover and refrigerate for at least 3 hours. Makes about 1⅔ cups.

Fish in Paper

Look in kitchenware shops for the parchment paper you need to make this New Orleans classic.

Poaching Liquid (recipe follows)
6 boneless lingcod or rockfish fillets (6 to 8 oz. *each*)
Dry white wine
½ cup (¼ lb.) butter or margarine
½ pound mushrooms, sliced
⅓ cup finely chopped shallots
⅓ cup all-purpose flour
¼ cup whipping cream
6 pieces parchment paper (about 15 inches square *each*)
¼ pound *each* small cooked shrimp and shredded crabmeat

Prepare Poaching Liquid and pour into a wide frying pan over medium-high heat; bring to a boil. Add fish fillets in a single layer without crowding (a few at a time, if necessary). Liquid should barely cover fish; add equal amounts of water and wine to pan, if needed. Cover, reduce heat, and simmer until fish feels firm and is almost done (5 to 6 minutes for ¾-inch-thick fillets).

With a wide spatula, carefully lift out fish and set aside. Boil liquid until reduced to 2½ cups and set aside in a measuring cup; rinse pan.

In pan over medium heat, melt 2 tablespoons of the butter. Add mushrooms and cook, stirring, until lightly browned. With a slotted spoon, remove mushrooms and set aside.

Reduce heat to low and add 4 tablespoons of the remaining butter. Add shallots and cook,

stirring, until soft; then add flour and cook, stirring, until bubbly.

Gradually stir in reserved 2½ cups liquid and continue cooking and stirring until sauce thickens. Stir in cream and mushrooms and let cool.

Fold each piece of parchment paper in half and cut so each piece of parchment forms a heart shape about 11 inches long and 14 inches wide. Melt remaining 2 tablespoons butter.

Open each paper heart and lightly brush with butter. Place a fish fillet lengthwise next to center crease of each heart. Distribute shrimp and crabmeat equally over fillets, then top with sauce.

Fold other half of heart over filling. Starting at top, roll and crimp edges together; twist point of heart to seal. Place on baking sheets and brush tops with remaining melted butter. (At this point, you may cool, cover, and refrigerate until next day.)

Bake, uncovered, in a 450° oven for 7 to 10 minutes or until paper is lightly browned. (If refrigerated, bake in a 400° oven for about 20 minutes.)

To serve, cut a cross in top of each packet; pull back paper. Makes 6 servings.

POACHING LIQUID. In a 3 to 4-quart pan over medium-high heat, combine 1 quart (4 cups) **water,** 1 large **onion,** sliced, 6 **whole black peppercorns,** 2 **whole allspice,** 1 **bay leaf,** and 1 teaspoon **salt.** Add ½ cup **dry white wine,** if desired. Bring to a boil; cover, reduce heat, and simmer for 20 minutes. Strain, reserving liquid; discard onion and spices.

Fish-in-a-Fish

(Pictured on page 74)

Encased in a buttery pastry shell, this seafood extravaganza makes elegant company fare. You can assemble it up to a day in

advance; then bake to a golden brown just before serving.

Buttery Pastry (recipe follows)
1½ pounds lean mild fish fillets (such as rockfish, sole, or flounder), about 1 inch thick
½ teaspoon salt
2 tablespoons lemon juice
4 tablespoons butter or margarine
1 medium-size onion, chopped
¾ cup long-grain rice
½ cup lightly packed chopped parsley
Shrimp and Clam Sauce (recipe follows)
1 egg

Prepare Buttery Pastry, wrap well, and refrigerate for at least 1 hour or until next day.

Place fillets in a single layer in a shallow baking pan, overlapping thin edges. Sprinkle with salt and lemon juice.

Bake, covered, in a 450° oven for 10 to 15 minutes or until fillets are opaque throughout. Let cool, then pour juices into a pint measuring cup. Set fish and juices aside. (At this point, you may cover and refrigerate fish and juices until next day.)

In a 2 to 3-quart pan over medium heat, melt butter. Add onion and cook, stirring, until soft. Stir in rice. Add enough water to reserved fish juices to make 1½ cups; add to rice mixture. Bring to a boil; cover, reduce heat, and simmer until rice is tender (about 20 minutes). Stir in parsley. (At this point, you may cool, cover, and refrigerate until next day.)

Prepare Shrimp & Clam Sauce and let cool. (At this point, you may cover and refrigerate until next day.)

To make fish pattern, cut a piece of paper or cardboard into a fish shape about 4 by 7 inches. Using a well-floured rolling pin, roll half the pastry on a floured board to a thickness of ⅛ inch. Place fish pattern on pastry and, with a small sharp knife, cut around edges. Transfer fish-shaped pastry to a lightly greased

baking sheet; repeat until you have 8 fish (you'll need 2 baking sheets).

Distribute two-thirds of the rice mixture evenly among pastry fish, spreading to within ½ inch of pastry edges. Arrange fish fillets over rice mixture. Spoon sauce over fillets, spreading to within ½ inch of pastry edges; cover with remaining rice mixture. In a small bowl, beat egg lightly and brush over edges of pastry.

Roll remaining pastry and pastry scraps and cut into 8 ovals, *each* about 5 by 8 inches. Drape an oval over each fish and trim edges to extend ½ inch beyond bottom pastry. Tuck top pastry under bottom pastry.

If desired, roll any remaining pastry and cut into fin-shaped pieces. To attach to fish, brush edge of fin with beaten egg and place slightly underneath fish.

Press edges of pastry together with tines of a fork, sealing well. Cut through pastry top to make scales and other decorative details. (At this point, you may cover and refrigerate until next day.)

Bake, uncovered, in a 425° oven for 10 minutes, then reduce heat to 375° and bake for 40 to 50 more minutes or until golden (if fins and tail brown too quickly, cover them with foil). Makes 8 servings.

BUTTERY PASTRY. In a large bowl, combine 4½ cups **all-purpose flour** and ¾ teaspoon **salt.** Using a pastry blender or 2 knives, cut in 1½ cups (¾ lb.) **butter** or margarine until particles are about the size of very small peas. Add 1 cup plus 2 tablespoons cold **water,** mixing with a fork until pastry clings together. Press firmly into a ball.

MASQUERADING as a denizen of the deep, this endearing creature is actually sculptured from pastry. Inside Fish-in-a-Fish (page 73) are fish fillets, seasoned rice, and a rich shrimp and clam sauce.

SHRIMP & CLAM SAUCE. Drain juice from 1 can (6½ oz.) **chopped clams** into a pint measuring cup; set clams aside. Add enough **whipping cream** or half-and-half (light cream) to clam juice to make 1½ cups; set aside.

In a small pan over medium heat, melt 2 tablespoons **butter** or margarine. Stir in 2 tablespoons **all-purpose flour** and cook until bubbly. Gradually stir in clam juice mixture. Reduce heat to medium-low and cook, stirring, until sauce thickens.

Add a dash of **ground nutmeg;** then stir in chopped clams and ½ pound small cooked **shrimp;** season to taste with **salt.** Let cool.

Vegetable-topped Fish Fillets

Oven-baked fillets of fish are topped with a flavorful tomato-mushroom mélange in this quick and easy entrée. Serve with potatoes or seasoned rice.

2 pounds red snapper or lingcod fillets (1 inch thick *each*), cut into serving-size pieces, if large
   Salt, pepper, and dry tarragon
   Salad oil
3 tablespoons butter or margarine
1 medium-size onion, chopped
¼ pound mushrooms, sliced
1 medium-size tomato, seeded and chopped
¼ cup *each* dry white wine and tomato-based chili sauce
⅓ cup grated Parmesan cheese

Sprinkle fillets lightly with salt, pepper, and tarragon. Place in a greased 9 by 13-inch baking dish and drizzle about ½ teaspoon oil over each fillet. Bake, uncovered, in a 500° oven for 10 to 12 minutes or until fish flakes readily when prodded in thickest portion with a fork.

Meanwhile, in a wide frying pan over medium heat, melt butter. Add onion and mushrooms and cook until onion is soft.

Remove from heat and stir in tomato, wine, and chili sauce.

Remove fish from oven; spoon out and discard juices. Spoon onion mixture evenly over each fillet, then sprinkle with cheese. Broil about 4 inches from heat until cheese begins to melt. Makes 4 to 6 servings.

Poached Fish & Vegetables in Cheese Sauce

Money-saving frozen fish can taste almost as moist and tender as today's catch if prepared properly. The secret? Cook the fish without defrosting.

1½ tablespoons lemon juice
1 bay leaf
¼ cup dry white wine or water
3 whole black peppercorns
2 whole allspice
¼ teaspoon salt
1 package (1 lb.) frozen fish fillets (sole, perch, cod, or haddock)
4 to 6 *each* small thin-skinned potatoes and small boiling onions (about 1½ inches in diameter *each*; cut in half, if larger)
1 cup frozen peas
   Cheese Sauce (recipe follows)

In a 10-inch frying pan, combine lemon juice, bay leaf, wine, peppercorns, allspice, and salt. Add fish fillets, potatoes, and onions. Pour in just enough water to cover fish. Bring to a boil over high heat; cover, reduce heat, and simmer until fish is almost opaque throughout (about 18 minutes).

Add peas; cover and simmer until fish flakes readily when prodded in thickest portion with a fork (4 to 6 more minutes). With a slotted spatula, lift out fish and vegetables and arrange on a serving platter; cover and keep warm. (If potatoes aren't done, continue cooking until tender; then remove from pan.)

Boil poaching liquid until

reduced to ¾ cup; strain and set aside.

Prepare Cheese Sauce and pour over fish and vegetables. Makes 2 servings.

CHEESE SAUCE. In a wide frying pan over medium heat, melt 2 tablespoons **butter** or margarine. Blend in 1½ tablespoons **all-purpose flour** and cook until bubbly.

Gradually stir in reserved ¾ cup **poaching liquid**, ¼ cup **milk** or half-and-half (light cream), and ¼ teaspoon **dry mustard.** Continue cooking and stirring until sauce boils and thickens. Reduce heat to low and add ⅔ cup shredded **Swiss cheese** and a dash of **ground nutmeg;** cook, stirring, until cheese is melted. Season with **salt** and **pepper** to taste.

Sweet & Sour Fish

A piquant sweet and sour sauce tops crisply fried fish and stir-fried vegetables in this Chinese-inspired recipe.

    Sweet-Sour Sauce (recipe follows)
    About ⅓ cup cornstarch
2   pounds Greenland turbot or
    halibut fillets (thawed, if frozen),
    cut into 2-inch squares
    Salad oil
1   clove garlic, minced or pressed
1   onion, cut into 1-inch squares
1   medium-size green pepper, cut
    into 1-inch squares
1   medium-size tomato, cut into
    1-inch cubes

Prepare Sweet-Sour Sauce and set aside.

Place cornstarch in a bag and add fish pieces, shaking to coat completely; shake off excess.

Pour oil into a wide frying pan to a depth of about ¼ inch; place pan over medium-high heat. When oil is hot, add fish, a few pieces at a time, and cook until fish is browned on all sides and flakes readily when prodded

with a fork (about 5 minutes). Drain; arrange on a platter and keep warm.

In another pan, heat 2 tablespoons oil over high heat. Add garlic, onion, and pepper; cook, stirring, for 2 minutes. Stir Sweet-Sour Sauce and add to pan along with tomato. Bring to a boil, stirring; then pour over fish. Makes 4 to 6 servings.

SWEET-SOUR SAUCE. In a small bowl, mix 1 tablespoon **cornstarch** with ¼ cup **sugar.** Stir in 2 tablespoons *each* **soy sauce** and **catsup,** ¼ cup **vinegar,** and ½ cup regular-strength **chicken broth.**

Oven-fried Herbed Shark Fillets

Shark? It's delicious—a firm, white-fleshed fish that's low in fat and free of small bones.

2   pounds shark fillets, cut into
    serving-size pieces, if desired,
    or steaks
¼   cup *each* white vinegar and
    water
1   tablespoon lemon juice
1   egg
1   tablespoon milk
⅔   cup all-purpose flour
2   teaspoons parsley flakes
1½ teaspoons dry basil
1   teaspoon *each* grated lemon peel
    and garlic salt
¾   teaspoon thyme leaves
¼   teaspoon pepper
2   tablespoons butter or margarine
2   tablespoons salad oil
    Lemon wedges

Place shark fillets in a shallow pan. Pour vinegar, water, and lemon juice over fish; cover and refrigerate, turning once, for 1 to

2 hours. Remove fish from marinade and pat dry.

In a pie pan, beat together egg and milk. In another pie pan, combine flour, parsley, basil, lemon peel, garlic salt, thyme, and pepper.

Place a large shallow baking dish or broiler pan in oven while it preheats to 500°. Meanwhile, dip fish in egg mixture, then in flour mixture to coat; set aside in a single layer on wax paper.

When dish is hot, remove from oven and add butter and oil, swirling until butter is melted (fat should be about ⅛ inch deep). Turn fish in butter mixture to coat, then arrange fish slightly apart in dish.

Return dish to oven and bake, uncovered, until fish is browned and opaque throughout when split in thickest portion (allow about 10 minutes per inch of thickness at thickest part). Serve with lemon wedges. Makes 4 to 6 servings.

Sole with Curried Rice & Papaya

Accent delicately flavored fresh sole with hot, gingery papaya slices; then serve over curried rice and garnish with lime.

    About 4 tablespoons butter or
    margarine
1   bunch green onions
2   to 3 teaspoons curry powder
1½ cups long-grain rice
2   cans (14 oz. *each*) regular-
    strength chicken broth
1½ to 2 pounds sole fillets,
    separated along lengthwise
    seam, if large
    Salt, pepper, paprika, and all-
    purpose flour
    About 2 tablespoons salad oil or
    olive oil
1   teaspoon *each* sugar and ground
    ginger
1   large or 2 small papayas,
    peeled, seeded, and cut into
    thick slices
2   tablespoons lime juice
2   limes, cut into wedges

Place 1 tablespoon of the butter in a 9 by 13-inch baking dish and melt in a 350° oven. Meanwhile, slice green onions, keeping white part separate from green tops; set tops aside.

Remove dish from oven and stir in white part of onions, curry powder, and rice. In a 2-quart pan over high heat, combine chicken broth with enough water to make 4 cups; bring to a boil and pour over rice mixture. Bake, covered, for 25 minutes or until rice is tender and liquid is almost absorbed.

Meanwhile, sprinkle fillets lightly on both sides with salt, pepper, and paprika. Dredge in flour to coat completely; shake off excess and set fish aside in a single layer on wax paper.

Heat about 1 tablespoon *each* of the butter and oil in a wide frying pan over medium heat until frothy. Add fillets in a single layer without crowding (a few at a time, if necessary) and cook, turning, until lightly browned on both sides (2 to 4 minutes on each side). Add butter and oil as needed. As fillets are cooked, remove from pan and arrange in a single layer on a baking sheet; keep warm.

In another frying pan over medium heat, melt 1 tablespoon of the remaining butter. Stir in sugar and ginger; add papaya slices and drizzle with lime juice. Cook, turning as needed, just until heated through and glazed.

Arrange fillets and papaya over rice. Garnish with lime wedges and reserved onion tops. Makes 6 servings.

Coquilles St. Jacques au Gratin

Tender and succulent scallops are truly one of the sea's most valuable treasures. Here, they're enveloped in a bubbling hot cheese sauce; if you like, serve them in scallop shells.

2 pounds scallops (thawed, if frozen), cut into bite-size pieces, if large
   About 1 cup regular-strength chicken broth
4 tablespoons butter or margarine
¾ pound mushrooms, sliced
1 tablespoon lemon juice
1 large onion, finely chopped
6 tablespoons all-purpose flour
½ cup whipping cream
⅛ teaspoon ground nutmeg
1½ cups (6 oz.) shredded Swiss cheese
¼ cup lightly packed chopped parsley
   Salt

In a 3 to 4-quart pan over medium-high heat, combine scallops and 1 cup of the broth. Bring to a boil; cover, reduce heat, and simmer until scallops are just opaque throughout (about 5 minutes). Let scallops cool in liquid.

Drain cooled liquid into a pint measuring cup. Add broth, if necessary, to make 2 cups liquid; set aside. Cover scallops and refrigerate.

In a wide frying pan over medium-high heat, melt 2 tablespoons of the butter. Add mushrooms and lemon juice and cook, stirring, until mushrooms are golden brown and liquid has evaporated. Spoon into a small bowl and set aside.

To pan, add onion and remaining 2 tablespoons butter. Cook, stirring, until onion is soft. Add flour and cook, stirring, until bubbly.

With a wire whisk, gradually stir in reserved 2 cups liquid. Continue cooking and stirring until sauce boils and thickens (about 10 minutes). Add mushrooms, cream, nutmeg, and ½ cup of the cheese; stir until blended. Cover sauce and refrigerate until chilled.

Stir scallops and parsley into sauce; season with salt to taste. Spoon scallop mixture into 4 to 6 individual 2-cup ramekins or scallop shells (commercially prepared for baking) and sprinkle

with remaining 1 cup cheese. (At this point, you may cover and refrigerate until next day.)

Bake, uncovered, in a 400° oven for 12 to 15 minutes or until sauce is bubbly and edges are lightly browned. Makes 4 to 6 servings.

Shrimp-Scallop Teriyaki

Quick cooking in a very hot wok or frying pan allows this seafood and vegetable medley to retain ultrafresh color and flavor.

¼ cup teriyaki sauce
3 tablespoons dry sherry
1½ teaspoons finely chopped fresh ginger or ¾ teaspoon ground ginger
2 cloves garlic, minced or pressed
1½ teaspoons cornstarch
½ pound medium-size (30–32 per lb.) raw shrimp, shelled and deveined
½ pound scallops (thawed, if frozen), cut into bite-size pieces, if large
¼ cup peanut oil or salad oil
¼ pound Chinese pea pods or 1 package (6 oz.) frozen pea pods, thawed
½ pound mushrooms, sliced
5 green onions (including tops), cut into 2-inch lengths

In a deep bowl, mix teriyaki sauce, sherry, ginger, garlic, and cornstarch; add shrimp and scallops. Cover and refrigerate for at least 30 minutes.

Place a wok or wide frying pan over high heat. When wok is hot, add 2 tablespoons of the oil. When oil is hot, add pea pods and cook, stirring quickly, until bright green. Remove pea pods and set aside.

Add remaining 2 tablespoons oil to wok. When oil is hot, add mushrooms and cook, stirring quickly, until soft (about 3 minutes). Add shrimp mixture and onions and cook, stirring, until shrimp turn pink (about 2 minutes). Stir in pea pods. Makes 2 or 3 servings.

Layered Clam & Noodle Casserole

A lemon-garlic sauce with minced clams binds layers of lasagne noodles, spinach, and cheese in this informal dinner entrée.

8 ounces lasagne noodles
   Boiling salted water
2 cans (6½ oz. *each*) minced clams
4 tablespoons butter or margarine
¼ cup all-purpose flour
1 bottle (8 oz.) clam juice
2 cloves garlic, minced or pressed
1 teaspoon Italian herb seasoning *or* ¼ teaspoon *each* dry basil and oregano, thyme, and marjoram leaves
¼ cup lightly packed finely chopped parsley
3 tablespoons lemon juice
   Pepper
1 pint (2 cups) small curd cottage cheese or ricotta cheese
1 package (10 oz.) frozen chopped spinach, thawed
½ pound jack cheese, thinly sliced
   About ¼ cup grated Parmesan cheese

Cook noodles in boiling salted water according to package directions; drain, rinse with cold water, and drain again. Set aside. Drain clams, reserving liquid, and set clams aside.

In a 2 to 3-quart pan over medium heat, melt butter. Add flour and cook, stirring, until bubbly. Gradually stir in reserved clam liquid and clam juice. Continue cooking and stirring until mixture boils and thickens (about 5 minutes). Remove from heat and stir in clams, garlic, herb seasoning, parsley, and lemon juice; season to taste with pepper.

Line a greased 9 by 13-inch baking dish with a third of the noodles. Spoon cottage cheese evenly over noodles and top with a third of the clam sauce. Add a second layer of noodles.

Squeeze out as much moisture from spinach as possible and arrange over noodles. Cover with half of the jack cheese slices, then spread with half the remaining clam sauce. Top with remaining noodles, cheese slices, and clam sauce. (At this point, you may cover and refrigerate until next day.)

Sprinkle with Parmesan cheese and bake, uncovered, in a 350° oven for 30 minutes (45 minutes, if refrigerated) or until bubbly and heated through. Let stand for 10 minutes before cutting. Makes 6 to 8 servings.

San Francisco-style Cioppino

(Pictured on facing page)

Cioppino is a crab-based stew, invented by fishermen in turn-of-the-century San Francisco.

¼ cup olive oil or salad oil
1 large onion, chopped
2 cloves garlic, minced or pressed
1 large green pepper, seeded and chopped
⅓ cup lightly packed chopped parsley
1 can (15 oz.) tomato sauce
1 can (1 lb. 12 oz.) tomatoes
1 cup dry red or white wine *or* ¾ cup water combined with ¼ cup lemon juice
1 bay leaf
1 teaspoon dry basil
½ teaspoon oregano leaves
1 dozen small hard-shell clams, scrubbed well
1 pound medium-size (30–32 per lb.) raw shrimp, shelled and deveined
   About 5 pounds large blue or medium-size Dungeness crabs, cooked, cleaned, and cracked

Heat oil in a 6 to 8-quart kettle over medium heat. Add onion, garlic, pepper, and parsley; cook, stirring, until onion is soft.

Stir in tomato sauce, tomatoes (break up with a spoon) and their liquid, wine, bay leaf, basil, and oregano. Cover, reduce heat, and simmer until slightly thickened (about 20 minutes). (At this point, you may cool, cover, and refrigerate until next day; reheat broth before continuing.)

Add clams, shrimp, and crabs. Cover and simmer until clams pop open and shrimp turn pink (about 20 more minutes). Ladle into wide soup bowls. Makes about 6 servings.

Oven-fried Oysters

It's the cornmeal in the coating that gives these juicy baked oysters their crispy crust.

2 jars (10 oz. *each*) small Pacific oysters
½ cup (¼ lb.) butter or margarine
¾ cup baking mix (biscuit mix)
3 tablespoons yellow cornmeal
½ teaspoon *each* garlic salt and paprika
¼ teaspoon pepper
2 eggs
2 tablespoons chopped parsley
   Lemon wedges

Drain oysters and cut in half, if large; pat dry and set aside. Put butter in a foil-lined 10 by 15-inch baking pan and melt in a 425° oven. Remove pan from oven.

In a pie pan, combine baking mix, cornmeal, garlic salt, paprika, and pepper. In another pie pan, lightly beat eggs. Dip each oyster in egg, then in crumb mixture, and roll in melted butter to coat well. Arrange oysters in a single layer in pan.

Return pan to oven and bake, uncovered, for 15 to 20 minutes or until oysters are crisp and browned. Transfer to a serving platter and sprinkle with parsley. Serve with lemon wedges. Makes 4 servings.

ALL HANDS ON DECK for a seafaring supper featuring San Francisco-style Cioppino (recipe on this page), a tomatoey seafood stew; offer French bread for dunking and plenty of extra napkins. Complete this floating picnic with Crisp Spinach Salad (page 20) and red wine.

EGGS & CHEESE

Solo or ensemble

Creamy Eggs & Sweet Onions

A golden brunch centerpiece that has inspired numerous compliments, this French presentation of eggs needs only a few accompaniments—crusty bread, fresh fruit, and cheese.

2½ **pounds small boiling onions (about 10)**
4 **tablespoons butter or margarine**
1 **quart (4 cups) milk**
½ **cup all-purpose flour**
1 **dozen hard-cooked eggs**
   Salt and pepper

Cut each onion in half lengthwise through stem; then cut each half into thin slices. In a 5-quart Dutch oven over medium heat, melt butter. Add onions and cook, stirring, until soft but not browned (about 25 minutes).

Meanwhile, in a 2-quart pan over medium heat, scald milk (*do not boil*). Gradually stir flour into onion mixture until well blended. Slowly pour in hot milk and cook, stirring, until sauce boils and thickens.

Slice eggs ½ inch thick; reserving about 10 slices for garnish, gently stir remaining egg slices into sauce. Season to taste with salt and pepper. Spoon egg mixture into a warm large rimmed platter. Garnish with reserved egg slices. Makes 8 to 10 servings.

Scotch Baked Eggs

Hard-cooked eggs snug in a blanket of savory sausage—what a novel presentation of a favorite breakfast combination. You can prepare this delicious British pub snack a day in advance, then pop it into the oven just before serving.

1¼ **pounds bulk pork sausage**
4 **hard-cooked eggs, chilled and shelled**

Divide sausage into 4 equal portions. On wax paper, flatten each portion into a round, flat patty about ⅜ inch thick. Loosen patties from paper with a spatula.

Moisten your hands for easier handling of sausage and wrap an egg in each sausage patty; smooth surfaces until free from cracks. (At this point, you may cover and refrigerate until next day.)

Place sausage-wrapped eggs slightly apart in a shallow pan. Bake in upper third of a 450° oven for 30 minutes or until meat is richly browned and no longer pink when slashed. Drain briefly and serve hot. Makes 4 servings.

Make-ahead Layered Mushrooms & Eggs

Eighteen eggs get together with mushrooms, cheese, and a hearty splash of sherry for this extravaganza of crowd-pleasing proportions. What's best, you can prepare it a day ahead.

- 1 **can (10¾ oz.) condensed cream of mushroom soup (undiluted)**
- 3 **tablespoons dry sherry or milk**
- 1½ **cups (6 oz.)** *each* **shredded sharp Cheddar cheese and jack cheese**
- 18 **eggs**
- 2 **tablespoons milk**
- 1 **teaspoon parsley flakes**
- ½ **teaspoon dill weed**
- ⅛ **teaspoon pepper**
- 4 **tablespoons butter or margarine**
- ¼ **pound mushrooms, sliced**
- ¼ **cup chopped green onions (including tops)**
  Paprika

In a small pan over medium heat, combine soup and sherry and cook, stirring, until smooth and heated through. Remove from heat and set aside. In a small bowl, lightly mix Cheddar and jack cheeses; set aside. In another bowl, beat eggs with milk, parsley, dill weed, and pepper; set aside.

In a wide frying pan over medium-low heat, melt butter. Add mushrooms and onions and cook, stirring, until onions are soft. Add egg mixture and cook, gently lifting cooked portion to let uncooked egg flow underneath, until eggs are softly set.

Spoon half the egg mixture into a 7 by 11-inch baking dish and cover with half the soup mixture; then sprinkle evenly with half the cheese mixture. Repeat layers; sprinkle top with paprika. (At this point, you may cool, cover, and refrigerate until next day.)

Bake, uncovered, in a 300° oven for 30 to 35 minutes (1 hour, if refrigerated) or until bubbly and heated through. Let stand for 10 minutes before cutting. Makes 8 to 10 servings.

South-of-the-Border Brunch Eggs

Brighten your next brunch with the wide-awake flavors and colors of these Latin-style scrambled eggs. For easy preparation, use a wide electric frying pan.

- 6 **corn tortillas**
- ½ **cup thinly sliced green onions (including tops)**
- 1 **can (4 oz.) whole green chiles, seeded and chopped**
- 1 **can (6 oz.) white sauce**
- 1 **cup milk**
- 8 **eggs**
- 2 **tablespoons salad oil**
- 4 **tablespoons butter or margarine**
- 3 **medium-size tomatoes, peeled, seeded, and chopped**
- 1 **can (2¼ oz.) sliced ripe olives, drained**
- 2 **cups (8 oz.) shredded jack cheese**

With scissors, snip tortillas into short strips and set aside. In a large bowl, mix onions, chiles, white sauce, and milk; beat in eggs and set aside.

Heat oil and 2 tablespoons of the butter in an electric frying pan set at 350° (or use a wide frying pan over medium-high heat). When hot, add tortilla strips and cook, stirring often, until crisp. Reduce temperature to 250° (or medium-low).

In pan, melt remaining 2 tablespoons butter, then pour in egg mixture and cook, gently lifting cooked portion to let uncooked egg flow underneath, until eggs are set to your liking.

Evenly distribute tomatoes, olives, and cheese over eggs. Cover, turn off heat, and let stand until cheese is melted. Makes 6 to 8 servings.

Country Omelet

Served in wedges directly from the pan, this open-faced omelet is lavish with such extra taste treats as crunchy bacon, bits of potato and onion, cheese, sour cream, and crisp sautéed walnuts.

- 4 **strips bacon**
  About 8 walnut halves
- 1 **small thin-skinned potato, peeled and cut into ¼-inch cubes**
- ¼ **cup finely chopped onion**
- 2 **tablespoons butter or margarine**
- 3 **or 4 eggs, lightly beaten**
- ¼ **cup diced Swiss cheese**
- 2 **tablespoons shredded Swiss cheese**
- 1 **tablespoon minced parsley**
  About ¼ cup sour cream
  Salt

In a wide frying pan over medium heat, cook bacon until crisp. Remove bacon from pan, drain, and crumble; set aside.

Add walnuts to drippings; cook, stirring, until lightly browned (1 to 2 minutes—take care, as they scorch easily). Lift out and set aside.

Discard all but 2 tablespoons drippings. Add potato and onion to pan, reduce heat to medium-low, and cook, stirring, until potato is soft but only lightly browned (about 10 minutes). Remove potato mixture from pan and keep warm.

Wipe pan clean, then melt butter over medium-low heat. Pour in eggs and cook, gently lifting cooked portion to let

uncooked egg flow underneath, until eggs are set but top still looks moist and creamy. Sprinkle evenly with bacon, potato mixture, diced cheese, shredded cheese, and parsley.

Mound sour cream in center of omelet and garnish with walnuts. Season with salt to taste. Cut into wedges and serve from pan. Makes 2 to 4 servings.

Spanish Omelet Picnic Loaf

Tucked inside a big round bread loaf that can stay warm for hours, this hearty sausage and potato omelet makes perfect picnic fare.

- 1 **large round loaf sourdough French bread (about 10 to 12 inches in diameter)**
  About 4 tablespoons olive oil
  About 10 ounces chorizo sausage
- 1 **large thin-skinned potato, cooked**
- 1 **medium-size onion, finely chopped**
- 1 **clove garlic, minced or pressed**
- 1 **medium-size green pepper, seeded and chopped**
- 1 **medium-size red bell pepper, seeded and chopped, or 1 jar (4 oz.) roasted red bell pepper or pimentos, drained and chopped**
- 9 **eggs**
- ¾ **teaspoon salt**
- ¼ **teaspoon pepper**

With a long serrated knife, cut bread in half horizontally. Partially hollow out center of each half (reserve bread chunks for other uses), leaving a 1-inch-thick rim. Brush cut surfaces with about 1 tablespoon of the oil. Reassemble loaf, wrap in foil,

and warm in a 300° oven while preparing omelet.

Remove sausage casings; crumble meat into a 10-inch non-stick omelet or frying pan over medium heat and cook, stirring, until lightly browned. Remove sausage with a slotted spoon and drain; discard drippings from pan.

Peel and thinly slice potato. Heat 1 tablespoon of remaining oil in pan over medium-high heat. Add potato, onion, and garlic; cook, stirring, until potato is browned (about 3 minutes). Stir in green and red peppers and cook for 1 more minute; then stir in sausage and remove pan from heat.

In a large bowl, beat eggs with salt and pepper. Return pan to medium heat and push potato mixture to one side. Drizzle 1 tablespoon of remaining oil over pan bottom, then redistribute potato mixture in pan.

Pour in eggs. As edges begin to set, lift with a spatula and shake or tilt pan to let uncooked egg flow underneath. Cook until eggs are softly set but top still looks moist and bottom is lightly browned (about 5 minutes).

To turn omelet, run a wide spatula under edge of omelet to loosen; invert a plate over omelet, then quickly invert pan, turning omelet out onto plate.

Add remaining 1 tablespoon oil to pan. Gently slide omelet back into pan and cook until lightly browned on second side (about 2 minutes); set aside.

Remove bread from oven, unwrap, and lift off top. Slide omelet out of pan into bottom of loaf. Replace top of bread.

If made ahead, wrap loaf in several thicknesses of foil to keep warm for up to 4 hours. Or let cool, wrap, and refrigerate; to reheat, place wrapped loaf in a 400° oven for 25 to 30 minutes or until omelet is heated through.

To serve, cut into wedges. Makes 6 to 8 servings.

Chile-Egg Puff

Here's a spirited egg and chile casserole that has won rave reviews again and again. For a party of four, prepare half the recipe and bake in an 8-inch square pan.

- 10 **eggs**
- ½ **cup all-purpose flour**
- 1 **teaspoon baking powder**
- ½ **teaspoon salt**
- 1 **pint (2 cups) small curd cottage cheese**
- 4 **cups (1 lb.) shredded jack cheese**
- ½ **cup (¼ lb.) butter or margarine, melted and cooled**
- 2 **cans (4 oz. *each*) diced green chiles, drained**
  Butter or margarine

In a large bowl, beat eggs until light and lemon colored. Add flour, baking powder, salt, cottage cheese, jack cheese, and the ½ cup butter; mix until smooth. Stir in chiles.

Pour egg mixture into a well-buttered 9 by 13-inch baking dish. Bake, uncovered, in a 350° oven for about 35 minutes or until top is browned and center appears firm. Serve immediately. Makes 8 servings.

Cheese Soufflé for Two

Soufflés, those prima donna delicacies, sometimes deflate disappointingly before you get them to the table. To avoid such a calamity, serve the soufflé the minute you take it out of the oven.

- 1 **tablespoon butter or margarine**
- 1 **tablespoon all-purpose flour**
  Dash of ground red pepper (cayenne)
- ⅛ **teaspoon dry mustard**
- ⅓ **cup milk**
- ¾ **cup shredded sharp Cheddar cheese**
- 2 **tablespoons grated Parmesan cheese**
- 2 **eggs, separated**
  Butter or margarine

(Continued on next page)

CREAMY MOUNTAIN of homemade Fresh Cheese (page 84) pairs perfectly with fresh fruit for a summery dessert. The cheese tastes like cream cheese, but has only half the calories.

In a wide frying pan over medium heat, melt the 1 tablespoon butter. Stir in flour, pepper, and mustard and cook, stirring, until bubbly. Gradually pour in milk and continue cooking and stirring until sauce boils and thickens.

Add Cheddar cheese and 1 tablespoon of the Parmesan cheese; cook, stirring, until cheese is melted. Remove from heat and beat in egg yolks.

In a small bowl, beat egg whites until soft, moist peaks form; fold into cheese mixture.

Generously butter a 1-quart soufflé dish or 2 individual 1¼-cup soufflé dishes; coat inside with remaining 1 tablespoon Parmesan cheese. Pour in soufflé mixture; with tip of a knife, draw a circle on surface about an inch from rim of dish.

Bake in a 350° oven for 18 to 20 minutes for a 1-quart dish, 12 to 15 minutes for individual dishes or until center feels firm when touched and crack looks fairly dry. Serve immediately. Makes 2 servings.

Mushroom-crust Quiche

A novel crust made with sautéed mushrooms cradles the custard filling of this savory quiche and enhances its egg-and-cheese goodness.

- 5 tablespoons butter or margarine
- ½ pound mushrooms, coarsely chopped
- ½ cup finely crushed saltine crackers
- ¾ cup chopped green onions (including tops)
- 2 cups (8 oz.) shredded jack or Swiss cheese
- ½ pint (1 cup) small curd cottage cheese
- 3 eggs
- ¼ teaspoon *each* ground red pepper (cayenne) and paprika

In a wide frying pan over medium heat, melt 3 tablespoons of the butter; add mushrooms and cook until soft. Stir in crushed crackers, then turn crust mixture into a well-greased 9-inch pie pan. Press evenly over bottom and sides.

In pan, melt remaining 2 tablespoons butter; add onions and cook until soft. Spread over crust and sprinkle evenly with jack cheese. In a blender or food processor, whirl cottage cheese, eggs, and red pepper until smooth. Pour into crust and sprinkle with paprika.

Bake, uncovered, in a 350° oven for 25 to 30 minutes or until a knife inserted just off center comes out clean. Let stand on a rack for 10 to 15 minutes before cutting. Makes 4 to 6 servings.

Bacon & Cheese Breakfast Pizza

Here's a version of pizza for those mornings—or other times— when a change of fare is likely to tickle everyone's fancy.

- Pastry for single-crust 9-inch pie
- ½ pound sliced bacon
- 2 cups (8 oz.) shredded Swiss cheese
- 4 eggs
- 1⅓ cups sour cream
- 2 tablespoons chopped parsley

Roll pastry and fit into a 12-inch pizza pan, ¾ inch deep; press against pan sides and trim even with top. Bake on lowest rack of a 425° oven for 5 minutes. Gently press bubbles down.

In a wide frying pan over medium heat, cook bacon until crisp; drain and crumble. Sprinkle bacon and cheese evenly over crust.

In a bowl, lightly beat eggs with sour cream and parsley until smooth; pour over pizza. Return to lowest oven rack and bake for 20 to 25 more minutes or until puffy and lightly browned. Makes 4 servings.

Fresh Cheese

(Pictured on page 82)

This homemade cheese tastes like cream cheese, but it has twice as much protein and only half the calories. And it's perfectly simple to make—the only ingredients are milk and buttermilk. You won't need much in the way of equipment, either—just a large kettle, a candy or deep-frying thermometer, a colander, and some cheesecloth.

This recipe makes 1 quart (2 lbs.) of cheese, but you can freeze any that won't be used within a week. It does become a little granular when frozen, so it's best to beat it with a rotary beater or whirl it in a food processor before serving. The recipe can be cut in half for a smaller quantity.

You can enjoy this cheese while it's still warm; just sprinkle it with salt, pepper, or sugar. Chilled, it's delicious with sweetened or unsweetened fruit.

- 4 quarts whole milk
- 1 quart cultured buttermilk
  Salt, pepper, or sugar (optional)

In a 6 to 8-quart kettle over medium heat, combine milk and buttermilk. Set a candy or deep-frying thermometer into milk. Heat until temperature reaches 180° (about 40 minutes, if milk was refrigerated).

Reduce heat to low and continue to cook, watching temperature on thermometer; it can range from 185° to 200° (remove from heat if temperature goes above

200°; return to heat when temperature falls within proper range). *Do not* stir while cooking—it breaks up curd and produces poor yield and texture.

Cook for about 20 more minutes for very soft-curd cheese or about 35 more minutes for more firm-curd cheese. Cheese will form a clot surrounded by clear whey. A small scorched area will probably develop on pan bottom, but don't be concerned about it. To test curd, use back of a spoon, gently pressing top of clot; it should feel like baked custard.

Line a colander with 3 or 4 thicknesses of cheesecloth that have been dipped in cold water and wrung dry; let edges of cloth hang over sides of colander.

(Continued on next page)

YOUR OWN YOGURT

The important factor in making successful yogurt is keeping the milk culture at a fairly constant temperature (about 115°) until it thickens. Yogurt bacteria are killed by higher temperatures; below 90°, they become inactive.

Today, many commercial yogurt makers are available that provide the right amount of heat. Also, a variety of home methods will keep the milk warm.

Homemade Yogurt

Readers have expressed much appreciation for these easy-to-follow directions and their delicious results. Take your choice between two reliable techniques.

Electric frying pan method. Preheat several canning jars or a bowl by filling them with warm water (about 115°). Set inside a deep kettle and fill kettle with water (about 115°). Place a candy or deep-frying thermometer in water surrounding jars and set kettle in an electric frying pan or on an electric griddle. Turn appliance setting to warm (or a setting that will keep water at 115°).

Cover kettle with a lid or a tent of foil. (You can also set a folded bath towel on top of foil to help hold in heat.) Let stand; meanwhile, prepare **Thick Homemade Yogurt Mixture** (recipe follows).

When mixture is ready, remove jars, pour out their water, and replace with milk mixture. Cover jars and return to kettle. (Yogurt will develop most even consistency if surrounding water is at same level as mixture in jars.) Cover kettle with lid or foil tent.

Leave undisturbed for 3½ hours or until yogurt is set. If water temperature should go as high as 120°, ladle out some of the water, replace with cold water, and lower heat setting as needed. To test yogurt, lift out a jar, uncover, and gently tip—yogurt should be firm and not move.

If not set, cover, replace in kettle, and test again every half-hour. When yogurt is set, remove jars, cover loosely, and refrigerate until yogurt is cold. Makes 1 quart.

Thermos bottle method. Preheat a wide-mouthed 1-quart thermos bottle by filling it with warm water (about 115°). Cap bottle and let stand; meanwhile, prepare **Thick Homemade Yogurt Mixture** (recipe follows).

When mixture is ready, pour water out of bottle and immediately replace with milk mixture. Cover tightly and leave undisturbed for 4 hours or until set. To test, uncover and gently tip bottle—yogurt should be firm and not move.

If not set, cover and test again every half-hour. When yogurt is set, remove cap, cover loosely, and refrigerate until yogurt is cold. Makes 1 quart.

Thick Homemade Yogurt Mixture. Pour 2 cups **low-fat milk** into a pan and place over medium heat. Heat to scalding (185°). Remove from heat and let cool; discard skin. Meanwhile, in a bowl, combine 1¼ cups **water** and 1⅓ cups **instant nonfat dry milk powder** and stir until smooth. Add to milk.

As soon as mixture cools to 115°, add ¼ cup **plain yogurt,** purchased or homemade (if homemade, yogurt should be no more than a week old); stir until smooth. Transfer mixture to preheated yogurt container and keep warm as directed.

Yogurt Cheese. Line a colander with a clean dishcloth or 3 or 4 thicknesses of cheesecloth (cut 20 inches square) that have been dipped in cold water and wrung dry. Spoon in 1 quart (4 cups) **Homemade Yogurt.** Twist ends of cloth together to close. Place colander in sink (or set in a larger bowl) and let drain at room temperature for 24 hours or until yogurt is consistency of cream cheese. Cover and refrigerate. Makes 1½ cups.

Slowly pour cheese into colander; *do not* scrape pan. Let cheese drain for at least 30 minutes.

Serve warm, sprinkled with salt, pepper, or sugar, if desired. Or cover and refrigerate for up to a week. Makes about 1 quart (2 lbs.) cheese.

Zucchini Jack Casserole

When your zucchini patch overwhelms you with the abundance of its yield, consider this spirited way to use some of the surplus. Serve squares of this chile-cheese casserole with barbecued chicken for a summer supper on the patio.

8 small zucchini (about 2 lbs. *total*)
4 eggs
½ cup milk
1 teaspoon salt
2 teaspoons baking powder
3 tablespoons all-purpose flour
¼ cup chopped parsley
1 clove garlic, minced or pressed
1 small onion, finely chopped
1 large can (7 oz.) diced green chiles
4 cups (1 lb.) shredded jack cheese
1 cup seasoned croutons, homemade (page 25) or purchased
3 tablespoons butter or margarine, melted

Slice zucchini into ¼-inch-thick rounds (you should have about 7 cups); set aside.

In a large bowl, beat eggs with milk, salt, baking powder, and flour until smooth. Stir in parsley, garlic, onion, chiles, cheese, and zucchini. Spoon egg mixture into a greased 9 by 13-inch baking dish. Toss croutons in melted butter, then sprinkle over top.

Bake, uncovered, in a 350° oven for 35 to 40 minutes or until a knife inserted in center comes out clean and zucchini is tender when pierced. Let stand for 10 minutes before cutting. Makes about 10 servings.

Chiles Rellenos with Marinara Sauce

There are chiles rellenos and chiles rellenos. This particular rendition steals the show because of its piquant topping.

1 can (4 oz.) whole green chiles
¼ to ⅓ pound jack cheese, cut into wide strips
4 eggs
⅓ cup milk
½ cup all-purpose flour
½ teaspoon baking powder
1 cup (4 oz.) shredded sharp Cheddar cheese
2 cups Fresh Marinara Sauce (page 104) or 1 can (15 oz.) marinara sauce
Pitted ripe olives

Cut a slit down side of each chile; gently remove and discard seeds and pith. Fold or stuff equal amounts of jack cheese strips inside each chile. Arrange chiles, side by side, in a lightly greased shallow 1½-quart baking dish.

In large bowl of an electric mixer, beat eggs until thick and foamy. Add milk, flour, and baking powder; beat until smooth. Pour egg mixture evenly over chiles and sprinkle with Cheddar cheese.

Bake, uncovered, in a 375° oven for about 30 minutes or until egg topping is puffy and jiggles only slightly when gently shaken. Meanwhile, heat marinara sauce to simmering in a small pan over low heat, then pour into a serving bowl.

Quickly garnish hot casserole with olives and serve with marinara sauce. Makes 4 servings.

Ricotta-filled Blintzes

(Pictured on facing page)

These blintzes burst with a creamy ricotta cheese filling that's low in calories but high in protein. Embellish servings with fruit and sour cream or yogurt.

Sweet Crêpes (recipe follows)
2 cups (1 lb.) ricotta cheese
2 tablespoons honey
1 tablespoon lemon juice
½ teaspoon *each* grated lemon peel and ground cinnamon
⅛ teaspoon salt
About 4 tablespoons butter or margarine
Sweetened fresh fruit, jam, or preserves
½ pint (1 cup) sour cream or plain yogurt (optional)

Prepare Sweet Crêpes; if made ahead, bring to room temperature.

In a small bowl, stir together ricotta, honey, lemon juice, lemon peel, cinnamon, and salt. For each blintz, spoon about 2 tablespoons of the ricotta mixture in center of each crêpe (arranged browned side up). Fold opposite sides over filling so they overlap slightly at center; then fold top and bottom in toward center to form a packet. Arrange, seam side down, on a baking sheet. (At this point, you may cover and refrigerate for up to 4 hours.)

In a wide frying pan over medium heat, melt 2 tablespoons of the butter. Place blintzes, seam side down, in pan (without crowding) and cook, turning, until golden brown on both sides (about 2 minutes on each side). Transfer to a platter and keep warm until all are cooked. Add more butter to pan as needed.

Serve with fruit and sour cream, if desired, to spoon over individual portions. Makes 6 servings.

SWEET CRÊPES. Follow directions for Basic Crêpes (page 117), adding 1 tablespoon **sugar** to batter before mixing.

BUTTERY BUNDLES of honey-sweetened ricotta cheese wear a generous topping of sour cream and fruit. They're Ricotta-filled Blintzes (recipe on this page), a tempting choice for a buffet-style breakfast on a spring morning.

...Cauliflower Cheese-Dilly (cont'd.)

Break cauliflower into flowerets. Pour water into a 3-quart pan to a depth of 1 inch. Bring to a boil over high heat. Add cauliflower. Cover, reduce heat to medium, and cook until crisp-tender (5 to 7 minutes). Drain well and turn into a shallow 1-quart casserole or baking dish.

In a small bowl, combine butter, 2 tablespoons of the cheese, dill, and garlic. Add to cauliflower, stirring gently; season to taste with salt and pepper. Sprinkle with remaining 2 tablespoons cheese.

Broil about 6 inches from heat until golden brown (about 10 minutes). Makes 4 to 6 servings.

Crusty Eggplant

Sliced eggplant is the star here, encased in a crunchy crumb crust and browned in the oven. Plan to use the eggplant soon after you bring it home from the market, unless you have a cool (about 50°) storage area.

2 medium-size eggplants (about 1 lb. *each*)
¼ cup grated Parmesan cheese
½ cup fine dry bread crumbs
1 tablespoon chopped parsley
¼ teaspoon salt
⅛ teaspoon pepper
2 eggs
 About ¼ cup all-purpose flour
4 tablespoons butter or margarine, melted

Peel eggplants, if desired; cut into ½-inch-thick slices.

In a pie pan, combine cheese, bread crumbs, parsley, salt, and pepper. In another pan, beat eggs lightly. Dust each eggplant slice with flour and dip into beaten egg, coating both sides. Dredge in crumb mixture, shaking off excess.

Pour 2 tablespoons of the butter into each of two 10 by 15-inch rimmed baking sheets; tilt pans to coat evenly. Arrange eggplant slices in a single layer in pans.

Bake, uncovered, in a 400° oven for 25 minutes, turning once, or until browned on both sides. Makes about 6 servings.

Eggplant Parmesan with Fresh Marinara Sauce

Eggplant Parmesan is unbeatable when you make it with your own marinara sauce. Juicy red tomatoes, olive oil, and fresh herbs become spirited partners in this dish the Italians call *melanzane Parmigiano*.

1 large eggplant (about 1½ lbs.), cut into ½-inch-thick slices
⅓ cup olive oil or salad oil
3 cups Fresh Marinara Sauce (page 104)
2 cups (8 oz.) shredded mozzarella cheese
½ cup grated Parmesan cheese

Brush both sides of eggplant slices with oil and place in a single layer in a large shallow baking pan. Bake, uncovered, in a 450° oven for 30 to 40 minutes or until browned and very soft.

Place about half the eggplant slices in a shallow 1½-quart casserole or baking dish. Top with 1½ cups of the Fresh Marinara Sauce, then sprinkle with 1 cup of the mozzarella cheese and ¼ cup of the Parmesan cheese. Repeat layers.

Reduce oven temperature to 350° and bake, uncovered, for 25 minutes or until bubbly. Makes 4 to 6 servings.

REAP A BOUNTY of color and flavor with hors d'oeuvres made from versatile vegetables. For appetizers with a garden-fresh feeling, try Spinach Squares (page 94), Zucchini Flats (page 96), and Stuffed Cherry Tomato Halves with guacamole filling (page 7).

Spinach Squares

(Pictured on page 90)

Looking for a new, versatile way to serve spinach? You can offer these tasty squares hot or cold, as a side dish, appetizer, or first course.

2 packages (10 oz. *each*) frozen chopped spinach, thawed
3 tablespoons butter or margarine
1 small onion, chopped
¼ pound mushrooms, sliced
4 eggs
¼ cup fine dry bread crumbs
1 can (10¾ oz.) condensed cream of mushroom soup
¼ cup grated Parmesan cheese
⅛ teaspoon *each* pepper, dry basil, and oregano leaves

Squeeze out as much moisture from spinach as possible; set aside. In a wide frying pan over medium heat, melt butter. Add onion and mushrooms and cook, stirring, until soft.

In a large bowl, beat eggs lightly; stir in onion mixture, bread crumbs, soup, 2 tablespoons of the cheese, pepper, basil, oregano, and spinach. Turn into a well-greased 9-inch square baking pan; sprinkle with remaining 2 tablespoons cheese.

Bake, uncovered, in a 325° oven for 35 minutes or until edges are beginning to brown. Serve warm. Or let cool, cover, and refrigerate; serve cold. To reheat, place in a 325° oven for 10 to 12 minutes. Makes about 9 servings.

Summer Squash Bake

It's midsummer and your garden is overflowing with squash. What do you do? Try this festive side dish, which features three kinds of lightly cooked summer squash. Or, if you prefer, use only one or two varieties—just be sure you have about three pounds altogether.

4 medium-size crookneck squash (about 1½ lbs. *total*)
4 medium-size pattypan squash (about ½ lb. *total*)
3 medium-size zucchini (about 1 lb. *total*)
1 teaspoon salt
½ teaspoon *each* pepper and oregano leaves
1¼ cups (5 oz.) shredded jack cheese
½ cup grated Parmesan cheese
½ cup chopped pecans or almonds
2 tablespoons butter or margarine, melted

Cut each squash into ½-inch-thick slices. Pour water into a 4 to 5-quart pan to a depth of 1 inch. Bring to a boil over high heat. Add squash; cover, reduce heat to medium, and cook just until crisp-tender (4 to 5 minutes). Drain well.

In a small bowl, combine salt, pepper, and oregano. Arrange half the squash in a greased shallow 2-quart casserole or baking dish; sprinkle with half the salt mixture and half the jack cheese. Repeat layers, then sprinkle with Parmesan cheese. In a small bowl, mix nuts and butter; sprinkle over top.

Bake, uncovered, in a 350° oven for 15 minutes or until heated through. Makes 6 to 8 servings.

Seasoned Spaghetti Squash

After this unusual vegetable is cooked, its flesh comes out in strands just like spaghetti.

1 medium-size spaghetti squash (about 4 lbs.)
Herb-Cheese Butter *or* Spicy Butter (recipes follow)

With a fork, pierce squash in several places. Place on a rimmed baking sheet and bake in a 350° oven for 1½ hours or until shell gives to pressure; turn squash over after 45 minutes. Meanwhile, prepare seasoned butter

of your choice and set aside.

Split squash in half lengthwise; scoop out and discard seeds. Pull strands free with a fork, place in a serving bowl, and mix with seasoned butter. Makes 6 to 8 servings.

HERB-CHEESE BUTTER. In a small bowl, combine ½ cup (¼ lb.) **butter** or margarine, softened; 3 tablespoons finely chopped **parsley;** ½ teaspoon **Italian herb seasoning** *or* ¼ teaspoon *each* dry basil and marjoram leaves; ¼ teaspoon *each* **garlic salt** and **pepper;** and ¼ cup grated **Parmesan cheese.** Stir until well blended.

SPICY BUTTER. In a small bowl, combine ½ cup (¼ lb.) **butter** or margarine, softened; 3 tablespoons firmly packed **brown sugar;** ¼ teaspoon *each* **ground cinnamon** and **ground allspice;** and ⅛ teaspoon **ground nutmeg.** Stir until well blended.

Baked Tomatoes

The recipe for these garlicky baked tomatoes originated in Provence, a region of France known for its lively, spirited style of cooking.

8 to 10 medium-size tomatoes (about 3 lbs. *total*)
About ¼ teaspoon salt
2 tablespoons olive oil or salad oil
2 tablespoons *each* finely chopped garlic (about 7 large cloves), chopped parsley, and fine dry bread crumbs
Dash of pepper

Core tomatoes and cut in half horizontally. Gently squeeze out juice and seeds.

(Continued on page 96)

SWEET, MOIST, AND TENDER, sliced yams are especially dramatic when bathed in a glossy glaze, as in Fresh Yams Baked in Orange Sauce (page 96).

Sprinkle a 9 by 13-inch baking dish with salt. Arrange tomatoes, cut side up, in dish and drizzle with oil. Bake, uncovered, in a 400° oven for 10 minutes.

Meanwhile, in a small bowl, combine garlic, parsley, bread crumbs, pepper, and ¼ teaspoon of the salt. Sprinkle over tomatoes and continue baking for 15 more minutes or until tomatoes are soft throughout. Makes 8 to 10 servings.

Chile-Cheese Tomatoes

What a way to show off fresh, ripe, juicy tomatoes! Each thick slice makes a serving.

3 large tomatoes, peeled
½ pint (1 cup) sour cream
½ teaspoon salt
¼ teaspoon pepper
1 teaspoon sugar
1 tablespoon all-purpose flour
2 green onions (including tops), chopped
1 to 2 tablespoons diced canned green chiles
1 cup (4 oz.) shredded Cheddar cheese

Cut each tomato horizontally into 3 thick slices. Gently squeeze out some of the seeds. Arrange tomatoes on rack of a broiler pan.

In a small bowl, combine sour cream, salt, pepper, sugar, flour, onions, and chiles; stir until well blended. Spoon chile mixture evenly over tomatoes, then sprinkle with cheese.

Broil about 4 inches from heat just until cheese is bubbly and golden brown (about 4 minutes). Makes 9 servings.

Fresh Yams Baked in Orange Sauce

(Pictured on page 95)

There's something undeniably homey about fresh yams, hot from the oven. And when they're glazed with orange sauce and garnished with thin orange slices, their natural moist sweetness becomes irresistible.

About 4 pounds yams or sweet potatoes
1¼ cups sugar
2 tablespoons cornstarch
1 teaspoon salt
2 cups orange juice
4 tablespoons butter or margarine
1½ teaspoons grated orange peel
1 orange, thinly sliced

Peel yams and cut into ½-inch-thick slices, discarding thin ends. Overlapping slices, arrange in rows in a shallow 3-quart casserole or baking dish; set aside.

In a small pan, combine sugar, cornstarch, and salt; stir in orange juice until well blended. Bring to a boil over high heat and cook, stirring, until sauce thickens and becomes clear (about 1 minute).

Remove from heat, add butter and orange peel, and stir until butter is melted. Pour over yams.

Bake, covered, in a 400° oven for 45 minutes. Uncover and baste tops of yams thoroughly with sauce.

Continue baking, uncovered, basting with sauce several more times, for 15 more minutes or until yams are tender when pierced and tops are well glazed. Garnish with orange slices. Makes 12 to 14 servings.

Zucchini Lasagne

Sliced zucchini replaces the pasta in this lighter and less starchy version of lasagne.

Meat Sauce (recipe follows)
6 medium-size zucchini (about 2 lbs. *total*), cut into ⅛-inch-thick slices
½ pound mozzarella cheese, thinly sliced
1 cup (8 oz.) ricotta cheese
½ cup grated Parmesan cheese

Prepare Meat Sauce; set aside.

Arrange half the zucchini slices in a greased shallow 3-quart casserole or baking dish. Evenly top with half the mozzarella, half the ricotta, and half the sauce. Repeat layers; then sprinkle with Parmesan cheese.

Bake, uncovered, in a 350° oven for 35 minutes or until zucchini is tender when pierced and cheese is lightly browned. Makes 6 to 8 servings.

MEAT SAUCE. Heat 2 tablespoons **salad oil** in a wide frying pan over medium heat. Add 2 cloves **garlic,** minced or pressed, and 1 large **onion,** chopped. Cook, stirring, until onion is soft. Add ¼ pound **mushrooms,** sliced, and ½ pound lean **ground beef.** Cook, stirring, until meat is lightly browned (about 5 minutes).

Stir in 1 can (1 lb.) **tomatoes** (break up with a spoon) and their liquid, 1 can (6 oz.) **tomato paste,** ¾ cup **dry red wine** or regular-strength beef broth, 1½ teaspoons **oregano leaves,** ½ teaspoon **dry basil,** and **salt** and **pepper** to taste. Boil gently, uncovered, until thick (about 25 minutes).

Zucchini Flats

(Pictured on page 90)

Use large zucchini for this dish —that way, you'll come out with wide, flat, succulent strips.

About ¾ cup grated Parmesan cheese
2 eggs
2 tablespoons *each* all-purpose flour and finely chopped parsley
¾ teaspoon salt
¼ teaspoon pepper
2 cloves garlic, minced or pressed
¼ cup milk
2 large zucchini (about 7 inches long *each*)
All-purpose flour
¼ cup salad oil

In a shallow bowl, combine ¾ cup of the cheese, eggs, the 2 tablespoons flour, parsley, salt, pepper, garlic, and milk. With a wire whisk or rotary beater, beat until smooth. Cover and refrigerate for at least 15 minutes.

Cut zucchini in half crosswise, then into lengthwise slices about ¼ inch thick. Lightly dust each piece with flour.

Heat oil in a wide frying pan over medium heat. Using a fork, dip each zucchini slice into cheese mixture, thickly coating both sides. Place in pan, a few pieces at a time, and cook, turning once, until golden brown on both sides.

Drain briefly on paper towels, then transfer to a serving plate and keep warm until all are cooked. Sprinkle to taste with additional cheese. Makes 4 to 6 servings.

Tender-Crisp Vegetable Medley

These stir-fried vegetables make a crunchy, vitamin-rich side dish when served alone, or a complete meal when combined with meat and served over rice. For a change of pace, add tofu cubes instead of meat, or spoon the mixture into the center of a big Dutch Baby pancake (see page 128).

1¼ pounds broccoli
  Cooking Sauce (recipe follows)
3 tablespoons salad oil
1 clove garlic, minced or pressed
1 medium-size onion, chopped
2 stalks celery, cut into ½-inch-thick slanting slices
2 carrots, cut into ¼-inch-thick slanting slices
1 red or green bell pepper, seeded and cut into ¼-inch strips
3 tablespoons water
¼ pound mushrooms, sliced
1 cup cooked chicken, turkey, or ham, cut into strips (optional)
½ cup toasted slivered almonds or cashews

Cut off broccoli stems, peel, then cut into ¼-inch-thick slices; set aside. Slice large broccoli flowerets in half lengthwise through stems. Prepare Cooking Sauce and set aside.

Place a wok or wide frying pan over high heat. When pan is hot, add 2 tablespoons of the oil. When oil is hot, add garlic, onion, celery, carrots, bell pepper, and broccoli stems. Cook, stirring quickly with a wide spatula, for 2 minutes. Add water; cover and cook, stirring often, for 3 more minutes.

Add remaining 1 tablespoon oil, broccoli flowerets, and mushrooms. Cook, stirring quickly, for 1 minute. Stir sauce and add to vegetable mixture, along with chicken, if desired.

Continue cooking and stirring until sauce boils and thickens. Turn into a serving dish and sprinkle with nuts. Makes about 4 servings.

COOKING SAUCE. In a small bowl, combine 3 tablespoons **cornstarch,** 1 teaspoon **garlic powder,** 1 teaspoon *each* **dry basil** and **oregano leaves,** ¼ cup **dry sherry,** and 2½ cups regular-strength **chicken broth.** Stir until blended.

Armenian Vegetable Casserole

In the cuisines of the Middle East, fresh vegetables have a special importance, playing a leading role in many dishes. Armenian cooks often combine several vegetables to create a stew-like casserole. This one is called *tourlu*. If you like, you can serve it with yogurt spooned on top.

½ pound green beans (optional)
1 medium-size eggplant (about 1 lb.), unpeeled, cut into 1-inch cubes
2 large onions, cut into 1-inch cubes
3 medium-size carrots, cut into ¾-inch-thick slanting slices
2 large stalks celery, cut into ½-inch-thick slanting slices
1 large red or green bell pepper, seeded and cut into 1-inch squares
1 or 2 large thin-skinned potatoes, peeled and cut into 1-inch cubes
1 can (1 lb.) Italian-style tomatoes
½ cup *each* olive oil and catsup
  About 2 teaspoons salt
1½ teaspoons *each* sugar and dry basil
¼ teaspoon pepper
3 or 4 small zucchini, cut into ½-inch-thick slices
  Chopped parsley (optional)

If beans are used, cut into 2-inch lengths. Place in a 5-quart casserole or baking dish along with eggplant, onions, carrots, celery, bell pepper, and potatoes.

Drain juice from tomatoes into casserole. Chop tomatoes and add to casserole with oil, catsup, 2 tablespoons of the salt, sugar, basil, and pepper; stir gently.

Bake, covered, in a 350° oven for 1½ to 2 hours or until vegetables are almost tender; baste vegetables with juices about every 30 minutes.

Gently stir in zucchini and continue baking, uncovered, for 20 to 30 more minutes or until vegetables are tender when pierced. Season with salt to taste. Garnish with parsley, if desired, and serve hot or at room temperature.

If made ahead, cool, cover, and refrigerate until next day. To reheat, cover and place in a 350° oven for 30 to 40 minutes or until heated through. Makes 12 to 15 servings.

PASTA & GRAINS

Stuffed, tossed, or in a casserole

Fresh Noodles with Four Cheeses

A quartet of distinctive Italian cheeses—fontina, Bel Paese, Gorgonzola, and Parmesan—gives character to the dish the Italians call *fettucine a quattro formaggi*. Three of the cheeses blend into a rich sauce; the fourth—Parmesan—is tossed with the noodles and also sprinkled on individual servings.

You can serve this dish as a first course or as an entrée. In either case, balance its richness with a crisp salad and a light, fruity dessert.

3 tablespoons butter or margarine
1½ tablespoons all-purpose flour
⅛ teaspoon ground nutmeg
    Dash of white pepper
1 cup half-and-half (light cream)
½ cup regular-strength chicken broth
⅓ cup *each* shredded fontina cheese and Bel Paese cheese
⅓ cup crumbled Gorgonzola cheese
    Homemade Noodles (page 101) or 8 ounces packaged wide noodles
½ cup grated Parmesan cheese
    Grated Parmesan cheese

In a 2-quart pan over medium heat, melt 1½ tablespoons of the butter. Blend in flour, nutmeg, and pepper; cook, stirring, until bubbly. Gradually pour in half-and-half and broth; continue cooking and stirring until sauce boils and thickens.

Stir in fontina and Bel Paese cheeses; cook, stirring, until cheeses are melted and sauce is smooth. Add Gorgonzola, stirring until blended. Cover and place over simmering water to keep warm; or let cool, cover, and refrigerate. To reheat, place over simmering water and stir until smooth and heated through.

Cut fresh noodles, if used, into strips about 10 inches long. Cook noodles according to recipe or package directions. Drain and

return to pan. Stir noodles lightly with remaining 1½ tablespoons butter and the ½ cup Parmesan cheese. Spoon noodles onto plates and top each serving with cheese sauce. Pass Parmesan cheese at the table. Makes 4 to 6 servings.

Fettuccine Verde

Verde means "green," and it's the spinach noodles that give this dish its festive color. If you don't want to make your own pasta and can't find spinach noodles at the store, you can use plain ones instead. Prepare the fettuccine just before serving; if allowed to cool, it becomes gummy.

> Spinach Noodles (page 101) or 8 ounces packaged wide spinach noodles
> 6 tablespoons butter or margarine
> 1 cup sliced green onions (including tops)
> 2 cloves garlic, minced or pressed
> ½ pint (1 cup) whipping cream
> 1½ cups (4½ oz.) grated Parmesan cheese
> ⅛ teaspoon ground nutmeg
> Salt and pepper

Cook noodles according to recipe or package directions. Drain well.

Meanwhile, in a wide frying pan over medium-high heat, melt butter. Add onions and garlic and cook, stirring, for 2 minutes. Add cream and cook until bubbling.

Add hot noodles to pan; using 2 forks, stir gently. Add ½ cup of the cheese and stir until noodles are evenly coated. Add ½ cup of the remaining cheese and stir again. Add nutmeg and season to taste with salt and pepper; then stir again. Serve immediately. Pass remaining cheese at the table. Makes 4 servings.

Lasagne Swirls

Instead of layering the noodles for this meatless lasagne, you wrap them around a spinach and ricotta filling and stand them on end. The result: a platter of pinwheels that taste old-world Italian, but look excitingly different. Serving is easier this way, too.

> 8 packaged lasagne noodles
> 1 package (10 oz.) frozen chopped spinach, thawed
> 1 cup (3 oz.) grated Parmesan cheese
> 1⅓ cups ricotta cheese
> ¼ teaspoon ground nutmeg
> 1 teaspoon salt
> ½ teaspoon pepper
> 2 tablespoons salad oil
> 2 cloves garlic, minced or pressed
> 1 large onion, chopped
> 1 large can (15 oz.) tomato sauce
> 1 teaspoon sugar
> ½ teaspoon *each* dry basil and oregano leaves

Cook noodles according to package directions. Drain, rinse under cold water, and drain again. Set aside.

Squeeze out as much moisture from spinach as possible. In a large bowl, stir together spinach, ¾ cup of the Parmesan cheese, ricotta cheese, nutmeg, ½ teaspoon of the salt, and ¼ teaspoon of the pepper. Spread about ¼ cup of the spinach mixture along entire length of each noodle; roll up noodles. Grease a 9 by 13-inch baking dish. Stand rolled noodles on end and slightly apart in dish. Set aside.

Heat oil in a wide frying pan over medium heat. Add garlic and onion and cook until onion is soft. Add tomato sauce, sugar, basil, oregano, remaining ½ teaspoon salt, and remaining ¼ teaspoon pepper. Simmer, uncovered, for 5 minutes. Pour over noodles. (At this point, you may cool, cover, and refrigerate until next day.)

Bake, covered, in a 350° oven for 30 minutes (45 minutes, if refrigerated) or until heated through. Sprinkle with remaining ¼ cup Parmesan cheese. Makes 4 servings.

Ricotta-stuffed Giant Shells

These stuffed shells proudly display the colors of Italy—green spinach, pearly white pasta, and a robust red tomato sauce.

> 4 cups Italian Mushroom Gravy (recipe follows)
> 1 package (10 oz.) frozen chopped spinach, thawed
> 3 tablespoons butter or margarine
> 1 small onion, finely chopped
> 1 clove garlic, minced or pressed
> 2 eggs
> 2 cups (1 lb.) ricotta cheese
> ¼ cup grated Parmesan cheese
> 1 tablespoon chopped parsley
> ½ teaspoon *each* oregano leaves and salt
> Dash of pepper
> 24 giant-size pasta shells

Prepare Italian Mushroom Gravy and set aside.

Squeeze out as much moisture from spinach as possible. In a wide frying pan over medium heat, melt butter. Add onion and garlic and cook, stirring, until onion is soft. Add spinach and cook for 3 minutes.

In a large bowl, stir together eggs and ricotta cheese until well blended; then stir in spinach mixture, Parmesan cheese, parsley, oregano, salt, and pepper. Set aside.

Cook pasta shells according to package directions. Drain, rinse under cold water, and drain again. Stuff each shell with 3 tablespoons of the spinach-cheese mixture.

Pour 2 cups of the gravy into a very large baking dish. Arrange filled shells side by side in gravy. Spoon remaining 2 cups gravy over shells. (At this point, you may cover and refrigerate until next day.)

Bake, covered, in a 350° oven for 30 minutes (40 to 50 minutes, if refrigerated) or until bubbly and heated through. Makes 4 to 6 servings.

(Continued on next page)

ITALIAN MUSHROOM GRAVY.
In a small bowl, pour 1½ cups hot **water** over 1 cup (about ½ oz.) **dried mushrooms;** set aside.

Heat 3 tablespoons **olive oil** or salad oil in a wide frying pan or 5-quart kettle over medium heat. Add 1½ cups chopped **parsley;** 2 or 3 stalks **celery,** chopped; 2 cloves **garlic,** minced or pressed; and ½ teaspoon *each* **dry rosemary, thyme leaves,** and **sage leaves.** Cook, stirring, until vegetables are soft.

Stir in 2 large cans (15 oz. *each*) **tomato sauce,** 2 cans (about 1 lb. *each*) **tomatoes** (break up with a spoon) and their liquid, and ¼ teaspoon **crushed red pepper.**

Chop mushrooms and add to pan along with mushroom-soaking liquid. Cover and simmer for 3 hours. Season with **salt** to taste. Makes 1½ to 2 quarts.

Tomato Manicotti

Among the larger tubes of pasta are manicotti—"little muffs." This recipe calls for manicotti shells that don't require precooking before they're stuffed. Look for packages with directions to stuff uncooked shells.

    1 large can (15 oz.) tomato sauce
    ½ pound lean ground beef
    2 tablespoons chopped parsley
    2 teaspoons instant minced onion
    ¼ teaspoon *each* oregano leaves and marjoram leaves
    ½ pint (1 cup) small curd cottage cheese
    2 cloves garlic, minced or pressed
    1 package (3¾ oz.) manicotti shells (quick-cooking type)
    2 cups (8 oz.) shredded jack cheese
    ½ cup grated Parmesan cheese

Pour ½ cup of the tomato sauce into a 7 by 11-inch baking dish; set aside.

In a large bowl, combine beef, parsley, onion, oregano, marjoram, cottage cheese, and garlic. Mix until combined. Divide beef mixture equally among 8 shells, carefully stuffing mixture into shells from each end. Place shells in baking dish; pour remaining sauce over manicotti.

Bake, covered, in a 350° oven for 30 minutes or until pasta is almost tender. Remove from oven and sprinkle with jack and Parmesan cheeses. Return to oven and bake, uncovered, for 10 more minutes. Makes 4 servings.

Cannelloni Roma

Cannelloni appears in many forms and many flavors—some delicate, some hearty. This version uses crêpes instead of pasta.

    14 to 16 Basic Crêpes (page 117)

Filling

    4 tablespoons butter or margarine
    1 small clove garlic, minced or pressed
    1 large onion, coarsely chopped
    1¼ pounds chicken thighs, skinned, boned, and cut into 2-inch cubes
    ½ pound boneless veal, cut into 2-inch cubes
    1 cup ricotta cheese
    ½ cup grated Parmesan cheese
    ¾ teaspoon salt
    ⅛ teaspoon ground nutmeg
    1 egg

White sauce

    4 tablespoons butter or margarine
    1½ tablespoons all-purpose flour
    1½ cups regular-strength chicken broth
    1 cup milk

Tomato sauce

    1½ tablespoons butter or margarine
    2 tablespoons chopped shallots or green onion (white part only)
    1 can (about 1 lb.) Italian-style tomatoes
    ½ cup regular-strength chicken broth
    ½ teaspoon *each* dry basil and salt

    1½ pounds thinly sliced teleme or jack cheese

Bring crêpes to room temperature, if refrigerated or frozen.

To make filling, melt butter in a wide frying pan over medium heat. Add garlic and onion and cook until onion is soft. Add chicken and veal and stir to coat each piece with butter. Cover, reduce heat, and simmer until meat is tender (about 35 minutes).

Using a food processor or finest blade of a meat grinder, finely chop meat mixture. Mix in ricotta cheese, Parmesan cheese, salt, and nutmeg. (At this point, you may cover and refrigerate until next day.)

Mix in egg just before spooning filling on crêpes.

To make white sauce, melt butter in a 2-quart pan over medium heat. Blend in flour and cook, stirring, until bubbly. Gradually pour in broth and milk; continue cooking and stirring until sauce boils and thickens. Set aside.

To make tomato sauce, melt butter in a 2-quart pan over medium-high heat. Add shallots and cook until soft. Cut tomatoes in half and squeeze out seeds, reserving juice; discard seeds. Finely chop tomatoes. Add tomatoes and juice to pan along with broth, basil, and salt. Reduce heat and simmer, uncovered, stirring occasionally, until sauce thickens (about 30 minutes).

Lightly grease a shallow baking dish about 12 by 15 inches; 2 shallow baking dishes, each at least 6 by 15 inches; *or* 6 to 8 shallow baking dishes, each about 3 by 6 inches. Combine tomato sauce and white sauce and spoon into dish.

Spoon about ¼ cup of the meat filling down center of each crêpe; roll to enclose. Place filled crêpes, seam side down, slightly apart in sauce. Evenly distribute cheese slices over cannelloni, covering completely. (At this point, you may cover and refrigerate until next day.)

Bake, uncovered, in a 450° oven for 12 to 15 minutes (about 20 minutes, if refrigerated) or un-

(Continued on page 102)

MAKING PASTA AT HOME

Homemade noodles require a little extra time and effort, and you may need some practice before you achieve perfect results. But it's definitely worth the trouble. Not only does making your own pasta yield the most tender and flavorful noodles you can get, but it also can provide a hands-on diversion for your family or guests. If you enjoy the kind of cooking that allows everyone to lend a helping hand, by all means have a pasta party—this is one instance when too many cooks won't spoil the broth.

Homemade Noodles

- 2 cups all-purpose flour
- 2 large eggs
- 3 to 6 tablespoons water
  Additional all-purpose flour for kneading, rolling, and cutting

Mound flour on a work surface or in a large bowl and make a well in center. Break eggs into well. With a fork, beat eggs lightly and stir in 2 tablespoons of the water.

Using a circular motion, begin to draw flour from sides of well. Add 1 tablespoon of the remaining water and continue mixing until flour is moistened. Add more water, a tablespoon at a time, if needed. When dough becomes stiff, use your hands to finish mixing. Pat dough into a ball and knead a few times to help flour absorb liquid.

Clean work surface and sprinkle lightly with flour. If you plan to use a rolling pin, knead dough by hand, sprinkling with flour if needed, until smooth and elastic (about 10 minutes). Cover dough and let rest for 20 to 30 minutes. If you plan to use a pasta machine, knead dough by hand, sprinkling with flour if needed, just until dough is no longer sticky (3 to 4 minutes). Divide dough into 4 equal portions; roll and cut a portion at a time, keeping remaining dough covered.

To roll and cut by hand, roll a portion of dough on a floured board into an 8 by 10 to 12-inch rectangle about ¹⁄₁₆ inch thick. If dough feels sticky, turn and flour both sides as you roll. Lay dough flat on a lightly floured cloth or sheet of wax paper. Repeat for remaining portions. Let rolled dough dry, turning once, until dough has feel and flexibility of soft leather (5 to 10 minutes—don't let dough become brittle).

Starting at a narrow end, roll up each rectangle jelly roll style and cut into ¼-inch-wide slices. Unfurl coiled noodles as soon as they're cut and sprinkle lightly with flour, if sticky.

To roll and cut with pasta machine, slightly flatten a portion of dough and sprinkle with flour. Feed through smooth rollers set at widest setting. Fold dough into thirds and feed through again; repeat folding and rolling 8 to 10 more times or until dough is smooth and elastic. If dough feels sticky, flour both sides each time dough is rolled.

Set rollers one notch closer together and, without folding dough, feed through machine. Repeat rolling, setting rollers closer each time, until dough is about ¹⁄₁₆ inch thick (on most machines, roller will be on second from narrowest notch).

Cut strip in half crosswise for easier handling; lay dough flat on a lightly floured cloth or sheet of wax paper. Repeat for remaining portions of dough.

Let rolled dough dry, turning once, until dough has feel and flexibility of soft leather (5 to 10 minutes).

To cut noodles, change machine to ¼-inch blade setting. Flour both sides of each dough strip and feed through. Sprinkle lightly with flour, if sticky.

If made ahead, arrange slightly apart on a cloth or sheet of wax paper. Let stand, uncovered, for up to an hour. Or place in a plastic bag and refrigerate for up to 2 days; for longer storage, freeze for up to a month.

To cook noodles, place 4 to 6 quarts water in a large kettle over high heat. Add 1 tablespoon salt and bring to a boil. Drop in fresh pasta (do not thaw, if frozen) and stir with a fork. Cook, uncovered, just until tender to bite (2 to 3 minutes). Drain well. Makes about 4 servings, 1 cup each.

Spinach Noodles. Cook half of a 10-ounce package frozen **chopped spinach** according to package directions. Let cool, then squeeze out as much moisture as possible. Mince spinach finely (you should have ¼ cup). Follow recipe for Homemade Noodles (preceding), omitting water and stirring spinach in with eggs.

til sauce is bubbly and filling is heated through. Serve immediately. Makes 14 to 16 cannelloni; allow 2 or 3 for each main-dish serving.

Lemon Rice

This lemony mushroom-and-rice pilaf is a sensational accompaniment for fish—or, if you like, a stuffing. The recipe makes enough to fill an 8-pound fish.

    6 tablespoons butter or margarine
    1 cup sliced celery
    1 small onion, chopped
    ¼ teaspoon thyme leaves
    2 teaspoons grated lemon peel
    ¼ cup lemon juice
  2½ cups water
  1¼ cups long-grain rice
    ½ to ¾ pound mushrooms, thinly
        sliced
    1 teaspoon salt
    ⅛ teaspoon pepper

In a wide frying pan over medium heat, melt 3 tablespoons of the butter. Add celery and onion and cook, stirring, until soft. Stir in thyme, lemon peel, lemon juice, and water; bring to a boil. Add rice; cover, reduce heat, and simmer until rice is tender and liquid is absorbed (about 20 minutes).

Meanwhile, in another frying pan over medium heat, melt remaining 3 tablespoons butter. Add mushrooms and cook, stirring, until soft. When rice is done, stir in mushrooms along with salt and pepper. Makes about 5 cups.

Tomato Fried Rice

Because the Oriental stir-fry technique cooks food quickly over intense heat, colors remain bright and few nutrients are lost. To vary the flavor of the rice, omit the salt and add about a tablespoon of soy sauce with the sherry.

    2 tablespoons salad oil
    2 tablespoons butter or margarine
    1 small onion, finely chopped
    3 cups cold cooked rice
    ½ teaspoon *each* salt and sugar
        Dash of pepper
    1 small jar (2 oz.) sliced pimentos,
        drained
        About 2 tablespoons dry sherry,
        white wine, or water
    2 medium-size tomatoes, peeled,
        seeded, and diced
        Chopped parsley or sliced green
        onion tops

Heat a wok or wide frying pan over medium-high heat. When pan is hot, add oil and butter. When butter is melted, add onion and cook, stirring, until golden (about 2 minutes).

Add rice and continue cooking and stirring until rice is golden (about 7 minutes). Stir in salt, sugar, pepper, pimentos, and 2 tablespoons of the sherry. Continue cooking and stirring, adding a little more liquid if needed, for about 1 more minute. Stir in tomatoes and cook for 1 to 2 more minutes.

Turn out into a serving dish and garnish with parsley. Makes 4 to 6 servings.

Brown Rice & Vegetable Casserole with Salsa

The recipe for this nutritional powerhouse comes to us from a restaurant in Sonoma, California. A wholesome hodgepodge of brown rice, cheese, sunflower seeds, and plenty of steamed vegetables, this casserole is a high-protein one-dish meal.

  2½ cups water
    2 chicken bouillon cubes
    1 cup long-grain brown rice
        About 1 pound broccoli
        About 1 pound cauliflower
    2 medium-size crookneck squash
        or zucchini
    ¼ cup sliced celery
    ¼ pound mushrooms, sliced
    ¼ cup *each* shredded carrot and
        chopped green onions
        (including tops)
    ½ teaspoon soy sauce
    1 can (about 7 oz.) mild green
        chile salsa
        About 20 cherry tomatoes, cut in
        half
    3 slices (1 oz. *each*) jack cheese,
        cut in half
    3 slices (1 oz. *each*) Cheddar
        cheese, cut in half
    3 tablespoons roasted salted
        sunflower seeds

In a 2-quart pan over high heat, bring water to a boil. Add bouillon cubes and boil until dissolved. Add rice; cover, reduce heat, and simmer until tender (about 45 minutes).

Meanwhile, break broccoli into bite-size flowerets with 2-inch stems (reserve remainder of stems for other uses). Break cauliflower into bite-size flowerets. Slice squash into ½-inch-thick rounds.

Pour water into a 5-quart kettle to a depth of 1½ inches. Bring to a boil over high heat. Place broccoli, cauliflower, squash, and celery on a rack above water. Cover, reduce heat to medium, and cook until vegetables are almost tender (8 to 10 minutes). Add mushrooms; cover and cook for 2 more minutes; set aside.

When rice is done, add carrot, onions, and soy; stir lightly with a fork. Spread rice mixture evenly in a greased shallow 2-quart casserole or baking dish. Spoon salsa over rice and top with steamed vegetables and tomatoes.

Cover with alternating slices of jack cheese and Cheddar cheese, overlapping edges slightly. (At this point, you may cover and refrigerate until next day.)

Bake, uncovered, in a 350° oven for 15 to 20 minutes (25 to 30 minutes, if refrigerated) or until heated through. Sprinkle with sunflower seeds and serve immediately. Makes 6 servings.

Mixed-grain Pilaf

A mélange of barley, brown rice, and bulgur wheat, this slightly chewy pilaf is accented with vegetables and topped with toasted nuts. It's a refreshing change from more ordinary rice dishes.

- 4 tablespoons butter or margarine
- ⅓ cup chopped almonds or walnuts
- 1 large onion, chopped
- 1 large carrot, chopped or shredded
- 1 clove garlic, minced or pressed
- ⅓ cup chopped parsley
- ⅓ cup *each* barley, brown rice, and bulgur wheat
- 2½ cups regular-strength beef or chicken broth
- ¼ cup dry sherry or water
- ¾ teaspoon *each* dry basil and oregano leaves
  Salt and pepper

In a 3-quart pan over medium heat, melt butter. Add nuts and stir until lightly toasted; with a slotted spoon, lift out nuts and set aside.

Increase heat to medium-high and add onion, carrot, garlic, and parsley. Cook, stirring, until vegetables are soft. Stir in barley, rice, and bulgur; continue cooking and stirring until grains are lightly browned.

Stir in broth, sherry, basil, and oregano. Bring to a boil; cover, reduce heat, and simmer until grains are tender (about 45 minutes).

Let stand, covered, for 10 minutes. Season to taste with salt and pepper. Garnish with toasted nuts. Makes about 6 servings.

Wheat Berry Pilaf

Wheat berries require soaking and then long, slow cooking to achieve tenderness. Once cooked, though, these plump, nutty whole wheat kernels lend themselves to use in many nourishing dishes.

- 1 cup wheat berries
- 5 cups water
- ¼ cup salad oil
- 1 large onion, chopped
- ½ pound mushrooms, thinly sliced
- 2 teaspoons beef stock base or 2 beef bouillon cubes
- ½ cup hot water
- ½ teaspoon dry basil
- ¼ teaspoon pepper
- 2 medium-size zucchini, thinly sliced
  Salt
- 1 cup (4 oz.) shredded Cheddar cheese or jack cheese
- 2 tablespoons minced parsley

In a 4-quart pan, combine wheat berries and the 5 cups water. Cover and let stand for 8 hours or until next day. (Or cover pan, bring to a boil over high heat, and boil for 2 minutes; then remove from heat and let stand, covered, for 1 hour.)

Without draining wheat berries, bring to a boil over high heat. Reduce heat and simmer, covered, until tender (about 1½ hours). Drain well, reserving liquid if desired; let cool. (At this point, you may cover and refrigerate for up to 2 weeks.)

Heat oil in a wide frying pan over medium heat. Add onion and mushrooms and cook, stirring, until soft. In a small bowl, combine beef stock base and the ½ cup hot water (or use ½ cup of the reserved liquid). Stir into pan with basil, pepper, and wheat berries.

Cover and bring to simmering. Stir in zucchini; cover and continue simmering until liquid is absorbed and wheat berries are heated through (about 10 minutes).

Season with salt to taste. Transfer pilaf mixture to a shallow 2-quart casserole or pan and sprinkle with cheese. Broil about 4 inches from heat until cheese is melted (about 2 minutes). Garnish with parsley. Makes about 6 servings.

Medford Oats

This recipe for quick and inexpensive granola comes from a woman in Medford, Oregon. "With my four children plus their friends raiding the granola canister all day, I felt an economical and speedy version was worth devising," she told us. It's a good choice for family breakfasts and after-school snacks.

- 8 cups regular rolled oats
- 1½ cups *each* regular wheat germ and firmly packed brown sugar
- 1 large package (8 oz.) shredded coconut
- 1½ cups roasted salted sunflower seeds or cashews
- ½ cup salad oil
- ¾ cup honey
- 2 teaspoons vanilla

In a large bowl, stir together oats, wheat germ, sugar, coconut, and sunflower seeds; set aside.

In a small pan over medium heat, combine oil, honey, and vanilla. Cook, stirring, until bubbly. Pour over oat mixture and mix thoroughly.

Grease two 10 by 15-inch rimmed baking pans and spread mixture evenly in pans. Bake, uncovered, in a 325° oven for 15 to 20 minutes, stirring two or three times, or until coconut is lightly browned.

Stir granola several times as it cools. Let cool thoroughly; then store in an airtight container. Makes 16 cups.

SAUCES

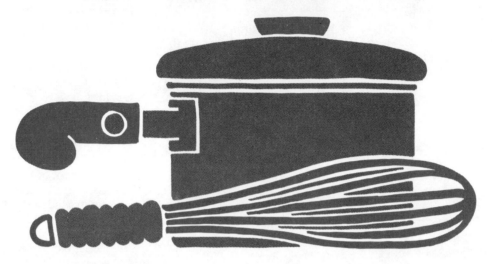

Flavor accents with international appeal

Fresh Marinara Sauce

The natural sweetness of carrots curbs the acid bite of tomatoes in this marinara sauce. It's delicious over pasta, hot vegetables, steaks, or omelets. Keep some on hand in your freezer; this is an especially useful recipe if you have a big tomato harvest to cope with.

- 6 pounds (about 15 medium-size) tomatoes
- ⅓ cup olive oil or salad oil
- 6 cloves garlic, minced or pressed
- 2 large onions, chopped
- 3 or 4 large carrots, finely chopped
- 2 tablespoons dry basil or ⅓ cup finely chopped fresh basil leaves
- 1 tablespoon dry oregano leaves or 3 tablespoons finely chopped fresh oregano leaves
- 2½ teaspoons salt
- ¾ to 1 teaspoon pepper

Immerse tomatoes, a few at a time, in boiling water to cover for about 1 minute. Lift out with a slotted spoon and plunge into cold water. Peel off and discard skins. Coarsely chop tomatoes (you should have 11 to 12 cups). Set aside.

Heat oil in a 5 to 6-quart kettle over medium heat. Add garlic, onions, and carrots and cook, stirring occasionally, until onions are translucent.

Add tomatoes, basil, oregano, salt, and pepper. Bring to a boil; reduce heat and simmer, uncovered, stirring occasionally, until sauce is very thick and reduced by about half (about 1½ hours).

If made ahead, cool, cover, and refrigerate for up to 3 days; for longer storage, freeze for up to 4 months. To reheat (thaw first, if frozen), simmer over low heat, stirring occasionally; add water if needed. Makes 1½ to 2 quarts.

Yogurt Hollandaise Sauce

Dieters won't have to pass up this hollandaise sauce—it's made with yogurt instead of butter. If you use low-fat yogurt and whole eggs, a tablespoon contains only about 22 calories, half the number in traditional hollandaise.

- ½ pint (1 cup) plain yogurt, homemade (page 85) or purchased
- 4 egg yolks or 2 whole eggs
- ¾ teaspoon salt
- 2 teaspoons sugar
- ¼ teaspoon liquid hot pepper seasoning

In top of a double boiler, stir together yogurt and egg yolks (or whole eggs) with a wire whisk; add salt, sugar, and hot pepper seasoning. Place over barely simmering water and cook, stirring with whisk, until sauce thickens (8 to 10 minutes).

104

Serve hot. If made ahead, cool, cover, and refrigerate for up to 2 days. To reheat, place in top of a double boiler and cook, stirring, over hot (not boiling) water until heated through. Makes about 1⅓ cups.

Oriental Sauce Mix

With a supply of this seasoning shortcut in the refrigerator, you'll always be ready for stir-fry dishes. Try it with beef, chicken, shrimp, or pork, or experiment with other ingredients—even leftovers—to create your own stir-fry combinations. This sauce keeps for up to 4 weeks.

¼ cup cornstarch
1 teaspoon *each* garlic powder and ground ginger
¼ cup *each* white vinegar and dry sherry
½ cup *each* soy sauce and dark corn syrup
1 can (14 oz.) regular-strength beef broth
¼ teaspoon pepper

In a 1-quart measuring cup or small bowl, stir together cornstarch, garlic powder, and ginger until well combined. Add vinegar and sherry and stir until cornstarch mixture is dissolved. Add soy, corn syrup, broth, and pepper and mix well. Stir in enough water to make 4 cups total.

Pour sauce into a jar with a tight-fitting lid. Cover and refrigerate for up to 4 weeks. Stir well before using. Makes 4 cups.

Aïoli

In southern France, the pungent garlic mayonnaise known as *aïoli* highlights a help-yourself meal of the same name when served with an array of vegetables, fish, and hard-cooked eggs. To complete a light summertime supper, offer French bread and butter, and fresh fruit for dessert.

6 to 8 medium-size cloves garlic
1½ tablespoons lemon juice
½ teaspoon salt
3 egg yolks
½ cup *each* olive oil and salad oil
1 to 2 tablespoons water
Accompaniments (suggestions follow)

In a blender or food processor, combine garlic, lemon juice, salt, and egg yolks; whirl until smooth (about 1 minute). Combine olive oil and salad oil in a small measuring cup; with motor on high, add oil mixture in a slow, steady stream. As mixture thickens, add oil a little faster, if you like, but never so quickly that it stands in puddles.

When sauce becomes too thick to incorporate oil, blend in water, a spoonful at a time; then slowly add remaining oil. Cover and refrigerate for at least 3 hours or up to 4 days.

Meanwhile, prepare accompaniments. Spoon aïoli over foods, or serve in individual bowls for dipping. Makes about 1¾ cups, enough for 6 to 8 servings.

ACCOMPANIMENTS. Choose several raw or cooked **vegetables** such as zucchini, tomatoes, mushrooms, cauliflower, radishes, green peppers, cabbage, turnips, small inner romaine leaves, hot boiled small thin-skinned potatoes, or hot or cold cooked green beans and artichokes.

Include cold cooked **shrimp,** lobster, or crab; hot or cold poached lean white-fleshed **fish,** such as halibut or lingcod; and hard-cooked **eggs.**

Cut large vegetables and fish into bite-size pieces; then reassemble to preserve their whole appearance.

For each serving, allow 1 artichoke, 1 turnip, 1 green pepper, and 1 or 2 potatoes, or equivalent amounts of other vegetables; ⅓ to ½ pound fish and shellfish; and 1 egg.

Pesto Sauce

Fragrant, bright green basil, fresh Parmesan cheese, and garlic give a hearty flavor to Italy's renowned pesto sauce. Use it to flavor vinaigrette dressing; stir it into soups, dips, or other sauces; or blend it with butter to melt over meat, vegetables, or pasta.

2 cups firmly packed fresh basil leaves
1 cup (3 oz.) freshly grated Parmesan cheese
½ teaspoon salt
2 large cloves garlic
½ cup olive oil

In a blender or food processor, combine basil, cheese, salt, and garlic; whirl at high speed until smooth. With motor on high, gradually pour in oil and whirl until well blended.

Cover and refrigerate for up to a week. For longer storage, freeze in small premeasured batches.

Add to soups, sauces, or other dishes. To add pesto (if frozen, do not thaw) to foods that require cooking, stir in pesto during last few minutes of cooking time. Heat gently, stirring, just until thoroughly blended. Makes about 1⅓ cups.

Duxelles

Slow cooking intensifies the buttery, nutlike taste of fresh mushrooms in this classic French preparation. You need just a few spoonfuls to make elegant sauces for vegetables, fish, or chicken.

1 pound mushrooms
4 tablespoons butter or margarine
1 small onion, finely chopped
1 clove garlic, minced or pressed
Salt, pepper, and ground nutmeg

With a sharp knife or food processor, finely chop mushrooms (if using processor, add half the

mushrooms at a time and use short bursts to avoid puréeing mushrooms); set aside.

In a 3 to 4-quart pan over medium-high heat, melt butter. Add onion and cook, stirring, until soft (about 5 minutes). Add mushrooms and garlic and cook, stirring, until liquid has evaporated (about 15 minutes). Season to taste with salt, pepper, and nutmeg.

Let cool; then cover and refrigerate for up to a week; for longer storage, freeze in small premeasured batches. Thaw before using. Makes about 2 cups.

DUXELLES & CHIVE SAUCE. In a small bowl, combine ⅓ cup **sour cream**, 2 tablespoons **Duxelles** (preceding), and 1 teaspoon **freeze-dried chives.** Mix well. Season to taste with **salt, pepper,** and **ground nutmeg.** Refrigerate until chilled. Use as a dip for raw vegetables or as a sauce to spoon over lightly cooked green beans, zucchini, or red thin-skinned potatoes. Makes about ½ cup.

DUXELLES LEMON SAUCE. In a 2-quart pan over medium heat, melt 2 tablespoons **butter** or margarine; add ¼ cup **Duxelles** (preceding) and cook, stirring, until heated through. Add 2 tablespoons **all-purpose flour** and continue cooking, stirring, until bubbly.

Gradually add ⅔ cup regular-strength **chicken broth,** 2 tablespoons **lemon juice,** and 6 thin slices **lemon.** Continue cooking and stirring until sauce boils and thickens; season to taste with **salt** and **pepper.**

Serve hot, spooned over pan-fried or broiled fish fillets or chicken pieces; garnish with the lemon slices. Makes about 1¼ cups.

PARMESAN & DUXELLES SAUCE. In a small bowl, stir together ¼ cup grated **Parmesan cheese** and 2 tablespoons *each* **Duxelles** (preceding) and **mayonnaise.**

Spoon 2 to 3 tablespoons over baked chicken breasts or fish fillets about halfway through baking time. Or make appetizers by spooning about ½ teaspoon of the sauce on melba toast rounds or zucchini slices and broiling about 6 inches from heat just until cheese sizzles (2 to 3 minutes). Makes about ½ cup.

Garlic-Crumb Sauce

Bread crumbs soak up garlicky goodness in a sauce that adds distinction to leftover meats. You can use the sauce with roasted lamb, pork, beef, chicken, or turkey. Just slice the meat or cut it into bite-size pieces; then coat the meat with sauce as it reheats.

- 4 **tablespoons butter or margarine**
- ½ **cup fine dry bread crumbs**
  About 2 cups regular-strength chicken broth
- ½ **teaspoon dry thyme leaves or 1 teaspoon finely chopped fresh thyme leaves**
- 10 **large cloves garlic, coarsely chopped**
  Salt and pepper
- 3 **to 4 cups cooked lamb, pork, beef, chicken, or turkey, cut into slices or bite-size pieces**
  Parsley or mint sprigs (optional)

In top of a double boiler directly over medium heat, melt butter. Stir in bread crumbs until coated. Add 2 cups of the broth, ½ cup at a time, stirring until mixture comes to a boil.

Stir in thyme and garlic. Cover pan and place over simmering water; cook, stirring occasionally, for about 2 hours.

Season to taste with salt and pepper. Add meat and stir in a little more broth or water if needed so sauce coats meat generously. Cook until meat is heated through. Using a fork or tongs, transfer meat to a serving platter; garnish with parsley, if desired. Offer remaining sauce at the table. Makes 4 to 6 servings.

Homemade Mustard

You begin with dry mustard, adding vinegar for tartness and wine for mellowness; then you cook with egg yolks to give the spread its velvety smooth texture. You can season the mildly flavored mustard as suggested, or leave it plain.

For gift-giving, package the mustards in jars and identify them with decorative labels.

- ¼ cup *each* **dry mustard and white wine vinegar**
- ⅓ **cup dry white wine**
- 1 **tablespoon sugar**
- ½ **teaspoon salt**
- 3 **egg yolks**

In top of a double boiler, stir together mustard, vinegar, wine, sugar, and salt. Let stand, uncovered, for 2 hours.

Beat egg yolks into mustard mixture. Place over simmering water and cook, stirring with a wire whisk, until mixture thickens slightly (about 5 minutes). Pour into small jars and let cool. Cover tightly and refrigerate for up to a month. Makes about 1 cup.

LIME MUSTARD. Follow recipe for Homemade Mustard (preceding); when you remove mustard from heat, stir in ¾ teaspoon grated **lime peel** and 1½ teaspoons **lime juice.** Serve with roast lamb or chicken, shrimp, or sautéed fish.

TARRAGON MUSTARD. Follow recipe for Homemade Mustard (preceding); when you remove mustard from heat, stir in ½ teaspoon **dry tarragon.** Serve with roast lamb or chicken, shrimp, steaks, or as a sandwich spread.

SPICY MUSTARD. Follow recipe for Homemade Mustard (preceding), adding ¼ teaspoon *each* **ground turmeric** and **ground cloves** with egg yolks. Serve with baked ham, meat sandwiches, hamburgers, or frankfurters.

TOMATO MUSTARD. Follow recipe for Homemade Mustard (preceding), adding 1 teaspoon **paprika,** 1 tablespoon drained and chopped **pimento,** and ¼ cup **tomato paste** with egg yolks. Serve with seafood, hamburgers, frankfurters, or baked ham.

Belgian Coffee Sundae Syrup

Combining coffee with ice cream for dessert is a continental custom worth duplicating, and this brandy-laced coffee syrup does it to perfection—especially when poured over coffee ice cream, topped with whipped cream, and sprinkled with toasted nuts.

- 1 cup *each* firmly packed brown sugar and strong coffee
- ¼ teaspoon vanilla
- 1 tablespoon brandy
  Coffee ice cream
  Whipped cream
  Toasted almonds

In a small pan over medium-high heat, combine sugar and coffee; bring to a boil. Cook, uncovered, until mixture thickens (about 10 minutes). Remove from heat and stir in vanilla and brandy. Let cool.

Spoon syrup over scoops of ice cream; top each serving with whipped cream and nuts. Makes 4 servings.

Caramel Nut Sauce

This creamy nut sauce is a winner, no matter what you spoon it over. Add chocolate pieces for a delicious variation. Either way, the sauce is best served the same day it's made.

- 4 teaspoons butter or margarine
- ½ cup slivered almonds or coarsely chopped pecans
- 1 cup firmly packed brown sugar
- ½ pint (1 cup) whipping cream

In a wide frying pan over medium-low heat, melt butter. Add nuts and cook, stirring, until lightly toasted.

Stir in sugar and cream. Cook, stirring, over medium-high heat until sauce boils and sugar is dissolved. Let cool. Serve at room temperature. Makes 2 cups.

CARAMEL NUT & CHOCOLATE SAUCE. Follow recipe for Caramel Nut Sauce (preceding), stirring ¼ cup **semisweet chocolate chips** into cooled sauce.

Raspberry or Strawberry Sauce

Make either of these sauces in minutes from frozen and thawed presweetened berries. The ruby red raspberry sauce is slightly tart, the strawberry sauce mildly sweet. Both are good over ice cream, other fruits, or pancakes or waffles.

- 1 package (about 10 oz.) frozen presweetened raspberries or strawberries, thawed
- ½ teaspoon cornstarch
- 1 tablespoon light corn syrup

In a small pan over medium-high heat, combine berries, cornstarch, and corn syrup; bring to a boil. Cook, stirring, for 2 minutes. Let cool (the sauce thickens as it cools); then cover and refrigerate. Serve cold. Makes about 1 cup.

Orange Custard Sauce

Delicious over fresh or cooked fruits, this creamy sauce is accented with orange-flavored liqueur.

- ⅓ cup Vanilla Sugar (recipe follows); or use plain sugar and 1½ teaspoons vanilla
- 4 eggs
- 1 pint (2 cups) half-and-half (light cream) or milk
- 2 tablespoons orange-flavored liqueur

At least 2 days ahead, prepare Vanilla Sugar.

In top of a double boiler, combine sugar and eggs. In a small pan over medium-high heat, bring half-and-half to scalding; then stir into egg mixture. Place top of double boiler over simmering water and cook, stirring, until custard coats a metal spoon in a smooth velvety layer (10 to 15 minutes).

Immediately place top of double boiler in ice water to stop the cooking; stir often until custard has cooled. Stir in liqueur.

If made ahead, cover and refrigerate for up to 4 days. Makes about 2½ cups.

VANILLA SUGAR. Place 1 **vanilla bean** in a 1-quart jar and fill with **sugar.** Let stand for 2 days so flavor of bean permeates sugar. Replenish sugar as used; bean will give off flavor for several years.

Hot Chocolate Sauce

This rich chocolate sauce is the essence of sweet simplicity.

- 4 ounces semisweet chocolate, coarsely chopped
- 6 tablespoons whipping cream

In a small pan over lowest possible heat, combine chocolate and cream. Cook, stirring, until chocolate is melted and well blended with cream. Makes about 1 cup.

BREADS

Freshly baked to fill your breadbasket

Super Simple Refrigerator Bread

No kneading is necessary for these airy, tender loaves—they couldn't be simpler. After mixing the ingredients, you let the dough rise in the refrigerator for 3 hours; or, if you're pressed for time, the dough can wait there until the next day.

⅓ cup *each* sugar and solid shortening
1 tablespoon salt
2 cups boiling water
2 packages active dry yeast
1 teaspoon sugar
¼ cup warm water (about 110°)
2 eggs, well beaten
7½ to 8 cups all-purpose flour

In a large bowl, combine the ⅓ cup sugar and shortening with salt and the 2 cups boiling water;

let cool until lukewarm. In a small bowl, stir yeast into the 1 teaspoon sugar and the ¼ cup warm water; let stand until bubbly (5 to 15 minutes).

Add yeast mixture to lukewarm mixture; stir in eggs. Beat in 4 cups of the flour; then gradually stir in as much of the remaining flour as dough will absorb, mixing well. Place in a greased bowl; cover and refrigerate for at least 3 hours or until next day.

Divide dough in half. With greased hands, shape each portion into a smooth loaf. Place each in a greased 9 by 5-inch loaf pan. Cover and let rise in a warm place until almost doubled (about 2 hours).

Bake in a 350° oven for 30 to 35 minutes or until bread sounds hollow when tapped. Turn out onto racks and let cool. Makes 2 loaves.

Easy 100% Whole Wheat Bread

If you're impatient, this is the bread for you. Only one rising puffs it up to plump, grainy perfection. How is this possible? You warm the flour first, and use extra yeast. One reader calls it "the answer to a busy baker's prayers."

About 4⅓ cups whole wheat flour
2 packages active dry yeast
2 tablespoons molasses or honey
1¾ cups warm water (about 110°)
¼ cup salad oil
1½ teaspoons salt
⅓ cup regular wheat germ

Measure flour into a heat-resistant bowl; then place in a warm oven (about 150°) until warmed through (about 10 minutes).

Meanwhile, in a large bowl, stir together yeast, molasses, and ¾ cup of the water; let stand until bubbly (5 to 15 minutes). Mix in remaining 1 cup water, oil, and salt. Stir in wheat germ. Mix in flour, about 1 cup at a time, beating well after each addition.

When dough begins to clean sides of bowl, turn dough out onto a lightly floured board. Knead just enough to shape into a smooth loaf. Place in a greased 9 by 5-inch loaf pan. Cover and let rise in a warm place until dough is about 1 inch above rim of pan (30 to 40 minutes).

Bake in a 400° oven for 35 minutes or until loaf is well browned and sounds hollow when tapped. Turn out onto a rack and let cool. Makes 1 loaf.

Three-wheat Batter Bread

This briskly beaten batter needs no kneading. Baked in coffee cans, the finished loaves are a nutrition-packed taste sensation that has brought us numerous compliments.

- 1 package active dry yeast
- ½ cup warm water (about 110°)
- ⅛ teaspoon ground ginger
- 3 tablespoons honey
- 1 large can (13 oz.) evaporated milk
- 1 teaspoon salt
- 2 tablespoons salad oil
- 2½ cups all-purpose flour
- 1¼ cups whole wheat flour
- ½ cup regular wheat germ
- ¼ cup cracked wheat

In a large bowl, stir together yeast, water, ginger, and 1 tablespoon of the honey; let stand until bubbly (5 to 15 minutes). Stir in milk, salt, oil, and remaining 2 tablespoons honey.

In another bowl, stir together all-purpose flour, whole wheat flour, wheat germ, and cracked wheat; add to liquid ingredients,

a cup at a time, beating well after each addition.

Spoon batter into a well-greased 2-pound coffee can or into 2 well-greased 1-pound coffee cans; cover with greased plastic lids. (At this point, you may freeze for up to 3 weeks.)

Let rise in a warm place until lids pop off (55 to 60 minutes for 1-pound cans, 1 to 1½ hours for 2-pound can). If frozen, let batter stand in covered cans at room temperature until lids pop off (4 to 5 hours for 1-pound cans, 6 to 8 hours for 2-pound can).

Bake, uncovered, in a 350° oven for about 45 minutes for 1-pound cans, about 1 hour for 2-pound can, or until bread sounds hollow when tapped. Let cool in cans on a rack for 10 minutes. Then, using a thin knife, loosen crust around edge of can; slide bread from can, and let cool in an upright position on rack. Makes 2 small loaves or 1 large loaf.

European Sour Bread

Flat beer—that's the secret ingredient used by European bakers to create an authoritative tartness in dark breads like this one.

- 2 cups flat beer
  About ⅔ cup yellow cornmeal
- 2 tablespoons butter or margarine
- 2 teaspoons salt
- ½ cup *each* dark molasses and warm water (about 110°)
- 2 packages active dry yeast
- 1 tablespoon sugar
- ½ cup *each* regular wheat germ and whole bran cereal
- 2 cups graham flour or whole wheat flour
- 1 cup gluten flour or all-purpose flour
  About 3½ cups all-purpose flour
- 1 egg yolk beaten with 1 tablespoon water

Heat beer in a pan over medium heat until steaming. Remove from heat and gradually stir in ½

cup of the cornmeal, butter, salt, and molasses; let cool until lukewarm.

Meanwhile, in a large bowl, stir together the ½ cup warm water, yeast, and sugar; let stand until bubbly (5 to 15 minutes). Gradually beat in cooled beer mixture, wheat germ, bran cereal, graham flour, and gluten flour. Gradually stir in enough of the all-purpose flour (about 3 cups) to make a stiff dough.

Sprinkle about ¼ cup of the remaining all-purpose flour on a board; turn dough out and knead until smooth and satiny (10 to 20 minutes), adding flour as needed to prevent sticking.

Turn dough over in a greased bowl; cover and let rise in a warm place until doubled (about 1 hour). Punch dough down, cover, and let rise again until doubled (about 45 minutes).

Evenly sprinkle 2 greased baking sheets (or 1 large sheet) with remaining cornmeal. Punch dough down, knead briefly on a lightly floured board to release air, and divide in half. Shape each half into a slightly flattened 8-inch round loaf; place each loaf on a baking sheet (or place 3 to 4 inches apart on one large sheet). Cover and let rise until almost doubled (about 40 minutes).

Using a floured sharp knife, make ½-inch-deep slashes on top of loaves, forming a tic-tac-toe design; brush tops and sides with egg yolk mixture.

Bake in a 375° oven for 40 minutes or until loaves are well browned and sound hollow when tapped. Transfer to racks and let cool. Makes 2 round loaves.

Basque Sheepherder's Bread

(Pictured on page 114)

"Very impressive-looking for a buffet" is the way one reader described this enormous round

loaf. To achieve its characteristic domed shape, you'll need to use a 10-inch cast-iron or cast-aluminum Dutch oven (5-quart size). Traditionally baked in a pit under a Basque shepherd's campfire, the bread bakes to the same crusty goodness (and a little more reliably) in your conventional oven at home.

  3 **cups very hot tap water**
  ½ **cup (¼ lb.) butter or margarine**
  ⅓ **cup sugar**
2½ **teaspoons salt**
  2 **packages active dry yeast**
  9 **to 9½ cups all-purpose flour**
     Salad oil

In a large bowl, combine water, butter, sugar, and salt. Stir until butter melts; let cool to about 110°. Stir in yeast, cover, and let stand until bubbly (5 to 15 minutes).

Beat in about 5 cups of the flour to make a thick batter. Stir in enough of the remaining flour (about 3½ cups) to make a stiff dough. Turn dough out onto a floured board; knead until smooth and satiny (10 to 20 minutes), adding flour as needed to prevent sticking. Turn dough over in a greased bowl; cover and let rise in a warm place until doubled (about 1½ hours).

Punch dough down and knead on a floured board to form a smooth ball. With a circle of foil, cover inside bottom of a 5-quart Dutch oven. Grease foil, inside of Dutch oven, and underside of lid with oil.

Place dough in pot and cover with lid. Let rise in a warm place until dough pushes up lid about ½ inch (about 1 hour—watch closely).

Bake, covered with lid, in a 375° oven for 12 minutes. Remove lid and bake for 30 to 35 more minutes or until loaf is golden brown and sounds hollow when tapped. Turn loaf out (you'll need a helper) onto a rack and let cool. Peel off foil. Makes 1 very large loaf.

Sourdough French Bread

Round or baguette-shaped, this tangy, crusty bread is much like San Francisco's best.

  2 **cups warm water (about 110°)**
  1 **cup Sourdough Starter (page 111), at room temperature**
7½ **to 8 cups all-purpose flour**
  2 **teaspoons** *each* **salt and sugar**
     Yellow cornmeal
     Boiling water
  1 **teaspoon cornstarch**
  ½ **cup water**

In a large bowl, combine the 2 cups warm water, starter, and 4 cups of the flour; stir until smooth. Cover lightly and let stand in a warm place (about 85°) until mixture is full of bubbles and spongy-looking (6 to 8 hours).

Stir in salt, sugar, and enough of the remaining flour (about 3 cups) to form a very stiff dough. Turn dough out onto a floured board; knead until smooth (10 to 20 minutes), adding flour as needed to prevent sticking. Turn dough over in a greased bowl; cover and let rise in a warm place until doubled (2 to 2½ hours).

Punch dough down and divide in half. Knead each piece gently on a floured board just until dough has a smooth surface. If you have only one oven, wrap one portion in plastic wrap and refrigerate.

For an oblong loaf, shape dough into a smooth log by rolling it back and forth, gently elongating loaf to about 14 inches. Sprinkle a piece of stiff cardboard (about 7 by 18 inches) with 3 tablespoons cornmeal and set loaf on top.

For a round loaf, shape dough into a smooth ball. Sprinkle a piece of stiff cardboard (12 inches square) with 3 tablespoons cornmeal and set loaf on top.

Cover lightly and let rise in a warm place until puffy and almost doubled (1 to 1½ hours). With oven racks in the 2 lowest positions, place a baking sheet on top rack as oven preheats to 400°. Just before bread is ready to bake, place a rimmed baking sheet on lowest rack and pour in boiling water to a depth of about ¼ inch.

Meanwhile, in a small pan over high heat, combine cornstarch and the ½ cup water; bring to a boil, stirring; let cool slightly. Using a floured sharp knife, cut ½-inch-deep slashes in top of loaf—3 slightly slanting slashes in oblong loaf, 4 slashes in a crisscross pattern in round loaf. Brush top and sides evenly with cornstarch mixture. Carefully slide loaf from cardboard onto baking sheet on top oven rack.

Bake at 400° for 10 minutes; brush evenly again with cornstarch mixture. Bake for 20 to 25 more minutes or until loaf is golden brown and sounds hollow when tapped. Transfer to a rack and let cool.

When you put first loaf in oven, remove other portion of dough from refrigerator and shape as directed (chilled dough may take slightly longer to rise). Bake as directed. Makes 2 loaves.

Buttery Sourdough Pan Rolls

Zesty sourdough flavors these fluffy, buttery pan rolls. To make your own sourdough starter, see the facing page.

  2 **packages active dry yeast**
  ½ **cup warm water (about 110°)**
  4 **cups all-purpose flour**
  ¼ **cup sugar**
  1 **teaspoon salt**
  ½ **cup (¼ lb.) plus 2 tablespoons butter or margarine, melted**
  1 **egg**
  1 **cup Sourdough Starter (page 111), at room temperature**
  ½ **cup warm milk (about 110°)**

(Continued on page 112)

STARTER FOR SOURDOUGH COOKERY

Since we first published the following sourdough starter recipe in 1978, we've received much praise for its delicious effect on bread, rolls, and pancakes. But a few readers have reported that their starters simply never got started. Unfortunately, success with sourdough starter can never be guaranteed, since too many uncontrollable factors are involved in its production.

Temperature is the main variable; you'll need to find a nice warm place to put your starter while it becomes sour and bubbly. Ideally, your nook should be between 80° and 100°. (Above 110°, the active bacteria may be killed—the starter can smell sour, but it won't get bubbly; below 70°, it doesn't grow well.)

Some good spots are on top of a water heater or refrigerator, near (but not directly over) a gas range burner or pilot light, or in any partially enclosed area where heat collects.

The light in an electric oven can provide enough heat, too. Adjust the oven racks so the top of the container will be 2 to 2½ inches under the oven light. Turn the oven on for a minute or so—just until the air inside feels a little warmer than room temperature; then turn the oven off. Place the starter inside, close the door, and turn on the light (or prop the door open just enough to keep the light on). If necessary, occasionally remove the container and repeat the oven-warming process.

If you're unsuccessful in your first attempt to make a starter, it may be because the necessary bacteria weren't present in the milk you used. Try again with milk from a different dairy.

One last thought to bear in mind: the older the starter, the better the results will be when you bake. Sometimes young starters (less than 6 months old) just don't have enough oomph—they're best used in breads that also call for yeast as well as sourdough starter, or in pancakes and waffles.

Sourdough Starter

Rinse a 1½-quart glass, ceramic, rigid plastic, or stainless steel container with hot water for several minutes; wipe dry.

In a pan, heat 1 cup **skim milk** or low-fat milk to 90°

to 100° on a thermometer. Remove from heat and stir in 3 tablespoons **plain yogurt.** Pour into warm container, cover tightly, and let stand in a warm place (see preceding suggestions).

After 8 to 24 hours, starter should be about the consistency of yogurt (a curd forms and mixture doesn't flow readily when container is slightly tilted). If some clear liquid rises to top of milk during this time, simply stir it back in. However, if liquid has turned light pink, it indicates that milk is beginning to break down; discard and start again.

After curd has formed, gradually stir 1 cup **all-purpose flour** into starter until smooth. Cover tightly and let stand in a warm place (80° to 100°) until mixture is full of bubbles and has a good sour smell (2 to 5 days).

If clear liquid forms during this time, stir it back into starter. But if liquid turns pink, spoon out and discard all but ¼ cup starter; then blend in a mixture of 1 cup *each* warm milk (90° to 100°) and flour. Cover tightly and let stand again in a warm place until bubbly and sour smelling—then it's ready to use. To store, cover and refrigerate. Makes about 1½ cups.

To maintain an ample supply, replenish your starter every time you use it with equal amounts of warm milk (90° to 100°) and flour. For example, if you used ½ cup of the starter in a recipe, blend in a mixture of ½ cup *each* warm milk and flour. Cover tightly and let stand in a warm place for several hours or until next day; mixture should be bubbly again; then cover and refrigerate.

For consistent flavor, continue using the same type of milk you used originally. Always bring your starter to room temperature before using it (this takes 4 to 6 hours). If you plan to bake in the morning, leave it out the night before.

If you bake regularly—about once a week—the starter should keep lively and active. You can check your starter occasionally to see if it's active by spooning out ¼ cup of the starter and blending it with a mixture of ½ cup *each* warm milk (90° to 100°) and flour. Cover and let stand in a warm place. Check often; it should bubble again in 4 to 8 hours. You can combine this mixture with the original starter after the test.

If you don't bake often, it's best to discard about half your starter and replenish it with warm milk and flour about every 2 months to keep it active.

In a small bowl, stir yeast into water; let stand until bubbly (5 to 15 minutes). In a large bowl, stir together 2 cups of the flour, sugar, and salt; add yeast mixture, 6 tablespoons of the butter, egg, starter, and milk.

Using a heavy-duty mixer or wooden spoon, beat until well blended and smooth (about 5 minutes). Gradually beat in remaining 2 cups flour. Cover and let rise in a warm place until doubled (about 45 minutes).

Pour 2 tablespoons of the remaining butter into a 9 by 13-inch baking pan, tilting pan to coat bottom. Punch dough down and drop by large spoonfuls into pan, making 15 rolls. Cover and let rise in a warm place until light and puffy (about 30 minutes).

Drizzle remaining 2 tablespoons butter over rolls. Bake in a 425° oven for 15 to 20 minutes or until browned. Turn out onto a plate and serve hot; pull rolls apart to separate. Makes 15 rolls.

Four-way Refrigerator Rolls

This special yeast dough yields a surprising number of rolls—four to six dozen. The dough rises in the refrigerator and keeps its stamina for a remarkably long time. You can mix it one day, then bake a batch of rolls the next day, or up to 5 days later.

Remarkably versatile, the dough can be used in four different ways.

- **2 packages active dry yeast**
- **2½ cups warm water (about 110°)**
- **1 cup (½ lb.) butter or margarine**
- **¾ cup sugar**
- **1 tablespoon salt**
- **2 eggs**
  About 8¼ cups all-purpose flour

In a small bowl, stir yeast into 1½ cups of the water; let stand until bubbly (5 to 15 minutes).

Meanwhile, in large bowl of an electric mixer, beat together butter, sugar, and salt until fluffy. Add eggs, one at a time, beating well after each addition. With mixer on low speed, add yeast mixture. Add 4 cups of the flour, a cup at a time, beating well after each addition. Beat on medium speed for 5 minutes, scraping bowl frequently. Stir in remaining 1 cup water.

Using a heavy-duty mixer or wooden spoon, gradually beat in enough of the remaining flour (about 4 cups) to make a soft dough. Turn dough over in a large, greased bowl; cover and refrigerate for at least 8 hours or up to 5 days.

To shape for baking, punch dough down and divide into 4 equal portions. Using a portion at a time, shape and bake in any of the ways suggested below; cover and refrigerate unused dough. Makes 4 to 6 dozen rolls.

PERFECT DINNER ROLLS. Divide a portion of dough into 12 equal pieces. With oiled or greased hands, shape each piece into a smooth ball and place in a well-greased 2½-inch muffin cup. Cover and let rise in a warm place until doubled (1½ to 2 hours).

Bake in a 375° oven for 15 to 18 minutes or until browned. Turn out onto racks and let cool. Makes 1 dozen.

BUTTERY CASSEROLE ROLLS. Divide a portion of dough into 18 equal pieces. With oiled or greased hands, shape each into a smooth 1½-inch ball. Dip top of each in melted **butter** or margarine (use 2 tablespoons *total*). Arrange without touching, buttered side up, in a well-greased 9-inch round cake pan. Cover and let rise in a warm place until doubled (1½ to 2 hours).

Bake in a 375° oven for 25 minutes or until golden. Turn out onto racks and let cool. Makes 1½ dozen.

CINNAMON-NUT SWEET ROLLS. In a small pan over low heat, combine 4 tablespoons **butter** or margarine, ¼ cup firmly packed **brown sugar,** and 1 tablespoon **light corn syrup.** Stir until melted; mix in ¼ cup **chopped nuts.** Spoon equally into 12 well-greased 2½-inch muffin cups; set aside.

Remove a portion of dough from refrigerator. On a lightly floured board, roll dough out into a 10 by 12-inch rectangle. Brush with 1½ tablespoons **butter** or margarine, melted, and sprinkle with ¼ cup **sugar** mixed with 1 teaspoon **ground cinnamon.** Starting at a narrow end, roll up jelly roll style; pinch edge to seal. Cut into 12 equal slices and place a slice, cut side up, in each muffin cup. Cover and let rise in a warm place until doubled (1½ to 2 hours).

Bake in a 375° oven for 20 to 25 minutes or until golden. Invert pan onto a serving plate, hold in place for a few minutes, then lift off pan. Serve warm or at room temperature. Makes 1 dozen.

ORANGE SWEET ROLLS. In a small pan over medium-low heat, mix ½ cup **sugar,** ⅓ cup **orange juice,** 4 tablespoons **butter** or margarine, and 2½ teaspoons grated **orange peel.** Cook, stirring, until syrupy (8 to 10 minutes). Spoon equally into 12 well-greased 2½-inch muffin cups; set aside. Shape and finish a portion of dough as for Cinnamon-Nut Sweet Rolls (preceding).

Honey-Wheat Buns

When the specialty of the day is a sandwich made with a honey-wheat bun, even a humble paper-bag lunch becomes a gourmet banquet-for-one. Moist and wholesome, these plump little rolls taste terrific with ham and cheese—or just about any other filling.

1 cup *each* cracked wheat and boiling water
2 packages active dry yeast
¼ cup warm water (about 110°)
⅓ cup honey
2 tablespoons salad oil
1 tablespoon salt
1½ cups small curd cottage cheese
3 eggs
About 5½ cups whole wheat flour

In a large bowl, stir together cracked wheat and the 1 cup boiling water; let cool until lukewarm. Meanwhile, in another bowl, stir yeast into the ¼ cup warm water; let stand until bubbly (5 to 15 minutes). Stir into cracked wheat. Add honey, oil, salt, cottage cheese, and eggs; mix well. Gradually add 3 cups of the flour, beating well after each addition.

Using a heavy-duty mixer or wooden spoon, beat in enough of remaining flour (about 2 cups) to make a stiff dough. Turn dough out onto a lightly floured board and knead briefly, shaping dough into a smooth ball (dough will be a little sticky). Turn dough over in a greased bowl; cover and let rise in a warm place until doubled (about 1½ hours).

Punch dough down, turn out onto a lightly floured board, and divide into 20 equal pieces. Knead briefly, shaping each piece into a smooth ball (dough will still be a little sticky).

Place balls about 2 inches apart on greased baking sheets, and flatten slightly. Cover lightly and let rise in a warm place until puffy and doubled (about 45 minutes).

Bake in a 375° oven for 12 to 15 minutes or until lightly browned. Transfer to racks and let cool. Makes 20 buns.

Fennel Bread Sticks

(Pictured on page 119)

Aromatic fennel seeds add flavor to these crisp and tender Italian bread sticks. Wonderful served as appetizers with a pot of sweet butter, they're also very good with soups and salads.

1 package active dry yeast
¾ cup *each* warm water (about 110°) and salad oil
¾ cup beer, at room temperature
1½ teaspoons salt
1 tablespoon fennel seeds
About 4¾ cups all-purpose flour
1 egg beaten with 1 tablespoon water

In a large bowl, stir yeast into the ¾ cup warm water; let stand until bubbly (5 to 15 minutes). Add oil, beer, salt, and fennel seeds. Using a wooden spoon, beat in 4¼ cups of the flour.

Sprinkle ¼ cup of the remaining flour on a board or pastry cloth; turn dough out and knead until smooth and elastic, adding flour as needed to prevent sticking. Turn dough over in a greased bowl; cover and let rise in a warm place until doubled (1½ to 2 hours).

Knead briefly to release air. Pinch off lumps 1½ inches in diameter and roll each between your palms into an 18-inch-long rope. Cut each rope in half. Set lightly greased wire racks on baking sheets and place ropes, ½ inch apart, across racks. Brush ropes with egg mixture.

Bake in a 350° oven for 30 minutes or until evenly browned and crisp. Let cool on racks for 10 minutes; then invert racks and gently bend wires to release bread sticks. Let cool completely, then wrap airtight and store at room temperature. Makes about 4 dozen.

Basic Bagels

Legend has it that this unique bread was invented in 1683 by a Viennese baker as a tribute to Polish Prince John Soviesky, who had rescued the city from invaders. Originally called a "beugal," it was shaped like the prince's stirrup.

Bagels have enjoyed far-flung popularity ever since. *Sunset* readers have added their own fanfare to the bagel's fame.

2 packages active dry yeast
2 cups warm water (about 110°)
3 teaspoons salt
3 tablespoons sugar
5½ to 6 cups all-purpose flour
3 quarts water combined with 1 tablespoon sugar
Cornmeal
1 egg yolk beaten with 1 tablespoon water

In a large bowl, stir yeast into the 2 cups warm water; let stand until bubbly (5 to 15 minutes). Stir in salt and the 3 tablespoons sugar; gradually mix in 4 cups of the flour. Beat until smooth. Mix in about 1¼ cups of the remaining flour to make a stiff dough.

Turn dough out onto a floured board and knead until smooth and elastic (10 to 20 minutes), adding flour as needed to prevent sticking (dough should be firmer than for most other yeast breads). Turn dough over in a greased bowl; cover and let rise in a warm place until doubled (about 40 minutes).

Punch dough down; knead briefly on a lightly floured board to release air, then divide into 18 equal pieces.

To shape, knead each piece, forming it into a smooth ball.

(Continued on page 115)

Holding ball with both hands, poke your thumbs through center. With one thumb in hole, work around perimeter, shaping bagel like a doughnut, 2½ to 3 inches across. Place shaped bagels on a lightly floured board, cover lightly, and let stand in a warm place for 20 minutes.

In a 4 to 5-quart pan over high heat, bring water-sugar mixture to a boil; adjust heat to keep it boiling gently. Lightly grease a baking sheet and sprinkle with cornmeal. Gently lift bagels, one at a time, and drop into water; boil about 5 or 6 at a time, turning often, for 5 minutes. Lift out with a slotted spatula, drain briefly on a towel, and place on baking sheet.

Brush bagels with egg yolk mixture. Bake in a 400° oven for 25 to 30 minutes or until well browned and crusty. Transfer to racks and let cool. Makes 18 bagels.

WHOLE WHEAT BAGELS. Follow recipe for Basic Bagels, omitting the 3 tablespoons sugar; instead, use 3 tablespoons **honey.** In place of flour, use 2 cups **whole wheat flour,** ½ cup **regular wheat germ,** and about 2¾ cups **all-purpose flour.**

Mix in whole wheat flour, wheat germ, and 1¼ cups of the all-purpose flour before beating dough. Then mix in about 1½ cups of the remaining all-purpose flour; knead and finish as directed.

PUMPERNICKEL BAGELS. Follow recipe for Basic Bagels, omitting the 3 tablespoons sugar; instead, use 3 tablespoons **dark molasses.** In place of flour, use 2 cups **rye flour,** 2 cups **whole wheat flour,** and about 1¾ cups **all-purpose flour.**

Add rye flour and 1 cup *each* of the whole wheat and all-purpose flours before beating dough. Then mix in remaining 1 cup whole wheat flour and about ¾ cup of the remaining all-purpose flour; knead and finish as directed.

VARIATIONS. Add ½ cup **instant toasted onion** to Whole Wheat Bagels or Basic Bagels, stirring it into yeast mixture along with sugar and salt. Or sprinkle ½ teaspoon **poppy seeds** or sesame seeds *or* ¼ teaspoon **coarse salt** on each glazed bagel before baking. Or add 1 tablespoon **caraway seeds** to Pumpernickel Bagels, then sprinkle each glazed bagel with ½ teaspoon additional caraway seeds before baking.

Crumpets

Crumpets have holes for a reason. How else, ask the British, can a proper amount of butter permeate each moist and springy bite?

Whether due to butter, holes, or our unsurpassable recipe, these crumpets have proved to be one of our most popular breads. You'll need metal rings to contain this simple yeast batter as it cooks in a frying pan or on a griddle. You can use 3-inch flan rings or open-topped cooky cutters. Or do as we did—use tuna cans with tops and bottoms removed.

1 package active dry yeast
1 teaspoon sugar
¼ cup warm water (about 110°)
⅓ cup milk, at room temperature
1 egg
   About 4 tablespoons butter or margarine, melted
1 cup all-purpose flour
½ teaspoon salt

In a large bowl, stir together yeast, sugar, and water; let stand until bubbly (5 to 15 minutes). Blend in milk, egg, and 1 tablespoon of the butter. Add flour

and salt and beat until smooth. Cover and let stand in a warm place until almost doubled (about 45 minutes).

Brush bottom of a heavy frying pan or griddle and the inside of each 3-inch ring with butter. Heat rings in pan over low heat; pour about 3 tablespoons of the batter into each ring. Cook until holes appear and tops are dry (about 7 minutes). Remove rings and turn crumpets to brown other side lightly (about 2 minutes). Repeat with remaining batter.

Serve warm; or transfer to a rack and let cool; toast just before serving. Makes 7 or 8 crumpets.

Whole Wheat Croissants

Wholesome and subtly sweet, these rolls are as buttery as the traditional French breakfast rolls—but whole wheat flour gives them extra nutritional vigor. Our special refrigerator dough adapts well to a busy schedule.

1 package active dry yeast
1 cup warm water (about 110°)
¾ cup evaporated milk
1½ teaspoons salt
⅓ cup honey
1 egg
3 cups whole wheat flour
4 tablespoons butter or margarine, melted and cooled
3 cups all-purpose flour
1 cup (½ lb.) firm butter or margarine, cut into pieces
1 egg beaten with 1 tablespoon water

In large bowl of an electric mixer, stir yeast into the 1 cup warm water; let stand until bubbly (5 to 15 minutes). Add milk, salt, honey, the 1 egg, and 2 cups of the whole wheat flour. Beat on medium speed until smooth. Stir in the 4 tablespoons melted butter; set aside.

In another large bowl, stir together all-purpose flour and re-

CUSTOM DICTATES that the first piece of Basque Sheepherder's Bread (page 109) goes to the herder's invaluable dog. And why not? The voluminous golden-brown loaf can feed a full house, and then some.

maining 1 cup whole wheat flour. Using a pastry blender or 2 knives, cut in the 1 cup firm butter pieces until particles are the size of peas. Pour in yeast mixture and stir gently just until flour is evenly moistened. Cover tightly and refrigerate for at least 4 hours or up to 4 days.

Turn dough out onto a well-floured board and knead for about 5 minutes. Divide dough into 4 equal portions. Working with a portion at a time (keep remaining portions refrigerated), roll on a well-floured board into a 17-inch circle (dough will be stiff). Using a floured sharp knife, cut circle into 8 wedges.

Loosely roll each wedge from wide end toward point. Shape each roll into a crescent and place, point down, 1½ inches apart on an ungreased baking sheet. Cover and let rise in a draft-free place (do not speed rising by putting in a warm place) until almost doubled (about 2 hours).

Brush rolls with egg-water mixture. Bake in a 325° oven for 25 minutes or until lightly browned. Serve warm; or transfer to racks and let cool completely, wrap airtight, and freeze.

To reheat, arrange rolls (thawed, if frozen) on baking sheets and heat, uncovered, in a 350° oven for about 10 minutes. Makes 32 croissants.

Sopapillas

A classic treat from New Mexico, these fluffy pillows of golden-fried bread are as versatile as they are delicious. For a snack similar to a homemade doughnut, drizzle with honey or syrup, sprinkle with cinnamon-sugar, or dust with powdered sugar.

You can split sopapillas and stuff them with savory fillings for sandwiches or appetizers. Or fill them with fruit and sweetened whipped cream for dessert.

1   package active dry yeast
¼   cup warm water (about 110°)
1½ cups milk
3   tablespoons lard or solid shortening
1½ teaspoons salt
2   tablespoons sugar
1   cup whole wheat flour
    About 4 cups all-purpose flour
    Salad oil

In a large bowl, stir yeast into water; let stand until bubbly (5 to 15 minutes). In a pan, combine milk, lard, salt, and sugar; heat to 110° (lard need not melt completely), and add to dissolved yeast.

Beat in whole wheat flour and 3 cups of the all-purpose flour. Using a heavy-duty mixer or wooden spoon, add enough of the remaining all-purpose flour (about ½ cup) to make a stiff, sticky dough. Turn dough out onto a floured board and knead until smooth and no longer sticky, adding flour as needed.

Turn dough over in a greased bowl; cover and let rise at room temperature for an hour. Punch dough down. (At this point, you may cover and refrigerate dough until next day.)

Knead dough on a lightly floured board to release air. Working with a portion at a time (keep unused portion covered), roll dough slightly less than ⅛ inch thick. For large sopapillas, cut dough into rectangles 3½ by 5 inches; for small ones, cut dough into 3-inch squares.

Place on lightly floured baking sheets and cover lightly. You can let cut sopapillas stay at room temperature for up to 5 minutes; otherwise, refrigerate until all are ready to fry.

Pour oil into a deep, wide frying pan or 5 to 6-quart kettle to a depth of 1½ to 2 inches; heat to 350° on a deep-frying thermometer. Fry sopapillas, 2 or 3 at a time, until beginning to puff; with a slotted spoon, gently push portion where air bubble is form-

ing into hot oil several times (this helps it puff more evenly).

Cook, turning several times, just until pale gold on both sides (1 to 2 minutes total). Drain on paper towels.

Serve immediately; or place in a warm oven until all are fried. If made ahead, cool, wrap, and refrigerate or freeze. To reheat, arrange on baking sheets and heat, uncovered, in a 300° oven, turning once, for 5 to 8 minutes or just until warmed (do not overheat). Makes 2 dozen large or 4 dozen small sopapillas.

Sourdough Pancakes & Waffles

Here's a virtually foolproof use for a young sourdough starter.

1   cup *each* whole wheat flour and all-purpose flour
½   cup Sourdough Starter (page 111), at room temperature
2   cups warm buttermilk (about 110°)
2   eggs
¼   cup *each* milk and salad oil
2   tablespoons sugar
1   teaspoon baking soda
½   teaspoon salt

In a large bowl, combine whole wheat flour, all-purpose flour, starter, and buttermilk; beat until blended. Cover and let stand at room temperature for about 45 minutes, or cover and refrigerate until next day.

In another bowl, beat eggs, milk, and oil. Add to flour mixture and stir until blended. Combine sugar, baking soda, and salt. Stir into batter; let stand for 5 minutes.

For waffles, preheat an electric waffle iron. Bake according to manufacturer's directions until richly browned. Serve immediately; or let cool on racks, wrap airtight, and freeze. Reheat frozen waffles in a toaster. Makes 12 waffles, 4 inches square.

For pancakes, drop batter by spoonfuls onto a moderately hot greased griddle. Cook until tops are bubbly and appear dry; turn and cook other sides until browned. Makes about 2 dozen pancakes, about 4 inches in diameter.

SOURDOUGH BUCKWHEATS. Follow recipe for Sourdough Pancakes & Waffles, omitting whole wheat flour. Instead, use ¾ cup **buckwheat flour** and increase all-purpose flour to 1¼ cups.

SOURDOUGH BLUEBERRY PANCAKES. Follow recipe for Sourdough Pancakes & Waffles, stirring in ¾ cup fresh or well-drained frozen or canned **blueberries** just before cooking.

SOURDOUGH OATMEAL PANCAKES. Follow recipe for Sourdough Pancakes & Waffles, omitting 1 cup of either whole wheat or all-purpose flour; instead, use 1 cup **quick-cooking rolled oats.**

Anise Bread

Spicy fragrance fills the kitchen as this sweet and tender loaf bakes. A tradition for festive oc-casions in northeastern New Mexico, the bread is best served warm or toasted.

- 1 **package active dry yeast**
- ½ **cup *each* warm water (about 110°) and warm milk (about 110°)**
- 2 **tablespoons sugar**
- 1½ **tablespoons anise seeds**
- ½ **cup (¼ lb.) butter or margarine, melted and cooled**
- 2 **eggs**
- ½ **teaspoon salt**
- 4½ **to 5 cups all-purpose flour**
- ⅔ **cup firmly packed brown sugar mixed with ½ teaspoon ground cinnamon**
  Sugar Glaze (recipe follows)

(Continued on next page)

PAPER-THIN PANCAKES FROM FRANCE

The crêpe—the thinnest pancake of them all—is the ultimate in convenience and versatility. Though it takes time to make them, crêpes freeze well for weeks, even months. When you're ready to use them, bring them to room temperature so they won't stick together and tear when you separate them. Then wrap them around a savory filling and serve as a light entrée; or sweeten the batter with a tablespoon of sugar, spread the crêpes with butter and jam, and offer them for breakfast or dessert.

Basic Crêpes

- 3 **eggs**
- ⅔ **cup all-purpose flour**
- 1 **cup milk**
  About 4 teaspoons butter or margarine

In a blender or food processor, whirl eggs and flour until smooth. Then add milk and blend until thoroughly combined. Or combine eggs and flour in a medium-size bowl and blend with a wire whisk; add milk and mix until smooth. (At this point, you may cover and refrigerate until next day; bring batter to room temperature before cooking.)

Place a 6 or 7-inch crêpe pan or other flat-bottomed frying pan over medium heat. When pan is hot, add ¼ teaspoon of the butter and swirl to coat surface. Stir batter and pour in about 2 tablespoons, quickly tilting pan so batter flows over entire surface. If heat is correct and pan is hot enough, crêpe sets at once, forming tiny bubbles (don't worry if there are a few small holes); if pan is too cold, batter makes a smooth layer. Cook until surface is dry and edge is lightly browned.

Turn with a spatula and cook until other side is lightly browned. Turn out onto a plate. Repeat to make each crêpe; stir batter occasionally and stack crêpes. If made ahead, let cool; then place wax paper between crêpes, package airtight (in quantities you expect to use), and refrigerate for up to a week; freeze for longer storage. Bring crêpes to room temperature before separating.

To serve, wrap crêpes around a filling for a main-dish entrée. Makes about 18 crêpes.

In a large bowl, stir yeast into water; let stand until bubbly (5 to 15 minutes). Add milk, sugar, anise seeds, 3 tablespoons of the butter, eggs, salt, and 1½ cups of the flour. Beat for about 5 minutes, then gradually beat in about 2½ cups of the remaining flour to make a soft dough.

Turn dough out onto a floured board and knead until smooth and satiny (5 to 20 minutes), adding flour as needed to prevent sticking. Turn dough over in a greased bowl; cover and let rise in a warm place until doubled (about 1½ hours).

Punch dough down, knead briefly on a lightly floured board to release air, and roll into a 12 by 22-inch rectangle. Brush remaining 5 tablespoons butter over dough to within ½ inch of the edges.

Sprinkle brown sugar-cinnamon mixture evenly over butter. Starting with a wide side, roll up tightly jelly roll style, pinching edge to seal.

Without stretching roll, place it, seam side down, in a greased 10-inch tube pan; pinch ends together to close circle. Using a floured sharp knife, make 7 evenly spaced slashes, ½ inch deep, on top. Cover and let rise in a warm place until almost doubled (about 45 minutes).

Bake in a 350° oven for 50 to 60 minutes or until loaf is lightly browned and sounds hollow when tapped. Let cool in pan for 5 minutes; then turn out onto a rack. (At this point, you may cool, wrap airtight, and freeze. Before glazing, place thawed bread on a baking sheet and reheat in a 350° oven for about 10 minutes.)

Prepare Sugar Glaze and spoon on bread while still warm, letting glaze drizzle down sides. Makes 1 loaf.

SUGAR GLAZE. In a small bowl, blend ½ cup **powdered sugar** with 1 tablespoon **water** until smooth.

Portuguese Sweet Bread

This lightly sweetened and delectably tender bread originated in Portugal. But our version comes from Hawaii, where it has gained wide popularity since its introduction by Portuguese settlers in the late 19th century. Bake a batch—in one of the loaf or bun shapes described below—and you'll discover why its fame has spread so far.

¼ cup instant mashed potato granules or powder
⅔ cup *each* boiling water and sugar
¼ cup instant nonfat dry milk
½ cup (¼ lb.) butter or margarine
2 packages active dry yeast
⅓ cup warm water (about 110°)
4½ to 5 cups all-purpose flour
3 eggs
1 teaspoon salt
½ teaspoon vanilla
¼ teaspoon lemon flavoring
1 egg, beaten
Sugar (optional)

In a small pan, beat potato granules into the ⅔ cup boiling water. Stir in sugar, milk, and butter. Let cool to 110°.

Meanwhile, in a large bowl, stir yeast into the ⅓ cup warm water; let stand until bubbly (5 to 15 minutes). Stir in cooled potato mixture. Add 2 cups of the flour and beat until blended. Stir in the 3 eggs, salt, vanilla, and lemon flavoring until smoothly blended. Then beat in 1½ cups of the remaining flour.

Mix in enough of the remaining flour (1 to 1½ cups) to make a stiff dough. Turn dough out onto a floured board and knead until smooth and satiny (5 to 20 minutes), adding flour as needed to prevent sticking. Turn dough over in a greased bowl; cover and let rise in a warm place until doubled (about 1 hour).

Punch dough down and knead briefly on a lightly floured board to release air. Let dough rest for 10 minutes; then shape in one of the following ways.

For coiled loaves, divide dough in half. Roll each portion into a 30-inch-long rope. For each loaf, coil a rope into a greased 9-inch pie pan, starting at outside edge and ending in center; twist rope slightly as you lay it in pan.

For coiled buns, divide dough into 12 equal portions. Roll each into a 12-inch-long rope. On greased baking sheets, coil and twist each rope as described for coiled loaves, making buns 2½ to 3 inches in diameter and spacing them at least 2 inches apart.

For braided loaves, divide dough into 6 equal portions. Roll each into a 14-inch-long rope. For each loaf, arrange 3 ropes side by side on a greased baking sheet. Pinch together at top and loosely braid; pinch ends together and tuck underneath.

For round loaves, divide dough in half. Shape each half into a flattened round, about 8 inches in diameter, and place in a greased 9-inch pie pan.

Cover and let rise in a warm place until almost doubled (35 to 45 minutes for loaves, 20 to 30 minutes for buns). Brush with beaten egg; sprinkle with sugar, if desired.

Bake in a 350° oven for 25 to 30 minutes for loaves, 20 to 25 minutes for buns, or until browned. Transfer to racks and let cool. Serve warm or at room temperature. Or let cool completely, wrap airtight, and freeze.

To reheat, let thaw, unwrapped, at room temperature. Place on baking sheets, cover loosely with foil, and heat in a 350° oven for 10 to 15 minutes for buns, 25 to 30 minutes for loaves, or until heated through. Makes 2 loaves or 1 dozen buns.

TRANSPORT YOURSELF TO ITALY— it's easy when you're nibbling on fragrant Fennel Bread Sticks (page 113), sipping Chianti, and savoring a plateful of Antipasto Salad (page 27). If you can't lunch in Rome, this is surely the next best thing.

Vanocka

Filled with candied fruits and nuts, this plump, braided bread is a Czechoslovakian Christmas tradition. Our much-requested recipe yields two lovely and faintly lemony loaves—one to enjoy at home and one to give away.

2 packages active dry yeast
1 cup warm water (about 110°)
   About 5 cups all-purpose flour
½ cup *each* raisins and water
2 tablespoons rum or brandy (optional)
1 cup (½ lb.) butter or margarine
½ cup sugar
2 eggs
1 teaspoon *each* salt and grated lemon peel
½ cup *each* chopped blanched almonds and mixed chopped candied (glacé) fruit
1 egg beaten with 1 tablespoon water

In a large bowl, stir yeast into the 1 cup water; let stand until bubbly (5 to 15 minutes). Stir in 1 cup of the flour and beat until well blended. Cover and let stand in a warm place until bubbly (about 1 hour).

Meanwhile, in a small bowl, soak raisins in the ½ cup water for 1 hour. Pour off and discard water; add rum, if desired, and set aside.

In a large bowl, beat butter until creamy. Gradually add sugar, beating until light and fluffy. Add eggs, one at a time, beating well after each addition. Stir in salt and lemon peel. Add butter mixture to yeast mixture, stirring until blended.

Gradually beat in 2 cups of the remaining flour. Stir in raisins, almonds, and candied fruit. Gradually beat in enough of the remaining flour (about 1½ cups) to form a stiff dough.

Turn dough out onto a floured board and knead until smooth (about 10 minutes). Turn dough over in a greased bowl; cover and let rise in a warm place until doubled (about 1½ hours).

Punch dough down; knead briefly on a floured board to release air. Divide into 6 equal portions and roll each into a 10-inch-long rope. For each loaf, arrange 3 ropes side by side on a greased baking sheet. Pinch together at top and loosely braid; pinch ends together and tuck underneath. Cover and let rise in a warm place until almost doubled (30 to 40 minutes).

Brush loaves with egg-water mixture and bake in a 350° oven for 30 minutes or until browned. Transfer to racks and let cool. Makes 2 loaves.

Dresden-style German Stollen

Fruit and nut-laden *stollen* is as much a Christmas tradition in Germany as Herr Kringle himself. This version from the city of Dresden has brought something special to Christmas morning in America, too.

½ cup milk
1 cup (½ lb.) butter or margarine
½ cup granulated sugar
2 packages active dry yeast
½ cup warm water (about 110°)
½ teaspoon salt
1 teaspoon *each* almond extract and grated lemon peel
   About 5¼ cups all-purpose flour
2 eggs
⅓ cup finely chopped candied orange peel
½ cup *each* raisins, golden raisins, currants, and slivered almonds
1 egg white beaten with 1 teaspoon water
4 tablespoons butter or margarine, melted
⅓ cup powdered sugar

In a small pan over medium-low heat, combine milk, the 1 cup butter, and granulated sugar. Heat to scalding (120°), stirring to dissolve sugar and melt butter. Set aside; let cool to lukewarm.

In a large bowl, stir yeast into the ½ cup water; let stand until bubbly (5 to 15 minutes). Add cooled milk mixture, salt, almond extract, lemon peel, and 3 cups of the flour; beat until well blended. Add eggs, one at a time, beating well after each addition. Gradually stir in orange peel, raisins, currants, almonds, and 2 cups of the remaining flour.

Turn dough out onto a floured board and knead until smooth and elastic (about 10 minutes), adding more flour as needed to prevent sticking. Turn dough over in a greased bowl; cover and let rise in a warm place until doubled (about 1½ hours).

Punch dough down and divide in half. Place each portion on a lightly greased baking sheet and shape into a 7 by 9-inch oval about ¾ inch thick. Brush surface with some of the egg white mixture. Crease each oval lengthwise slightly off center and fold so top edge lies about an inch back from bottom edge. Brush evenly with remaining egg white mixture. Cover and let rise in a warm place until puffy and almost doubled (35 to 45 minutes).

Bake in a 375° oven for 25 minutes or until richly browned. Brush with the 4 tablespoons melted butter and sift powdered sugar over top. Return to oven and bake for 3 more minutes. Transfer to racks and let cool.

To reheat, place on baking sheets, cover loosely with foil, and heat in a 350° oven for 20 minutes. Makes 2 loaves.

Almond-Cherry Christmas Wreath

The colors of Christmas glow in the swirled red and green cherry filling of this festive wreath bread. A pot of soft sweet butter in the center of the wreath completes a gala holiday breakfast treat that may become an annual tradition in your home.

1 package active dry yeast
¼ cup warm water (about 110°)
½ cup warm milk (about 110°)
3 tablespoons sugar
4 tablespoons butter or margarine, softened
1½ teaspoons salt
½ teaspoon ground cardamom
2 eggs
1 teaspoon grated lemon peel
   About 3½ cups all-purpose flour
   Cherry-Almond Filling (recipe follows)
   Sugar Glaze (recipe follows)

In large bowl of an electric mixer, stir yeast into water; let stand until bubbly (5 to 15 minutes). Stir in milk, sugar, butter, salt, cardamom, eggs, and lemon peel. Beat in 2 cups of the flour, a cup at a time. Then beat on medium speed for 3 minutes, scraping bowl frequently.

Using a heavy-duty mixer or wooden spoon, beat in enough of the remaining flour (about 1¼ cups) to form a soft dough. Turn dough out onto a floured board and knead until smooth (5 to 10 minutes). Turn dough over in a greased bowl; cover and let rise in a warm place until doubled (about 1½ hours).

Meanwhile, prepare Cherry-Almond Filling and refrigerate.

Punch dough down and turn out onto a floured board; roll into a 9 by 30-inch rectangle. Crumble filling and scatter over dough to within 1 inch of edges. Starting with a long side, roll dough up tightly jelly roll style. Moisten edge with water; pinch to seal.

Using a floured sharp knife, cut roll in half lengthwise; carefully turn cut side up. Loosely twist ropes around each other, keeping cut sides up. Carefully transfer to a greased and flour-dusted baking sheet and shape into a 10-inch circle; pinch ends together firmly to seal. Let rise, uncovered, in a warm place until puffy (45 to 60 minutes).

Bake in a 375° oven for 20 minutes or until browned. Run

wide spatulas under wreath to loosen; then transfer to a rack. (At this point, you may cool, wrap airtight, and store at room temperature for up to 2 days. Before glazing, reheat, wrapped in foil, in a 350° oven for about 20 minutes.)

Prepare Sugar Glaze and drizzle over wreath while still warm. Makes 1 large wreath.

CHERRY-ALMOND FILLING. In large bowl of an electric mixer, beat 4 tablespoons **butter** or margarine, softened, ¼ cup **all-purpose flour,** and 2 tablespoons **sugar** until smooth. Stir in ⅔ cup finely chopped **blanched almonds,** ¼ cup *each* **red and green candied (glacé) cherries,** ½ teaspoon grated **lemon peel,** and ¾ teaspoon **almond extract.** Cover and refrigerate.

SUGAR GLAZE. In a small bowl, blend ⅔ cup **powdered sugar,** 1½ teaspoons **lemon juice,** and 3 teaspoons **water** until smooth.

Buttery Almond Bear Claws

(Pictured on page 122)

Our buttery bear claws rival the bakery's best.

1 cup (½ lb.) butter or margarine
1 package active dry yeast
¼ cup warm water (about 110°)
3 eggs
¼ cup sugar
½ teaspoon salt
1 small can (5⅓ oz.) evaporated milk
3⅓ cups all-purpose flour
   Almond Filling (recipe follows)
   About ¾ cup sliced almonds
   Sugar

Melt butter, then let cool to 110°. In a bowl, stir yeast into water; let stand until bubbly (5 to 15 minutes). Separate eggs, reserving 2 of the whites in a bowl and remaining egg white in another

bowl. Stir egg yolks into yeast mixture, along with the ¼ cup sugar, salt, evaporated milk, and cooled butter.

Place flour in a large bowl, pour in yeast mixture, and mix well. Cover and refrigerate for at least a day or up to 3 days. Prepare Almond Filling and refrigerate as directed.

To shape bear claws, roll dough on a well-floured board into a 13½ by 27-inch rectangle, using a ruler to straighten edges. Cut dough lengthwise into 3 long strips, each 4½ inches wide. Di-

(Continued on page 123)

SHAPING BEAR CLAWS

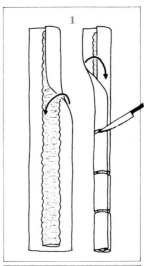

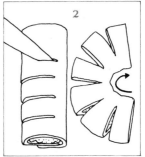

1 Fold long sides of strip over filling; then cut into 6 pieces.

2 On baking sheet, cut "claws" and fan out.

vide filling into 3 portions; on a floured board, roll each portion into a 27-inch-long rope. Lay an almond rope in center of each dough strip; then flatten rope slightly.

Fold long sides of each strip over filling, overlapping slightly as shown on page 121. Cut each filled strip into 6 pieces, each 4½ inches long. Arrange, seam side down, on 3 greased baking sheets. Using a floured sharp knife, make a row of cuts ½ inch apart halfway across each piece. Curve each bear claw so it fans, with cut sections facing out.

Lightly beat remaining egg white and brush over bear claws; top with sliced almonds and sprinkle lightly with sugar. Let rise, uncovered, in a warm place until puffy (about 20 minutes).

Bake in a 375° oven for 15 minutes or until golden brown. Transfer to racks and let cool. Wrap airtight and store at room temperature, or freeze. To reheat, unwrap and thaw, if frozen; place on baking sheets and heat, uncovered, in a 350° oven for about 10 minutes. Makes 18 bear claws.

ALMOND FILLING. In a bowl, smoothly blend ½ cup (¼ lb.) **butter** or margarine, softened, with 1⅓ cups **powdered sugar.** Add ⅔ cup **all-purpose flour** and 1 can (8 oz.) **almond paste.** Stir until crumbly and evenly mixed; then beat in 1 teaspoon grated **lemon peel** and 2 of the reserved egg whites. Stir in ¾ cup finely chopped **almonds.** Cover and refrigerate until firm (1 to 3 days).

Danish Coffee Cake

Choose, if you can, between two fanciful shapes—a heart or a butterfly—for this coffee cake.

⅓ cup milk
3 tablespoons sugar
½ teaspoon salt
4 tablespoons butter or margarine, cut into pieces
1 package active dry yeast
¼ cup warm water (about 110°)
3 to 3½ cups all-purpose flour
2 eggs
½ teaspoon almond extract
1 teaspoon grated lemon peel
  Cinnamon-Nut, Frangipane, *or* Apricot-Nut Filling (recipes follow)

In a small pan, combine milk, sugar, salt, and butter. Heat, stirring, to about 110° (butter need not melt completely).

In a large bowl, stir yeast into water; let stand until bubbly (5 to 15 minutes). Stir in milk mixture. Add 1½ cups of the flour and stir to moisten evenly. Beat in eggs, almond extract, and lemon peel until smoothly blended. Then stir in 1 cup of the remaining flour.

Turn dough out onto a floured board and knead until smooth and satiny (5 to 20 minutes), adding flour as needed to prevent sticking. Turn dough over in a greased bowl; cover and let rise in a warm place until doubled (about 1½ hours).

Punch dough down, knead briefly on a lightly floured board to release air, and roll into a 12 by 18-inch rectangle. Prepare filling of your choice and spread over dough to within 1 inch of edges.

Starting with a long side, roll up jelly roll style; pinch seam along top to seal. Then fold roll in half, pinch ends together tightly, and tuck under. Place on a lightly greased baking sheet; slash and shape for either butterfly or heart, as shown at right.

Cover and let rise in a warm place until almost doubled (about 45 minutes). Bake in a 350° oven for 25 minutes or until golden brown. Makes 1 large coffee cake.

CINNAMON-NUT FILLING. Brush dough with 3 tablespoons

butter or margarine, melted. In a small bowl, combine ¼ cup *each* **granulated sugar** and firmly packed **brown sugar** and 1½ teaspoons **ground cinnamon;** distribute evenly over buttered area of dough as directed; sprinkle with ¾ cup sliced **almonds.**

(Continued on next page)

SHAPING THE DOUGH

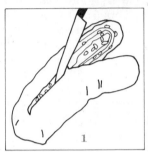

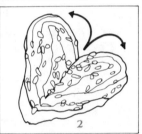

TO SHAPE HEART: 1. Cut through folded roll from center to one end; beginning 1 inch from other end, make a shallow slash to meet first cut.

2. Lift, pull, and spread out each side. Pinch end into a slight point.

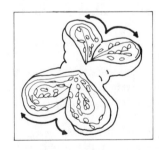

TO SHAPE BUTTERFLY: Cut toward center from each end of folded roll, leaving 1 inch uncut in center; then lift, pull, and spread out wings.

FRANGIPANE FILLING. In small bowl of an electric mixer, beat 4 tablespoons **butter** or margarine, softened, until creamy. Gradually add 1 can (8 oz.) **almond paste,** ½ cup **powdered sugar,** 1 **egg,** and ½ teaspoon grated **lemon peel;** continue beating until well blended and smooth. Spread over dough as directed; sprinkle with ¾ cup sliced **almonds.**

APRICOT-NUT FILLING. In a small pan over low heat, combine 1 cup (about 6 oz.) moist-pack **dried apricots,** chopped; ½ cup **raisins;** and ¼ cup *each* **water** and **sugar.** Cover and simmer, stirring occasionally, until mixture thickens (about 10 minutes). Spread over dough as directed; sprinkle with ½ cup chopped **pecans** or walnuts.

Giant Upside-down Pecan Rolls

Big enough for Paul Bunyan, these grand-scale breakfast rolls will elicit expressions of hungry anticipation—or at least surprise. Try the cinnamon version, too.

⅔ cup milk

1¾ cups sugar

1 teaspoon salt

½ cup (¼ lb.) butter or margarine, cut into pieces

2 packages active dry yeast

½ cup warm water (about 110°)

5½ to 6 cups all-purpose flour

2 eggs

4 tablespoons butter or margarine, melted

1 tablespoon ground cinnamon

1 cup coarsely chopped pecans

Brown Sugar Syrup (recipe follows)

1 cup pecan halves

1 teaspoon water

In a pan, combine milk, ¾ cup of the sugar, salt, and the ½ cup butter. Heat, stirring, to about 110° (butter need not melt completely).

In a large bowl, stir yeast into the ½ cup warm water; let stand until bubbly (5 to 15 minutes). Blend in milk mixture. Gradually mix in 3 cups of the flour, then beat for 5 minutes. Beat in 1 whole egg and 1 egg yolk (reserve remaining egg white); then gradually beat in enough of the remaining flour (about 2 cups) to make a stiff dough.

Turn dough out onto a floured board and knead until smooth and satiny (10 to 20 minutes), adding flour as needed to prevent sticking. Turn dough over in a greased bowl; cover and let rise in a warm place until doubled (about 2 hours).

Punch dough down. Knead briefly on a lightly floured board to release air; let dough rest for 10 minutes. Then roll and stretch dough into a 24 by 18-inch rectangle. Brush evenly with the 4 tablespoons melted butter.

In a small bowl, combine remaining 1 cup sugar with cinnamon; sprinkle evenly over dough, then sprinkle with chopped pecans. Starting with a narrow side, roll up jelly roll style. Moisten edge with water and pinch firmly to seal. Using a floured sharp knife, cut into 6 slices.

Prepare Brown Sugar Syrup, and immediately pour syrup into a 9 by 13-inch baking pan; tilt pan so syrup forms an even layer. Arrange pecan halves, flat side up, on syrup. Place dough slices, cut side up, over syrup and nuts. Cover and let rise in a warm place until almost doubled (about 1½ hours).

Brush surfaces of rolls with reserved egg white beaten with the 1 teaspoon water. Bake in a 350° oven for 30 to 35 minutes or until well browned. Immediately invert onto a serving tray. Makes 6 large rolls.

BROWN SUGAR SYRUP. In a pan over high heat, combine 4 tablespoons **butter** or margarine, 2 tablespoons **water,** and 1 cup firmly packed **dark brown sugar.** Boil for 1 minute.

GIANT UPSIDE-DOWN CINNA-MON ROLLS. Follow recipe for Giant Upside-down Pecan Rolls, brushing dough with butter and sprinkling with cinnamon-sugar mixture. Omit chopped pecans; instead, use ½ to 1 cup **currants** or raisins. Roll and cut as directed.

Omit syrup; instead, arrange slices, cut side up, in a well-greased 9 by 13-inch baking pan. Cover and let rise in a warm place until almost doubled (about 1½ hours).

Brush rolls with reserved egg white beaten with the 1 teaspoon water. Bake in a 350° oven for 30 to 35 minutes or until well browned.

Using a large spatula, transfer rolls to racks. (At this point, you may cool, wrap airtight, and freeze. Before glazing, place frozen rolls on a baking sheet and reheat in a 350° oven for 10 minutes or until heated through.)

In a bowl, beat 1½ cups **powdered sugar** with ⅛ teaspoon **vanilla,** 2 to 3 tablespoons warm **water,** and 1 tablespoon **butter** or margarine, softened, until smooth. Drizzle over rolls while still warm. Makes 6 large rolls.

Quick Focaccia

Similar to a thick, chewy pizza with only a hint of topping, *focaccia* is a flat Italian bread that soaks in seasonings as it bakes.

1 loaf (1 lb.) frozen bread dough, thawed

3 tablespoons olive oil or salad oil

1½ teaspoons onion salt

½ cup thinly sliced green onions (including tops)

Pull and stretch dough to fit in bottom of a well-greased 10 by 15-inch rimmed baking sheet. With your fingers, poke holes in dough at 1-inch intervals. Brush oil evenly over dough, sprinkle with onion salt, and top with onions.

Let rise, uncovered, in a warm place until almost doubled (25 to 35 minutes). Bake in a 450° oven for 12 to 15 minutes or until well browned.

Let cool slightly, then cut into squares. Serve warm or at room temperature. Makes 4 to 6 servings.

RAISIN FOCACCIA. Follow recipe for Quick Focaccia, kneading ⅓ cup **raisins** into dough until well distributed before fitting dough into pan. Omit onion salt and onions; instead, sprinkle evenly with 1 teaspoon **sugar.**

PIZZA FOCACCIA. Follow recipe for Quick Focaccia as far as spreading dough in pan and poking in holes. Spread dough with ½ cup canned or bottled **pizza sauce.** Omit onion salt; instead, sprinkle evenly with ⅓ cup grated **Parmesan cheese** and top with onions; drizzle oil over all.

Irish Soda Bread

Dubliners enjoy this crusty, almost cake-textured bread with breakfast and high tea. Thick, warm slices make delicious platters for butter and jam or honey.

 4 to 4¼ cups all-purpose flour
 1 teaspoon salt
 3 teaspoons baking powder
 1 teaspoon baking soda
 ¼ cup sugar (optional)
 ⅛ teaspoon ground cardamom or ground coriander (optional)
 4 tablespoons butter or margarine
 1 egg
 1¾ cups buttermilk

In a large bowl, stir together 4 cups of the flour, salt, baking powder, baking soda, sugar, and cardamom, if desired, until thoroughly blended. Using a pastry blender or 2 knives, cut in butter

until mixture resembles coarse crumbs.

In another bowl, beat egg lightly and mix with buttermilk; stir into flour mixture until blended. Turn out onto a floured board and knead until smooth (2 to 3 minutes).

Divide dough in half and shape each portion into a smooth, round loaf; place each loaf in a greased 8-inch cake or pie pan. Press down until dough fills pans. Using a floured sharp knife, cut crosses about ½ inch deep in tops of loaves.

Bake in a 375° oven for 35 to 40 minutes or until browned. Turn out onto racks and let cool. Makes 2 loaves.

WHOLE WHEAT SODA BREAD. Follow recipe for Irish Soda Bread, substituting 2 cups **whole wheat flour** for 2 cups of the all-purpose flour. After cutting in butter, add 1 to 2 cups **raisins** or chopped dates, if desired.

CURRANT SODA BREAD. Follow recipe for Irish Soda Bread, omitting cardamom. After cutting in butter, add 1¼ teaspoons **caraway seeds,** if desired, and 2 cups **currants** or raisins.

Civilized Cornbread

Neither Mom nor her apple pie is as exclusively American as cornbread, the austere but filling little cake that greeted Pilgrims and *conquistadores* when they got off their boats and horses. This version is lighter and more moist than the earlier, simpler fare.

 1 cup *each* yellow cornmeal and baking mix (biscuit mix)
 3 teaspoons baking powder
 2 eggs
 1 cup milk
 ⅓ cup honey
 4 tablespoons butter or margarine, melted
   Honey Butter (recipe follows)

In a large bowl, stir together cornmeal, baking mix, and baking powder. In a small bowl, beat eggs until blended; stir in milk, honey, and butter. Pour into cornmeal mixture and stir just until moistened.

Spoon batter into a well-greased 8-inch square baking pan. Bake in a 400° oven for 25 to 30 minutes or until a wooden pick inserted in center comes out clean.

Prepare Honey Butter and offer with warm cornbread, cut into squares. Makes about 9 servings.

HONEY BUTTER. In a bowl, beat ½ cup (¼ lb.) **butter** or margarine, softened, with ¼ cup **honey;** mound in a small crock. Makes about ¾ cup.

Brown Bread

Reminiscent of Boston, rain at the window, and a fire in the hearth, this moist, molasses-hued loaf tastes terrific with baked beans. Or, toast slices for breakfast.

 3 tablespoons butter or margarine
 ¾ cup firmly packed brown sugar
 2 cups buttermilk
 3 tablespoons light molasses
 2 cups whole wheat or graham flour
 1 cup unbleached all-purpose flour
 ½ cup regular wheat germ
 2 teaspoons baking soda
 1 teaspoon salt
 1 cup *each* raisins and chopped walnuts

In large bowl of an electric mixer, beat butter and sugar until creamy. Mix in buttermilk and molasses.

In a large bowl, stir together whole wheat flour, unbleached flour, wheat germ, baking soda, and salt. Add to buttermilk mixture and beat until well combined. Stir in raisins and chopped nuts.

(Continued on next page)

Spoon batter into a well-greased 9 by 5-inch loaf pan. Bake in a 350° oven for 1 hour and 20 minutes or until a wooden pick inserted in center comes out clean. Let cool in pan for 10 minutes, then turn out onto a rack and let cool completely. To serve, cut into thin slices. Makes 1 loaf.

Pushover Popovers

Soft and light as hot air balloons, these popovers are mixed in minutes from just four ingredients.

- 1 **cup all-purpose flour**
- 1 **cup milk**
- 4 **eggs**
  Dash of salt

In a bowl, combine flour, milk, eggs, and salt; using a fork, stir just until blended. (At this point, you may cover and refrigerate for up to 4 hours.)

Spoon batter into 8 well-greased 6-ounce custard cups, filling each half full. Place cups on a baking sheet in a cold oven; set temperature at 450° and bake for 30 minutes. Then reduce temperature to 300° and continue baking for 8 more minutes or until puffed and browned. Makes 8 popovers.

Cranberry Tea Bread

This moist, spicy bread is a perfect candidate for holiday gift-giving.

- ¾ **cup (¼ lb. plus 4 tablespoons) butter or margarine**
- 1½ **cups firmly packed brown sugar**
- 4 **eggs**
- 3 **cups all-purpose flour**
- 2 **teaspoons** *each* **baking powder, baking soda, and ground cinnamon**
- ½ **teaspoon ground cloves**
- 1 **can (1 lb.) whole berry cranberry sauce**
- ⅔ **cup** *each* **golden raisins and chopped walnuts**

In a large bowl, beat butter and sugar until creamy. Add eggs, one at a time, beating well after each addition. In another bowl, stir together flour, baking powder, baking soda, cinnamon, and cloves; add to butter mixture and stir until well blended. Mix in cranberry sauce, raisins, and nuts.

Spoon batter into 2 greased and flour-dusted 9 by 5-inch loaf pans. Bake in a 350° oven for 1 hour or until a wooden pick inserted in center comes out clean.

Let cool in pans for 10 minutes, then turn out onto racks to cool completely. To store, wrap airtight and refrigerate for up to a week. Freeze for longer storage. Makes 2 loaves.

Whole Wheat Banana Bread

Rich with full-bodied whole wheat flavor, this favorite snack loaf is just as nutritious as it is delectable. Spread it liberally with peanut butter for ideal after-school sustenance.

- ½ **cup (¼ lb.) butter or margarine, melted**
- 1 **cup sugar**
- 2 **eggs, lightly beaten**
- 1 **cup** *each* **mashed ripe bananas (about 3) and all-purpose flour**
- ½ **teaspoon salt**
- 1 **teaspoon baking soda**
- 1 **cup whole wheat flour**
- ⅓ **cup hot water**
- ½ **cup chopped walnuts**

In a large bowl, stir together butter and sugar. Mix in eggs and banana, blending until smooth.

In another bowl, stir together all-purpose flour, salt, baking soda, and whole wheat flour until thoroughly blended. Add to banana mixture alternately with hot water. Stir in nuts. Spoon batter into a greased 9 by 5-inch loaf pan.

Bake in a 325° oven for 1 hour

and 10 minutes or until bread begins to pull away from sides of pan and a wooden pick inserted in center comes out clean. Let cool in pan for 10 minutes; then turn out onto a rack and let cool completely. Makes 1 loaf.

All-season Quick Loaves

(Pictured on facing page)

Three seasonal ingredients lend three quite different flavors to this versatile, year-round bread. Oranges give it a tangy bite; apples create a sweet, spicy version; and the summer addition of vine-ripened tomatoes produces an unusual, savory result that's delicious with soup or salad.

- 3 **cups all-purpose flour**
- 1 **teaspoon** *each* **salt and baking soda**
- ½ **teaspoon baking powder**
- 2 **teaspoons ground cinnamon**
- 1 **cup chopped nuts**
- 2 **cups prepared fruit or vegetable (directions follow)**
- 3 **eggs**
- 1½ **cups sugar**
- 1 **cup salad oil**
- 1 **teaspoon vanilla**

In a large bowl, stir together flour, salt, baking soda, baking powder, cinnamon, and nuts; set aside.

Prepare fruit or vegetable of your choice; set aside.

In another bowl, lightly beat eggs with a wire whisk. Add sugar and oil and stir until blended. Stir in vanilla and prepared fruit or vegetable.

Add flour mixture all at once and stir just until evenly moistened. Spoon batter into 2

(Continued on page 128)

TEA FOR TWO was never quite so nice as with moist slices of apple bread spread with whipped cream cheese. Brighten an afternoon—or any other time of day—with this or another variation of All-season Quick Loaves (recipe on this page).

greased and flour-dusted 4½ by 8½-inch loaf pans.

Bake in a 350° oven for 50 to 60 minutes or until a wooden pick inserted in center comes out clean. Let cool in pans for 10 minutes; then turn out onto racks to cool completely. (Bread will be easier to slice if stored until next day.)

To store, wrap airtight and refrigerate for up to a week; freeze for longer storage. Makes 2 loaves.

ORANGE BREAD. Grate 1 tablespoon **orange peel.** Cut off and discard remaining peel and white membrane from about 4 large **oranges.** Remove seeds and finely chop pulp to make 2 cups. Combine pulp and grated peel.

APPLE BREAD. Peel, core, and shred 3 or 4 medium-size **tart apples** to make 2 cups. Stir 1 teaspoon **lemon juice** into apple.

TOMATO BREAD. Peel 3 or 4 medium-size **tomatoes.** Cut each in half and squeeze gently to remove seed pockets. Finely chop to make 2 cups firm tomato pulp.

SHOWSTOPPER PANCAKE

Spectacular, scrumptious, and surprisingly simple to make, the Dutch Baby is a puffy, oversized oven pancake that you can serve at almost any meal. For breakfast or brunch, offer it with powdered sugar, fruit, or syrup (see suggestions below); for a savory supper, accompany with sausages and a green salad, or top with Tender-Crisp Vegetable Medley (page 97) or vegetables of your choice.

For best results, you'll need to bake the pancake in a large container—a wide ovenproof frying pan, a large baking dish, or even a foil roasting pan. Any shape will do, but the container must be fairly shallow—not much more than 3 inches deep. Use the chart below to find the recipe proportions for the pan size you choose.

Dutch Baby

Pan Size	Butter	Eggs	Milk & Flour
2–3 qt.	¼ cup	3	¾ cup *each*
3–4 qt.	⅓ cup	4	1 cup *each*
4–4½ qt.	½ cup	5	1¼ cups *each*
4½–5 qt.	½ cup	6	1½ cups *each*

To make, place **butter** (or margarine—though it won't taste as good) in pan and set pan in a 425° oven until butter is melted and foamy. Meanwhile, quickly mix batter. In a blender or food processor, whirl **eggs** at high speed for 1 minute; with motor running, gradually pour in **milk,** then slowly add **flour;** continue whirling for 30 more seconds.

Or, in a bowl, beat eggs until blended; gradually beat in milk, then flour.

Remove pan from oven (butter should be foamy); then pour in batter. Return pan to oven and bake for 20 to 25 minutes (time depends on pan size) or until puffy and well browned. Serve immediately.

To serve as a sweet breakfast pancake, dust with **nutmeg,** if desired; then cut into wedges and serve with one of the following toppings. Makes 3 to 6 servings.

Powdered Sugar. Have a shaker or bowl of **powdered sugar** and thick wedges of **lemon** at the table. Sprinkle sugar on hot pancake, then squeeze on lemon juice.

Fruit. Arrange sliced **strawberries** or peaches, sweetened to taste, in pancake; or serve with any fruits in season, cut and sweetened. Or substitute canned or frozen fruit.

Hot Fruit. Glazed **apples** or pears make a good topping; offer with **sour cream** or yogurt. Or heat **banana** or papaya slices in melted **butter** or margarine over medium heat, turning until heated through; serve with **lime** wedges.

Canned Pie Filling. To **cherry** or **apple pie filling,** add **lemon juice** and **ground cinnamon** to taste. Serve warm or cold, topped with **yogurt** or sour cream.

Syrups. Pass warm or cold **honey,** maple syrup, or fruit syrup.

Spicy Pineapple-Zucchini Bread

Aromatic spices, crunchy walnuts, and tangy pineapple give this quick bread a lively flavor. Zucchini keeps it light, moist, and tender.

- 3 eggs
- 1 cup salad oil
- 2 cups sugar
- 2 teaspoons vanilla
- 2 cups coarsely shredded, unpeeled zucchini (about 4 medium-size)
- 1 can (8 oz.) crushed pineapple, drained well
- 3 cups all-purpose flour
- 2 teaspoons baking soda
- 1 teaspoon salt
- ½ teaspoon baking powder
- 1½ teaspoons ground cinnamon
- ¾ teaspoon ground nutmeg
- 1 cup *each* currants and finely chopped walnuts

In a large bowl, beat eggs until frothy. Add oil, sugar, and vanilla; beat until thick and foamy. Stir in zucchini and pineapple.

In another bowl, stir flour, baking soda, salt, baking powder, cinnamon, nutmeg, currants, and walnuts until thoroughly blended. Stir gently into zucchini mixture just until blended. Spoon batter into 2 greased and flour-dusted 9 by 5-inch loaf pans.

Bake in a 350° oven for 1 hour or until bread begins to pull away from sides of pan and a wooden pick inserted in center comes out clean. Let cool in pans for 10 minutes; then turn out onto racks and let cool completely. Makes 2 loaves.

Ready-bake Bran Muffins

Wholesome and delicious, these cakelike muffins are a boon to busy breakfast cooks. They're baked from a fruit-laced batter that keeps in the refrigerator for up to 2 weeks; make the batter ahead of time, then use only enough batter each morning for the number of freshly baked muffins you want.

- 3 cups whole bran cereal
- 1 cup boiling water
- 2 eggs, lightly beaten
- 2 cups buttermilk
- ½ cup salad oil
- 1 cup raisins, currants, chopped pitted dates, *or* chopped pitted prunes
- 2½ teaspoons baking soda
- ½ teaspoon salt
- 1 cup sugar
- 2½ cups all-purpose flour

In a large bowl, mix bran cereal with water, stirring until evenly moistened; set aside until cool.

Add eggs, buttermilk, oil, and raisins and mix well. In another bowl, stir together baking soda, salt, sugar, and flour until thoroughly blended; then stir into bran mixture. (At this point, you may cover tightly and refrigerate for up to 2 weeks, baking muffins at your convenience; before using, stir batter to distribute fruit evenly.)

To bake, spoon batter into greased 2½-inch muffin cups, filling each cup ⅔ to ¾ full. Bake in a 425° oven for about 20 minutes or until tops spring back when lightly touched. Serve hot. Makes 2 to 2½ dozen muffins.

Buttermilk Scone Hearts

Surprise someone with a plate of these buttery, fruit-laced scones on February 14. You'll be sure to please your valentine no matter how much toast you burn during the rest of the year.

- 3 cups all-purpose flour
- ⅓ cup sugar
- 2½ teaspoons baking powder
- ½ teaspoon baking soda
- ¾ teaspoon salt
- ¾ cup (¼ lb. plus 4 tablespoons) firm butter or margarine, cut into small pieces
- ¾ cup chopped pitted dates or currants
- 1 teaspoon grated orange peel
- 1 cup buttermilk
- About 1 tablespoon half-and-half (light cream) or milk
- ¼ teaspoon ground cinnamon mixed with 2 tablespoons sugar

In a large bowl, stir together flour, the ⅓ cup sugar, baking powder, baking soda, and salt until thoroughly blended. Using a pastry blender or 2 knives, cut butter into flour mixture until it resembles coarse cornmeal; stir in dates and orange peel.

Make a well in center of flour mixture; add buttermilk all at once. Stir mixture with a fork until dough cleans sides of bowl.

With your hands, gather dough into a ball; turn out onto a lightly floured board. Roll or pat into a ½-inch-thick circle. Using a 2½-inch heart (or other shape) cutter, cut into individual scones. Place 1½ inches apart on lightly greased baking sheets. Brush tops of scones with half-and-half; sprinkle lightly with cinnamon-sugar mixture.

Bake in a 425° oven for 12 minutes or until tops are lightly browned. Serve warm. Makes about 18 scones.

All-summer Fruit Coffee Cake

Heavenly for breakfast, this cake is also a luscious dessert when topped with ice cream or whipped cream. Vary the fruit according to whim or seasonal perfection.

(Continued on page 131)

...All-summer Fruit Coffee Cake (cont'd.)

2 cups all-purpose flour

1 cup sugar

2 teaspoons baking powder

1 teaspoon salt

1½ teaspoons grated orange peel

½ cup (¼ lb.) butter or margarine

2 eggs

1 cup milk

1 teaspoon vanilla

3½ cups prepared fresh fruit: blueberries; pitted sweet cherries; pitted apricots, nectarines, or plums, sliced ½ inch thick; peeled and pitted peaches, sliced ½ inch thick; *or* peeled and cored apples, sliced ¼ inch thick

   Streusel Topping (recipe follows)

In a large bowl, stir together flour, sugar, baking powder, salt, and orange peel. Using a pastry blender or 2 knives, cut butter into flour mixture until it resembles cornmeal.

In another bowl, beat eggs lightly, then stir in milk and vanilla. Make a well in center of flour mixture and pour in egg mixture; stir just until moistened.

Spoon batter into a well-greased 7 by 11-inch baking pan; arrange prepared fruit evenly on top, pressing in lightly. Prepare Streusel Topping and scatter over fruit.

Bake in a 350° oven for 1 hour or until a wooden pick inserted in center comes out clean. Let cool on a rack for 20 minutes; then cut into squares and serve warm. Or let cool completely, cover, and store at room temperature. To reheat, warm, uncovered, in a 300° oven for about 10 minutes. Makes 12 servings.

STREUSEL TOPPING. In a small bowl, combine ⅓ cup firmly packed **brown sugar,** ¼ cup **all-purpose flour,** and 1 teaspoon

ground cinnamon. With your fingers, work in 2 tablespoons **butter** or margarine until well distributed. Stir in ½ cup chopped **almonds** or walnuts.

Old-fashioned Oatmeal Pancakes

(Pictured on facing page)

Deserving of such old-fashioned praise as "sticks-to-the-ribs," these pancakes are hearty and tasty fare. Start the batter the night before to give the oats and buttermilk a chance to merge.

2 cups regular rolled oats

   About 2 cups buttermilk

2 eggs

4 tablespoons butter or margarine, melted and cooled

½ cup raisins (optional)

½ cup all-purpose flour

2 tablespoons sugar

1 teaspoon *each* baking powder and baking soda

½ teaspoon ground cinnamon

¼ teaspoon salt

In a bowl, combine oats and 2 cups of the buttermilk; stir until well blended. Cover and refrigerate until next day.

In a bowl, beat eggs lightly and add to oat mixture, along with butter and raisins, if desired; stir just until blended. In another bowl, stir together flour, sugar, baking powder, baking soda, cinnamon, and salt; add to oat mixture and stir just until moistened. If batter seems too thick, add more buttermilk (up to 3 tablespoons).

Preheat a griddle or wide frying pan over medium heat; grease lightly. Spoon batter, about ⅓ cup for each cake, onto griddle; spread batter out to make circles 4 inches in diameter. Cook until tops are bubbly and appear dry; turn and cook other sides until browned. Makes about 1½ dozen pancakes, about 4 inches in diameter.

Fresno French Toast

Worth waking up for, these golden-crisp toast triangles sparkle with cinnamon flavor. Dust them with powdered sugar just before presenting them at the breakfast table.

2 eggs

1 cup *each* all-purpose flour and milk

1½ teaspoons baking powder

½ teaspoon salt

1 teaspoon *each* ground cinnamon and vanilla

8 to 10 slices firm white bread

   About 6 tablespoons butter or margarine

   About 3 tablespoons salad oil

   Powdered sugar

   Apricot jam

In a blender or food processor, whirl eggs until blended; add flour, milk, baking powder, salt, cinnamon, and vanilla, and whirl until smooth. Pour mixture into a shallow baking dish.

Cut bread slices in half diagonally to form triangles. Lay in egg mixture, turning to soak both sides well.

Heat 2 tablespoons of the butter and 1 tablespoon of the oil in a wide frying pan over medium-high heat. Drain bread slices briefly and fry, a few pieces at a time, until golden brown on both sides; add remaining butter and oil as needed. Arrange toast on a serving platter and keep warm in a 150° oven until all are cooked.

To serve, dust with powdered sugar; pass apricot jam to spoon on top. Makes 4 or 5 servings.

HOT-FROM-THE-GRIDDLE breakfast of Old-fashioned Oatmeal Pancakes (recipe on this page) and sausages is like the one that nourished Grandpa after the milking was done, generations back. Heated maple syrup and cinnamon-topped applesauce are the final homey touches.

DESSERTS

Cakes, cookies, pies & other sweets

Sour Cream-Chocolate Bit Cake

Tote it to the PTA, potluck, or picnic—then watch the cake disappear as fast as you can cut it.

- 6 tablespoons butter or margarine, softened
- 1 cup sugar
- 2 eggs
- 1⅓ cups all-purpose flour
- 1½ teaspoons baking powder
- 1 teaspoon *each* baking soda and ground cinnamon
- ½ pint (1 cup) sour cream
- 1 small package (6 oz.) semisweet chocolate chips
- 1 tablespoon sugar

Grease and flour-dust a 9 by 13-inch baking pan; set aside.

In a large bowl, beat butter with the 1 cup sugar until creamy. Add eggs, one at a time, beating well after each addition. In another bowl, stir together flour, baking powder, baking soda, and cinnamon; stir into creamed mixture. Mix in sour cream and pour batter into prepared pan.

Sprinkle chocolate chips evenly over batter; then sprinkle with the 1 tablespoon sugar.

Bake in a 350° oven for 35 minutes or until cake begins to pull away from sides of pan. Serve warm or at room temperature (do not refrigerate). Makes 10 to 12 servings.

Frosted Brownie Cake

When a craving for chocolate creeps up on you, here's a most pleasant appeasement. It's almost as easy to whip up as a cake mix.

- 2 cups *each* all-purpose flour and sugar
- 1 teaspoon baking soda
- ¼ cup unsweetened cocoa
- 1 cup water
- 10 tablespoons (¼ lb. plus 2 tablespoons) butter or margarine
- ½ cup buttermilk
- 2 eggs
  Creamy Chocolate Frosting (recipe follows)

In a large bowl, stir together flour, sugar, baking soda, and cocoa. In a small pan over high heat, bring water and butter to a boil. Remove from heat and let cool slightly; then pour into flour mixture and beat until well blended. Beat in buttermilk; add eggs one at a time, beating well after each addition.

Pour batter into a well-greased 10 by 15-inch baking pan. Bake in a 350° oven for 25 minutes or until cake springs back when

132

lightly touched. Let cool in pan for 15 to 20 minutes.

Meanwhile, prepare Creamy Chocolate Frosting. Spread over warm cake. Let cool; then cut into 2½ to 3-inch squares. Makes 14 to 16 servings.

CREAMY CHOCOLATE FROST-ING. In a large bowl, combine 1 box (1 lb.) **powdered sugar,** ¼ cup unsweetened **cocoa,** ⅓ cup **milk,** and 1 teaspoon **vanilla.** Add ½ cup (¼ lb.) **butter** or margarine, melted, and beat with an electric mixer until light and fluffy and of spreading consistency (about 5 minutes).

Almond Fudge Torte

Its glossy, pastry-shop look belies the simple preparation of this sinfully delicious and undeniably rich dessert. Almond paste lends an extra burst of flavor.

Unsweetened cocoa
1   teaspoon instant coffee powder or granules
2   tablespoons hot water
4   squares (1 oz. *each*) semisweet baking chocolate, melted
3   eggs, separated
½   cup (¼ lb.) butter or margarine
¾   cup sugar
⅓   cup (about 2 oz.) almond paste, crumbled or shredded
½   cup all-purpose flour
Chocolate Glaze (recipe follows)

Grease an 8-inch round cake pan; lightly dust with cocoa and set aside.

Dissolve coffee in hot water; stir in melted chocolate. In a bowl, beat egg whites just until soft, moist peaks form.

In another bowl, beat butter with sugar until creamy. Beat in almond paste, egg yolks, chocolate mixture, and flour. Fold in beaten egg whites, a third at a time, just until blended. Spoon mixture into prepared pan; smooth top.

Bake in a 350° oven for 30

minutes or until lightly browned (do not overbake). Let cool in pan on a rack for about 10 minutes; then turn out of pan and let cool completely.

Meanwhile, prepare Chocolate Glaze; spread over top and sides of cooled cake. Let stand until glaze hardens (2 to 4 hours at room temperature; 30 to 45 minutes, if refrigerated). Serve at room temperature. Makes 10 servings.

CHOCOLATE GLAZE. In top of a double boiler, combine 4 squares (1 oz. *each*) **semisweet baking chocolate** and 1 tablespoon **butter** or margarine; stir over barely simmering water just until melted. Remove from heat and let cool, stirring occasionally, until slightly thickened.

Zucchini Fruitcake

Growing more mellow by the month, these summer-baked zucchini loaves wait patiently in your freezer until the autumn and winter holidays.

3   eggs
1   cup salad oil
2   cups firmly packed brown sugar
1   tablespoon vanilla
3   cups all-purpose flour
1   tablespoon ground cinnamon
2   teaspoons *each* baking soda and ground allspice
1   teaspoon *each* salt, ground nutmeg, and ground cloves
½   teaspoon baking powder
2   cups coarsely shredded unpeeled zucchini, lightly packed
2   cups *each* coarsely chopped walnuts and raisins
1   cup currants
2   cups mixed candied (glacé) fruit
8   tablespoons brandy or rum (optional)

In a large bowl, combine eggs, oil, sugar, and vanilla; beat until well blended. In another bowl, thoroughly stir together flour, cinnamon, baking soda, allspice,

salt, nutmeg, cloves, and baking powder. Stir into egg mixture.

With a wooden spoon, stir in zucchini, walnuts, raisins, currants, and candied fruit just until blended. Spoon batter into 2 greased and flour-dusted 5 by 9-inch loaf pans.

Bake in a 325° oven for about 1 hour and 10 minutes or until a wooden pick inserted in center comes out clean. If desired, spoon 4 tablespoons of the brandy over each loaf while still warm. Let cool in pans on racks.

When completely cooled, turn loaves out of pans. Wrap airtight and freeze. Or store wrapped loaves in refrigerator for at least 2 weeks before serving. Makes 2 loaves.

Chocolate Zucchini Cake

Zucchini bread is a fairly commonplace summertime staple among home vegetable gardeners. But zucchini-plus-chocolate was an unheard-of combination when this recipe first appeared in *Sunset* magazine. Even so, the recipe won praise from many undaunted readers, who wrote that the humble back-yard squash produced an unusually moist and tender cake.

2½   cups all-purpose flour
½   cup unsweetened cocoa
2½   teaspoons baking powder
1½   teaspoons baking soda
1   teaspoon *each* salt and ground cinnamon
¾   cup (¼ lb. plus 4 tablespoons) butter or margarine, softened
2   cups sugar
3   eggs
2   teaspoons *each* grated orange peel and vanilla
2   cups coarsely shredded unpeeled zucchini (about 4 medium-size), lightly packed
½   cup milk
1   cup chopped pecans or walnuts
Glaze (recipe follows)

(Continued on next page)

In a bowl, combine flour, cocoa, baking powder, baking soda, salt, and cinnamon; set aside.

In large bowl of an electric mixer, beat butter and sugar until fluffy. Add eggs, one at a time, beating well after each addition. Stir in orange peel, vanilla, and zucchini. Alternately stir flour mixture and milk into zucchini mixture, including nuts with last addition.

Pour batter into a greased and flour-dusted 10-inch tube or bundt pan. Bake in a 350° oven for about 1 hour or until a wooden pick inserted in center comes out clean. Let cool in pan for 15 minutes; then invert cake onto a rack to cool completely.

Prepare Glaze and drizzle over cooled cake; let Glaze harden. Makes 10 to 12 servings.

GLAZE. In a bowl, combine 2 cups **powdered sugar,** 3 tablespoons **milk,** and 1 teaspoon **vanilla.** Beat until smooth.

Carrot Cake

(Pictured on facing page)

Carrots, we learned in our nursery years, help us see in the dark; some say they also make our hair curl. What wonderful excuses for second helpings!

- 4 **eggs**
- 1½ **cups salad oil**
- 2 **cups** *each* **sugar and all-purpose flour**
- 1½ **teaspoons baking soda**
- 2 **teaspoons** *each* **baking powder and ground cinnamon**
- ½ **teaspoon ground nutmeg**
- 1 **teaspoon salt**
- 2 **cups shredded carrots**
- ½ **cup coarsely chopped walnuts or pecans**
- 1 **can (8 oz.) crushed pineapple, drained**
  Cream Cheese Frosting (recipe follows)

In a large bowl, beat eggs just until blended; add oil and sugar,

beating until thoroughly mixed. In another bowl, stir together flour, baking soda, baking powder, cinnamon, nutmeg, and salt. Add to egg mixture, stirring just until blended; then mix in carrots, nuts, and pineapple.

Pour batter into a greased and flour-dusted 9 by 13-inch baking pan or a 12-cup bundt or other fluted cake pan. Bake in a 350° oven for 45 minutes for a 9 by 13-inch pan, 55 minutes for a bundt or other fluted pan, or until a wooden pick inserted in center comes out clean.

Let cool (if you use a bundt or fluted pan, let cake cool in pan for 15 minutes; then invert onto a rack to cool completely).

Prepare Cream Cheese Frosting and spread over cooled cake. Makes 12 to 15 servings.

CREAM CHEESE FROSTING. In a bowl of an electric mixer, combine 2 small packages (3 oz. *each*) **cream cheese,** softened; 6 tablespoons **butter** or margarine, softened; and 1 teaspoon grated **orange peel;** beat until smooth. Add 1 teaspoon **vanilla** and 2 cups **powdered sugar;** beat until creamy. (Or put all ingredients into a food processor and whirl until blended.)

Cherry-glazed Sponge Cake

Plump, juicy cherries peek through the top of this light sponge cake that one reader called "a perfect remedy for wintry doldrums."

- 1 **cup (½ lb.) butter or margarine**
- 1½ **cups granulated sugar**
- 4 **eggs**
- 1 **teaspoon almond extract**
- 2 **cups all-purpose flour**
- 1 **can (21 oz.) cherry pie filling**
  Powdered sugar

In large bowl of an electric mixer, beat butter and granulated sugar

until fluffy. Add eggs, one at a time, beating well after each addition. Stir in almond extract and flour until well blended.

Spread batter in a well-greased 10 by 15-inch baking pan. With tip of a knife, lightly mark off batter into 15 equal pieces; then spoon equal portions of cherry pie filling into center of each piece.

Bake in a 350° oven for 35 to 40 minutes or until cake is lightly browned and a wooden pick inserted in center comes out clean. Let cool in pan. Dust with powdered sugar before serving. Makes 15 servings.

Eggnog Pound Cake

Rich Christmas flavors in this easy holiday favorite come from packaged cake mix and commercial eggnog. Who would believe it?

- About 2 **tablespoons butter or margarine, softened**
- ½ **cup sliced almonds**
- 1 **package (about 18½ oz.) yellow cake mix**
- ⅛ **teaspoon ground nutmeg**
- 2 **eggs**
- 1½ **cups purchased eggnog**
- 4 **tablespoons butter or margarine, melted**
- 2 **tablespoons rum or ¼ teaspoon rum flavoring**

Generously grease a 10-inch tube or bundt pan with the softened butter; press almonds on sides and bottom of pan; set aside.

In a large bowl, combine cake mix, nutmeg, eggs, eggnog, the melted butter, and rum. Using an

(Continued on page 136)

NOSTALGIC AS AN OLD-TIME NUTCRACKER, yet contemporary as a slick food processor, our moist Carrot Cake (recipe on this page) blends the appeal of old and new. Bake it in a pretty fluted pan and ice it with an orange-flavored cream cheese frosting.

electric mixer, beat until smooth and creamy (about 4 minutes at medium speed)—or beat for about 450 strokes with a wooden spoon. Pour batter into prepared pan.

Bake in a 350° oven for 45 to 55 minutes or until a wooden pick inserted in center comes out clean. Let cool in pan for 10 minutes; then invert cake onto a rack to cool completely. Makes 10 to 12 servings.

Ricotta Puffs

In flavor and appearance, these tempting puffs can pass for doughnuts—though they're plumped up with plenty of protein rather than calories.

½ pint (1 cup) ricotta cheese
3 eggs
¼ cup granulated sugar
1 cup all-purpose flour
4 teaspoons baking powder
¼ teaspoon salt
 Salad oil
 Powdered sugar

In a large bowl, beat ricotta with eggs and granulated sugar until blended and smooth. In another bowl, stir together flour, baking powder, and salt; add to ricotta mixture, beating until batter is smooth.

Pour oil into a deep pan to a depth of about 1½ inches; heat to 360° on a deep-frying thermometer. For each puff, drop a rounded teaspoon of batter into hot oil; fry several at a time, turning occasionally, until golden brown (about 1½ minutes). Lift out cooked puffs with a slotted spoon; drain well.

If made ahead, let cool, then wrap airtight and refrigerate. To reheat, arrange puffs in a single layer on a rimmed baking sheet; place in a 350° oven for about 10 minutes or until heated through.

Dust with powdered sugar and serve hot. Makes 3½ dozen.

Scotch Shortbread

Scotland's traditional cooky-cake has the charm of utter simplicity —there's practically nothing to it but flour, sugar, and butter. Still, the flavor keeps you coming back for more.

1¼ cups all-purpose flour
3 tablespoons cornstarch
¼ cup sugar
½ cup (¼ lb.) butter (do not substitute margarine), cut into chunks
1 tablespoon sugar

In a large bowl, combine flour, cornstarch, and the ¼ cup sugar; with your fingers, work in butter until mixture is crumbly and no large particles remain. Shape into a firm lump.

Place dough (it will still be crumbly) in an 8 or 9-inch springform pan; press firmly and evenly over bottom of pan. Impress edge of dough with tines of a fork (as you would a pie crust); prick surface evenly.

Bake in a 325° oven for about 40 minutes or until a pale golden brown. Using a sharp knife, cut into 8 to 12 wedges while still warm; sprinkle with the 1 tablespoon sugar. Let cool; then remove pan rim and lift out cookies.

Wrap airtight and store at room temperature for up to a week. Freeze for longer storage. Makes 8 to 12 cookies.

Chocolate-covered Almond Macaroons

A Swedish sweet tooth, when indulged, may sate itself with a cup of coffee and a confection of enchanting flavor like this one—an almond macaroon spread with chocolate buttercream, and dipped in still more chocolate.

 Almond Macaroons (recipe follows)
 Chocolate Buttercream (recipe follows)
5 squares (1 oz. *each*) semisweet baking chocolate
1 tablespoon plus 2 teaspoons solid shortening

Prepare Almond Macaroons; let cool completely. Prepare Chocolate Buttercream and spread 1 tablespoon of the buttercream over flat bottom of each macaroon. Place cookies, buttercream side up, in a single layer on a baking sheet; refrigerate until buttercream is firm (at least 15 minutes).

Meanwhile, in top of a double boiler, combine chocolate and shortening; stir over barely simmering water just until melted. Pour chocolate mixture into a small, shallow bowl and let cool, stirring occasionally, until lukewarm (80° to 85°).

Dip buttercream side of each cooky into chocolate mixture to coat buttercream. Return cookies to baking sheet, chocolate side up, and refrigerate until coating is set (at least 10 minutes).

Serve when chocolate is firm, or wrap airtight and store in refrigerator for up to 3 days. Freeze for longer storage. (If frozen, let thaw in refrigerator for at least 3 hours before serving.) Makes about 18 cookies.

ALMOND MACAROONS. In a blender or food processor, whirl 1½ cups **blanched almonds** until finely ground. In a bowl, mix nuts with 1½ cups sifted **powdered sugar** until all lumps disappear.

In a large bowl, beat 3 **egg whites** just until stiff, moist peaks form; fold nut mixture, a third at a time, into egg whites until blended.

For each cooky, drop a rounded tablespoon of the egg white mixture on a baking sheet lined with parchment paper or brown wrapping paper, spacing cookies about an inch apart.

Bake in a 350° oven for 15 to 18 minutes or until lightly browned. Let cool for 5 minutes; using a wide spatula, lift from pan and place on racks to cool completely.

CHOCOLATE BUTTERCREAM. In a small pan over high heat, stir together 7 tablespoons *each* **sugar** and **water.** Bring to a boil; continue boiling until syrup reaches 230° to 234° on a candy thermometer, or until syrup spins a 2-inch-long thread when dropped from a spoon.

In a small bowl, beat 4 **egg yolks** with an electric mixer until blended. Beating at high speed, slowly pour in hot syrup in a thin, steady stream; beat until mixture is thickened and lemon-colored, and has cooled to room temperature. Beat in ⅔ cup **butter,** softened, a tablespoon at a time, just until blended. Stir in 4 teaspoons unsweetened **cocoa.** (Refrigerate if mixture is too soft to hold its shape.)

Cooky Canvases

Smoothly glazed and sturdy, these cookies become edible canvases on which young (and older) artists can paint pictures with food coloring. Since the novel idea first appeared in *Sunset,* it has provided splashy entertainment at many a children's party.

You'll need to bake and glaze the cookies well in advance of a painting session. The glaze, applied while the cookies are still warm, takes 8 to 24 hours to dry.

For painting, have available

several sizes of water-color brushes, clear water for rinsing them, and small cups of food coloring, either undiluted (for bright colors) or slightly diluted with water (for lighter colors). Food coloring will flow, so allow each color to dry briefly before adding the next.

2   cups (1 lb.) butter or margarine, softened
2   cups granulated sugar
2   teaspoons vanilla
5   cups all-purpose flour
6   to 9 tablespoons warm water
1   to 1½ pounds powdered sugar
    Assorted food colors

In a large bowl, beat together butter, granulated sugar, and vanilla until well blended. Beat in flour until thoroughly blended (dough should hold together).

With a stockinet-covered rolling pin, roll out enough dough on an ungreased baking sheet to cover sheet in a ¼ to ⅜-inch-thick layer.

For rectangular or square cookies, use a sharp knife and a ruler to cut away a 1-inch margin of dough on all sides of baking sheet; make no other cuts.

For round or decorative shapes, flour cooky cutters (use a coffee can or tuna can with top and bottom removed for rounds); cut shapes, leaving at least 1 inch between cookies and lifting away excess dough. Combining excess with remaining dough, repeat rolling and cutting until all dough is used.

Bake in a 300° oven for 25 to 30 minutes or until dough is pale gold and center is set when lightly touched.

Meanwhile, in a large bowl, gradually add water to powdered sugar (you'll need about 6 tablespoons water per pound), beating constantly, until icing is smooth and thick; mixture should flow smoothly but set quickly.

Remove cookies from oven. If

making rectangles or squares, cut while still hot, using a sharp knife and a ruler; trim to straighten edges. Let cookies of all shapes cool on pan until just warm to the touch (about 7 minutes).

With a wide spatula, transfer cookies to a flat, foil-covered surface. With back of a spoon, quickly spread each cooky with enough icing to make a very smooth surface. Do not cover or disturb cookies until icing is dry to the touch (8 to 24 hours).

Paint with food coloring; or stack, unpainted, between pieces of foil and wrap airtight. Store at room temperature for up to 4 days. Freeze for longer storage. (If frozen, unwrap and let thaw at room temperature before painting.) Makes about 1 dozen 6-inch cookies or 2 dozen 3 to 4-inch cookies.

Cinnamon Pinwheel Cookies

A cinnamon-sugar filling swirls, pinwheel-fashion, through these crisp and delicate cookies. Baked from a sweet yeast dough, they resemble puff pastry in buttery flavor and flaky texture. Keep the dough cold and handle it as little as possible.

3   cups all-purpose flour
½   teaspoon salt
1   teaspoon ground cardamom (optional)
2   tablespoons sugar
1   cup (½ lb.) butter or margarine
1   package active dry yeast
¼   cup warm water (about 110°)
½   cup milk
1   egg, beaten
3   tablespoons salad oil
    Cinnamon Filling (recipe follows)
    About ⅓ cup sugar

In a large bowl, combine flour, salt, cardamom (if desired), and the 2 tablespoons sugar. Using a pastry blender or 2 knives, cut

(Continued on page 139)

butter into flour mixture until particles are about the size of peas.

Dissolve yeast in warm water; then stir in milk, egg, and oil. With a fork, stir yeast mixture into flour mixture just until flour is moistened. Cover with plastic wrap and refrigerate until firm (about 1 hour).

Meanwhile, prepare Cinnamon Filling and set aside.

Knead dough on a lightly floured board 4 times only. Roll into an 11 by 18-inch rectangle, keeping sides straight. Sprinkle filling evenly over surface to within ¼ inch of each edge. Starting with a long side, roll up tightly, jelly roll style; pinch seam to seal. Wrap well in plastic wrap and refrigerate until firm (about 1 hour).

Cut dough in half and return a portion to refrigerator. Cut remaining portion in ½-inch-thick slices. On a lightly floured board, pat each slice out into a circle about 5 inches in diameter.

Spread the ⅓ cup sugar on a plate; then dredge each dough circle in sugar to coat both sides. Place circles close together on an ungreased baking sheet.

Bake in a 350° oven for 15 minutes or until golden brown. With a spatula, transfer cookies to a rack and let cool.

Repeat with remaining dough.

Wrap cookies airtight and store at room temperature for up to a week. Makes 3 dozen cookies.

CINNAMON FILLING. In a bowl, stir together ¼ cup **dark brown sugar** and 2 tablespoons *each* **granulated sugar** and **ground cinnamon**.

WHAT'S COOL, CREAMY, AND SLIGHTLY SWEET? If you guessed ice cream, guess again. This enticing scoop of raspberry is Frozen Fruit Yogurt (page 149). Crank out a batch of your favorite flavor—or let an electric freezer do the work.

Fruitcake Cooky Cups

Miniature Christmas mouthfuls are perfect for nibbling by the fire—or for gift-giving in a pretty tin.

- 4 tablespoons butter or margarine, softened
- ½ cup firmly packed brown sugar
- ¼ cup apple or currant jelly
- 2 eggs
- 1 teaspoon vanilla
- 1½ cups all-purpose flour
- 2 teaspoons baking soda
- ½ teaspoon *each* ground allspice, ground cloves, ground cinnamon, and ground nutmeg
- 1 cup chopped walnuts or pecans
- 1 cup currants or raisins
- 1 cup chopped candied (glacé) cherries or mixed fruit

In a large bowl, beat together butter, sugar, and jelly until smooth. Add eggs and vanilla; mix well. In another bowl, combine flour, baking soda, allspice, cloves, cinnamon, and nutmeg; stir half the flour mixture into creamed mixture.

Add nuts, currants, and cherries to remaining flour mixture; then stir into creamed mixture, blending well.

Line 1½-inch mini-muffin cups with paper liners; spoon 1½ to 2 teaspoons of the batter into each cup. Or, for each cooky, drop a teaspoon of the batter on a lightly greased baking sheet, spacing cookies about 2 inches apart. Bake in a 300° oven for 17 to 20 minutes or until centers spring back when lightly touched.

Transfer to racks and let cool completely. Wrap airtight and

store in a cool place or refrigerate for up to 2 weeks; freeze for longer storage. Makes about 6 dozen.

Chocolate Chip Cookies at Their Best

Also known, immodestly, as "the best chocolate chip cookies in the universe," they positively skyrocketed in our cooky popularity poll. Don't skimp on their lavish proportions of chocolate pieces and walnuts if you want to understand their claim to cooky superiority.

- 1 cup solid shortening
- ½ cup (¼ lb.) butter or margarine, softened
- 1⅓ cups granulated sugar
- 1 cup firmly packed brown sugar
- 4 eggs
- 1 tablespoon vanilla
- 1 teaspoon lemon juice
- 2 teaspoons baking soda
- 1½ teaspoons salt
- 1 teaspoon ground cinnamon
- ½ cup regular or quick-cooking rolled oats
- 3 cups all-purpose flour
- 2 large packages (12 oz. *each*) semisweet chocolate chips
- 2 cups chopped walnuts

In large bowl of an electric mixer, beat shortening, butter, granulated sugar, and brown sugar at high speed until light and fluffy (about 5 minutes). Add eggs, one at a time, beating well after each addition. Beat in vanilla and lemon juice.

In another bowl, stir together baking soda, salt, cinnamon, oats, and flour. Beat into creamed mixture until well combined; stir in chocolate chips and nuts.

For each cooky, drop a scant ¼ cup dough on a lightly greased baking sheet, spacing cookies about 3 inches apart. Bake in a 350° oven for 16 to 18 minutes or until golden brown. Transfer to racks and let cool. Makes about 3 dozen large cookies.

Buttery Lemon Squares

(Pictured on page 34)

These rich bar cookies are after-school favorites.

 1 cup (½ lb.) butter or margarine, softened
 ½ cup powdered sugar
 2⅓ cups all-purpose flour
 4 eggs
 2 cups granulated sugar
 1 teaspoon grated lemon peel
 6 tablespoons lemon juice
 1 teaspoon baking powder
 3 tablespoons powdered sugar

In a large bowl, beat butter with the ½ cup powdered sugar until creamy. Add 2 cups of the flour and beat until blended. Spread evenly in a well-greased 9 by 13-inch baking pan. Bake in a 350° oven for 20 minutes.

Meanwhile, in a small bowl, beat eggs until light. Gradually add granulated sugar, beating until thickened and well blended. Add lemon peel, lemon juice, remaining ⅓ cup flour, and baking powder; beat until thoroughly blended. Pour lemon mixture over baked crust and return to oven. Bake for 15 to 20 more minutes or until pale gold.

Sprinkle evenly with the 3 tablespoons powdered sugar; let cool. To serve, cut into squares or bars. Makes about 20 squares.

Lemon-glazed Persimmon Bars

The regal flavor of persimmons blends with sharp, tangy lemon in these energy-rich bar cookies. Their already-chewy texture is enhanced by morsels of nut and date. Bake the thick batter until golden; then cool and glaze.

 1 cup frozen persimmon pulp, thawed, *or* 1 cup fresh persimmon pulp mixed with 1½ teaspoons lemon juice
 1 teaspoon baking soda
 1 egg
 1 cup sugar
 ½ cup salad oil
 8 ounces (about 1 cup) pitted dates, finely snipped
 1¾ cups all-purpose flour
 1 teaspoon *each* salt, ground cinnamon, and ground nutmeg
 ¼ teaspoon ground cloves
 1 cup chopped walnuts or pecans
 Lemon Glaze (recipe follows)

Lightly grease and flour-dust a 10 by 15-inch rimmed baking sheet; set aside.

In a small bowl, mix persimmon pulp with baking soda and set aside. In a large bowl, lightly beat egg; then stir in sugar, oil, and dates.

In another bowl, combine flour with salt, cinnamon, nutmeg, and cloves; add to date mixture alternately with persimmon mixture, stirring just until blended. Stir in nuts. Spread evenly in prepared pan. Bake in a 350° oven for 25 minutes or until lightly browned.

Let cool in pan on a rack for 5 minutes. Prepare Lemon Glaze and spread over cookies. Let cool completely; then cut into bars. Wrap airtight, separating layers with wax paper, and store at room temperature. Makes 30 bars.

LEMON GLAZE. In a small bowl, stir 1 cup **powdered sugar** with 2 tablespoons **lemon juice** until smooth.

Dried Fruit Newtons

Though the kids will care only about the taste of these cookies, mothers will appreciate the nutritional fuel that comes from wheat germ and whole wheat flour. Looking much like store-bought cookies, they're bigger, fresher, and more wholesome—and they offer a more interesting array of fillings, as well.

 1 cup whole wheat flour
 1¼ cups all-purpose flour
 ¼ cup regular wheat germ
 ¼ teaspoon *each* salt and baking soda
 ½ cup (¼ lb.) butter or margarine, softened
 ½ cup *each* granulated and firmly packed brown sugar
 2 eggs
 ½ teaspoon vanilla
 Dried fruit filling (recipes follow)

In a bowl, combine whole wheat flour, all-purpose flour, wheat germ, salt, and baking soda. In another bowl, beat butter until creamy; then gradually beat in granulated sugar and brown sugar until fluffy.

Beat in eggs and vanilla, then stir in flour mixture until blended. Knead dough lightly until smooth; cover and refrigerate for at least an hour or until next day. Meanwhile, prepare dried fruit filling of your choice and let cool completely.

Divide dough in half, returning one portion to refrigerator. On a floured board, roll dough out to make a 9 by 15-inch rectangle (use your fingers and a ruler to shape square corners and straight sides). Cut lengthwise into 3 strips, each 3 by 15 inches. Repeat with remaining portion of dough.

Divide filling into 6 equal portions; distribute a portion down center of each strip, spreading filling evenly out to ends. Using a long spatula, fold sides of each dough strip over filling so they overlap slightly on top. Press edges together lightly.

Cut strips in half, lift, and invert, seam side down, onto a greased baking sheet. Brush off excess flour; cover with plastic wrap and refrigerate for about 15 minutes.

Bake in a 375° oven for 15 to 20 minutes or until well browned. Let cool for 10 minutes on racks; then cut each strip into 4 equal portions. Let cool completely. Wrap airtight and store at room temperature for up to a week. Freeze for longer storage. Makes 4 dozen.

DRIED FIG FILLING. Using a food processor or food chopper fitted with a medium blade, grind 1 pound (about 2 cups) **dried figs** and ½ cup **walnuts** or almonds. Turn into a pan and add ⅓ cup **sugar,** ½ cup **water,** 1 teaspoon grated **lemon peel,** and 2 tablespoons **lemon juice.** Stir over medium heat until mixture boils and thickens (5 to 8 minutes). Let cool.

PRUNE FILLING. Follow recipe for Dried Fig Filling, substituting 1 pound (about 2 cups) **pitted prunes** for figs and adding ¾ teaspoon **ground cinnamon** with sugar.

APRICOT FILLING. Follow recipe for Dried Fig Filling, substituting 1 pound (about 3 cups) **dried apricots** for figs and 1 teaspoon grated **orange peel** for lemon peel.

DATE FILLING. Follow recipe for Dried Fig Filling, substituting 1 pound (about 2 cups) **pitted dates** for figs and increasing lemon peel to 2 teaspoons.

Crunchy Walnut Pie

For deluxe presentation, serve this exquisite dessert à la mode. The pie mellows to maximum richness if its flavors have a

chance to mingle quietly for a while—so bake it a day ahead.

> 3 eggs
> ½ cup firmly packed brown sugar
> 1 cup light corn syrup
> ¼ teaspoon salt
> 1 teaspoon *each* vanilla and ground cinnamon
> 4 tablespoons butter or margarine, melted
> 1 cup broken walnuts or walnut halves
> 9-inch unbaked pastry shell, 1½ inches deep

In a large bowl, beat eggs with sugar, corn syrup, salt, vanilla, cinnamon, and butter until well blended. Stir in walnuts; pour mixture into pastry shell.

Bake on the lowest shelf of a 375° oven for about 50 minutes or until filling jiggles only slightly when pan is gently shaken. Let cool on a rack for at least 2 hours before cutting.

If made ahead, cover with foil when completely cooled; store at room temperature until next day. Makes 6 to 8 servings.

Chocolate Swirl Eggnog Pie

Ripples of chocolate run through the rich rum filling of this festive holiday pie. To give it ample time to chill, make it a day ahead.

> Chocolate Crust (recipe follows)
> ¼ cup cold water
> 1 envelope (1 tablespoon) unflavored gelatin
> 2 tablespoons cornstarch
> ½ cup sugar
> 2 cups purchased eggnog
> 1½ squares (1½ oz.) semisweet baking chocolate, melted
> ½ pint (1 cup) whipping cream
> 6 tablespoons rum or ¾ teaspoon rum flavoring
> Semisweet baking chocolate

Prepare Chocolate Crust and let cool.

Pour water into a small bowl and sprinkle with gelatin; set aside. In a pan over medium heat, stir together cornstarch, sugar, and eggnog; cook, stirring, until thickened; stir in gelatin. Divide mixture in half and stir melted chocolate into one portion. Refrigerate both portions until thick but not set.

In a bowl, beat whipping cream until soft peaks form; fold whipped cream and rum into white portion; then spoon into cooled crust. Spoon chocolate portion over top. With a knife, gently swirl chocolate through cream layer. Refrigerate until well chilled.

Using a vegetable peeler, shave thin slices of semisweet chocolate into curls; sprinkle over top of pie. Makes 8 servings.

CHOCOLATE CRUST. In a large bowl, combine 1 cup **all-purpose flour,** ¼ cup firmly packed **brown sugar,** ¾ cup chopped **nuts,** and 1 square (1 oz.) **semisweet baking chocolate,** grated. Stir in ⅓ cup **butter** or margarine, melted; press mixture over bottom and sides of a 9-inch pie pan. Bake in a 375° oven for 15 minutes.

Pear & Almond Tart

(Pictured on front cover)

Similar to French *poires Bourda-loue* (poached pears with almond cream), this elegant tart looks as lovely as it tastes. Harmonizing with the pear and almond filling are a lemony crust and a tangy apricot glaze.

(Continued on next page)

Press-in Lemon Pastry (recipe follows)

Poached Pears (recipe follows) *or* 1 large can (29 oz.) pear halves

1 small package (3 oz.) cream cheese, softened

½ pint (1 cup) whipping cream

¼ cup powdered sugar

½ teaspoon grated lemon peel

1 teaspoon lemon juice

¼ teaspoon *each* almond extract and vanilla

2 tablespoons kirsch (optional)

⅔ cup apricot jam

¼ cup sliced almonds

Prepare Press-in Lemon Pastry and set aside to cool. Also prepare Poached Pears (or drain canned pear halves).

In small bowl of an electric mixer, beat cream cheese, then slowly blend in whipping cream. Add sugar, lemon peel, lemon juice, almond extract, vanilla, and kirsch, if desired. Beat until mixture is as thick as stiffly beaten cream. Spread filling evenly in pastry shell.

With stem ends pointing toward center, arrange pear halves, cavity side down, around tart (as many as will fit); gently push pears into filling. Cover and refrigerate until firm (about 1 hour).

Rub apricot jam through a wire strainer into a small pan; heat over low heat just until melted. Let cool for 5 minutes. Lightly brush or drizzle jam over pears and filling. Cover loosely with foil and refrigerate. Before serving, remove pan rim and distribute almonds around pears. Makes 10 to 12 servings.

PRESS-IN LEMON PASTRY. In a small bowl, combine 1⅓ cups **all-purpose flour,** ¼ cup **sugar,** and 1 teaspoon grated **lemon peel.** With your fingers, work in ½ cup (¼ lb.) firm **butter** or margarine (cut into pieces) until mixture is crumbly and no large particles remain. With a fork, stir in 1 **egg yolk** until blended; work dough with your hands until it holds together. Shape into a smooth ball.

Press dough evenly over bottom and sides of an 11-inch tart pan with removable bottom (or use a 10-inch spring-form pan, pressing dough 1¼ inches up sides). Bake in a 300° oven for 30 minutes or until golden brown.

POACHED PEARS. In a 4 to 5-quart pan over high heat, combine 1½ cups **water,** ¾ cup **sugar,** and 1 teaspoon *each* grated **lemon peel** and **vanilla.** Bring to a boil, stirring, and boil until sugar dissolves.

Cut 4 medium-sized **pears** in half lengthwise, peel, and sprinkle with **lemon juice.** Remove cores. Place halves, cavity side down, in sugar mixture; cover, reduce heat, and simmer until tender when pierced (about 10 minutes). Drain well (reserve syrup for other uses, if desired).

Upside-down Apple Nut Pie

Turned upside-down, this apple pie greets you with a rich and chewy caramel-glazed nut topping.

Rich Pie Crust (recipe follows)

4 to 5 large Golden Delicious apples

2 tablespoons butter or margarine

1 tablespoon lemon juice

½ teaspoon ground cinnamon

⅓ cup butter or margarine, melted

⅓ cup firmly packed brown sugar

About 1 cup pecan or walnut halves

Prepare Rich Pie Crust and refrigerate.

Peel, core, and thinly slice apples (you should have 8 cups). In a wide frying pan over medium heat, melt the 2 tablespoons butter. Add apples and cook, turning occasionally, until fruit is tender when pierced and juices have evaporated (about 15 minutes). Stir in lemon juice and cinnamon. Let cool.

Lightly grease sides of a 9-inch pie pan. With floured fingers, press half the pie crust dough evenly around pan sides (do not cover rim). Keep remaining dough chilled.

In a small bowl, stir together the ⅓ cup melted butter and brown sugar and pour into pan. Arrange nuts, flat side up, in a single layer in bottom of pan. Carefully lay apple slices over nuts.

Gather remaining dough into a ball. Place on well-floured wax paper. Flatten dough slightly, dust with flour, and cover with another piece of wax paper; with a rolling pin, roll to a 9-inch circle. Peel off top piece of wax paper; lift and invert pastry over apples, then peel off remaining paper. If pastry tears, press together gently with your fingers. Gently press edges of pastry circle to pastry on pan sides.

Bake in a 400° oven for 25 to 30 minutes or until browned. Remove from oven and run a spatula around sides to loosen. Immediately place a large heat-proof serving plate over pan and invert, letting pan rest briefly so caramel can drip down over apples.

Serve warm. If made ahead, cool and cover; to reheat, place in a 325° oven for 10 minutes. Makes 6 servings.

RICH PIE CRUST. In a large bowl, stir together 1¼ cups **all-purpose flour,** 1¼ teaspoons **baking powder,** ⅓ cup **sugar,** and ⅛ teaspoon **salt.** With a pastry blender or 2 knives, cut in ⅓ cup **solid shortening** until mixture resembles coarse cornmeal.

In another bowl, lightly beat together 1 **egg,** 1 tablespoon **milk,** and ½ teaspoon **vanilla.** Stir into flour mixture until well blended. Gather dough into a ball, cover, and refrigerate.

FROM SEASON TO SEASON, fresh fruit pies are always a crowd-pleaser. Try this cinnamon-scented apple version—or use any other seasonal fruit to make your favorite "Can't-Miss" Fruit Pie (page 146).

Pumpkin Pie Cheesecake

Everybody loves cheesecake—and pumpkin pie is just about as popular. This recipe brings out the best of both in a dessert that has a vocal and fiercely loyal fan club. Smooth texture makes it a cheesecake; spices and a gingery crust make it a pumpkin pie.

- 6 tablespoons butter or margarine, melted
- 2 cups finely crushed ginger cookies
- 2 large packages (8 oz. *each*) cream cheese, softened
- 1 cup *each* canned pumpkin and lightly packed brown sugar
- ¼ cup all-purpose flour
- 1½ teaspoons vanilla
- 1 teaspoon *each* ground cinnamon, ground ginger, and ground allspice
- ½ teaspoon *each* ground nutmeg and salt
- ¾ cup milk
- 4 eggs, lightly beaten
  Sour Cream Topping (recipe follows)

In a bowl, stir together butter and crushed cookies until well combined. Using a metal spatula, press butter mixture over bottom and halfway up sides of an ungreased 9 or 10-inch spring-form pan. Bake in a 350° oven for 10 to 12 minutes or until edges are well browned; let cool.

In large bowl of an electric mixer, beat cream cheese until smooth. Add pumpkin and sugar; beat until light and fluffy (3 to 5 minutes). Beat in flour, vanilla, cinnamon, ginger, allspice, nutmeg, and salt. Add milk and eggs, beating just until blended.

Pour mixture into cooled crust. Bake in a 350° oven for 1¼ to 1½ hours or until a knife inserted halfway between center and edge comes out clean. Turn oven off, set door slightly ajar, and leave cheesecake in oven for an hour; then place on a rack and let cool for at least 2 hours.

Remove pan rim. Prepare Sour Cream Topping and spread evenly over cooled cheesecake. Serve at room temperature or refrigerate and serve cold. Makes 10 to 12 servings.

SOUR CREAM TOPPING. In a small bowl, stir ½ pint (1 cup) **sour cream,** 2 tablespoons **sugar,** and 1 teaspoon **vanilla** until blended.

Frozen Chocolate-Peanut Pie

Yet another extravaganza for chocolate lovers, this chocolate-filled pie even has a chocolate crust. Crushed peanut brittle brightens the top.

- Chocolate-Nut Crust (recipe follows)
- 1 package (about 3½ oz.) chocolate fudge flavor pudding and pie filling
- 1¾ cups milk
- ½ cup crunchy peanut butter
- 1 teaspoon vanilla
- ½ pint (1 cup) whipping cream
- 1 cup sugar
- ½ cup crushed peanut brittle

Prepare Chocolate-Nut Crust; set aside.

In a pan over medium heat, combine pudding mix and milk. Cook, stirring constantly, until pudding boils. Remove from heat; stir in peanut butter and vanilla. Lay wax paper on surface of pudding and refrigerate for 30 to 40 minutes or until cool but not set.

In a bowl, beat whipping cream until soft peaks form; beat in sugar. Fold into cooled pudding and spoon filling into crust. Cover and freeze until firm.

Let thaw for 40 minutes before serving. Top with peanut brittle. Makes 6 servings.

CHOCOLATE-NUT CRUST. In a large bowl, mix 1 cup **chocolate wafer crumbs,** ⅓ cup chopped **peanuts,** 2 tablespoons **sugar,** and ⅓ cup **butter** or margarine, melted. Press over bottom and sides of a 9-inch pie pan. Bake in a 350° oven for 5 to 8 minutes. Let cool.

Frozen Strawberry Meringue Torte

Plump, pretty, sweet, and juicy, the season's first strawberries look and taste almost too good to be true. Celebrate their glory with this billowy meringue.

- Graham Cracker Crust (recipe follows)
- 4 cups sliced strawberries
- 1 cup sugar
- 2 egg whites
- 1 tablespoon lemon juice
- 1 teaspoon vanilla
- ⅛ teaspoon salt
- ½ cup whipping cream
  About 7 strawberries, cut in half

Prepare Graham Cracker Crust; let cool completely.

Place 2 cups of the sliced strawberries in a large bowl (refrigerate remaining berries). Add sugar, egg whites, lemon juice, vanilla, and salt. Using an electric mixer, beat on low speed to blend, then on high speed until firm peaks form when beaters are lifted (about 15 minutes).

In another bowl, beat whipping cream until very soft peaks form; gently fold whipped cream into berry mixture. Pour into cooled crust; cover and freeze until very firm (about 12 hours).

To serve, remove pan rim and arrange strawberry halves, cut side down, around top edge. Pass remaining sliced strawberries to spoon over individual servings. Return any leftover torte to freezer, removing berries first. Makes 8 to 10 servings.

GRAHAM CRACKER CRUST. In a small bowl, stir together 1 cup **graham cracker crumbs,** 3 tablespoons **sugar,** ½ cup chopped **pecans,** and 4 tablespoons **butter** or margarine, melted. Press crumb mixture over bottom of a 10-inch spring-form pan. Bake in a 325° oven for 10 minutes.

Chocolate-Coffee Freezer Torte

Some marriages are made in heaven—and the pairing of coffee with chocolate is one. In this candy-topped ice cream torte, the two sought-after flavors sing in heavenly harmony.

  Coconut Crumb Crust (recipe follows)
1 pint chocolate ice cream, slightly softened
½ cup chocolate-flavored syrup
1 pint coffee ice cream, slightly softened
  About 4 ounces chocolate-covered hard toffee candy bars, coarsely chopped

Prepare Coconut Crumb Crust; let cool completely.

Spread chocolate ice cream in an even layer over cooled crust; drizzle evenly with ¼ cup of the syrup. Freeze until firm.

Remove from freezer and top with an even layer of coffee ice cream; sprinkle evenly with chopped candy. Drizzle remaining ¼ cup syrup over top. Cover and freeze until firm. Before serving, remove pan rim. Makes 6 to 8 servings.

COCONUT CRUMB CRUST. In a small bowl, stir together 1 cup **macaroon cooky crumbs** and 2 tablespoons **butter** or margarine,

melted. Lightly press over bottom of a 9-inch spring-form pan. Bake in a 350° oven for 8 to 10 minutes or until lightly browned.

Chocolate Peppermint Torte

Sinfully rich, but worth every calorie, this delicious dessert is a chocolate-lover's delight, from its crumb crust to its decorative topping of grated chocolate.

  Chocolate Crumb Crust (recipe follows)
½ cup (¼ lb.) butter or margarine, softened
¾ cup sugar
3 squares (1 oz. *each*) unsweetened baking chocolate, melted
1 teaspoon vanilla
¾ teaspoon peppermint flavoring
3 eggs
½ cup whipping cream
  Grated unsweetened baking chocolate

Prepare Chocolate Crumb Crust and let cool.

In large bowl of an electric mixer, beat butter until creamy; gradually add sugar and beat until light and fluffy. Beat in melted chocolate, vanilla, and peppermint flavoring. Add eggs, one at a time, beating for 3 minutes after each addition.

In another bowl, beat whipping cream until soft peaks form; fold into chocolate mixture. Spoon into cooled crust and sprinkle generously with grated chocolate.

Cover and refrigerate for at least 4 hours or until next day. To serve, remove pan rim. Makes 10 to 12 servings.

CHOCOLATE CRUMB CRUST. In a small bowl, stir together 1 cup **chocolate wafer crumbs** and 2 tablespoons **butter** or margarine, melted. Press crumb mixture over bottom of a 9-inch spring-form pan. Bake in a 350° oven for 7 minutes.

Frosty Lemon Torte

Refreshingly cool and creamy, this lemon-coconut creation perfectly suits the after-dinner mood of a warm spring or summer evening. Though rich-tasting and satisfying, this torte is surprisingly low in calories.

  Coconut Crumb Crust (recipe follows)
2 eggs, separated
⅔ cup sugar
1 teaspoon grated lemon peel
⅓ cup lemon juice
  Dash of salt
⅔ cup *each* nonfat dry milk and water

Prepare Coconut Crumb Crust; let cool completely.

Place egg yolks in a bowl; using an electric mixer, beat until foamy. Gradually add ½ cup of the sugar and beat until thick and lemon-colored. Blend in lemon peel, lemon juice, and salt.

In another bowl, combine egg whites, dry milk, water, and remaining sugar. Beat (using clean beaters) on highest speed until stiff peaks form (about 5 minutes). Add yolk mixture and beat on lowest speed just until blended. Pour into prepared crust and sprinkle with remaining crumb mixture.

Cover and freeze until firm (at least 6 hours or until next day). Remove pan rim and let stand at room temperature for 10 minutes before serving. Makes 8 servings.

COCONUT CRUMB CRUST. In a small bowl, stir together 1 cup **macaroon cooky crumbs** and 2 tablespoons **butter** or margarine, melted. Lightly press about three-quarters of the crumb mixture over bottom of a 9-inch spring-form pan; set aside remaining crumb mixture.

Bake crust in a 350° oven for 8 to 10 minutes or until lightly browned.

"CAN'T-MISS" FRUIT PIES

Fresh, warm-from-the-oven pie with juicy morsels of fruit enveloped in tender, flaky pastry—who can resist such home-baked goodness? At any time of year, you can create delicious pies bursting with sugar and spice and pick-of-the-season fruit; and the best part of all is that it's so easy.

Even a novice can master the secrets of pie perfection by following the fruit filling chart on the opposite page and our easy recipe for pastry (or, if you prefer, simply use a pie crust mix). You can even choose between a traditional double-crust 9-inch pie and a single-crust pie with streusel topping.

Fresh Fruit Pie

(Pictured on page 143)

    Fruit filling (see chart on facing page)
    Flaky Pastry (recipe follows)
2 tablespoons butter or margarine (for double-crust pie)
    Streusel Topping (recipe follows), optional

Mix fruit of your choice with sugar, thickener, and suggested seasonings. Determine amount of sugar (within range indicated) by ripeness of fruit and taste. Sugar increases liquid in pie, so if fruit is juicy or you use maximum amount of sugar, use maximum amount of cornstarch or tapioca. Let mixture stand.

Meanwhile, prepare Flaky Pastry (for streusel-topped pie, prepare half the recipe). For double-crust pie, divide dough in half, rolling out a portion at a time.

On a lightly floured board or pastry cloth, flatten dough into a round. With a floured or stockinet-covered rolling pin, roll dough out from center in all directions with light, even strokes, making an 11-inch circle about ⅛ inch thick.

Gently fold dough into quarters; transfer to a 9-inch pie pan, placing point at center. Carefully unfold and, without stretching dough, ease from center out to rim, using fingertips to fit dough gently onto pan sides.

For double-crust pie, trim bottom pastry round, leaving ½ inch hanging over pan rim. Fill with fruit mixture and dot with butter. Roll remaining dough portion to same size circle as first; fold into quarters, transfer to pan, and gently unfold to cover filling. Trim, leaving a 1-inch overhang; fold edge of top pastry under edge of bottom pastry along rim. Flute edge decoratively between your fingers or press with tines of a fork to seal. Cut several slashes in top to allow steam to escape.

For streusel-topped pie, trim bottom pastry, leaving 1 inch hanging over pan rim. Fold edge under and flute between your fingers, hooking edge slightly over rim. Fill with fruit mixture. Prepare Streusel Topping and sprinkle evenly over fruit.

Set oven at temperature recommended on chart. To prevent excessive browning of rim, wrap edge with a strip of foil 2 to 3 inches wide. Set pie on a rimmed baking sheet and bake on lowest rack for recommended time. Check streusel-topped pie after 15 to 20 minutes; if it's browning too fast, cover loosely with foil.

Remove foil strip from edge 15 to 20 minutes before pie is done; uncover streusel-topped pie about 5 minutes before it's done. Bake until juices bubble vigorously and pastry is well browned.

Let cool on a rack. Serve warm; or refrigerate and serve cold. To reheat, place, uncovered, in a 350° oven for 10 to 15 minutes or until heated through.

Flaky Pastry. In a large bowl, combine 2¼ cups **all-purpose flour** with ½ teaspoon **salt.** Using a pastry blender or 2 knives, cut ¾ cup **solid shortening,** lard, or firm margarine into flour mixture until particles are about the size of peas.

Measure 5 tablespoons **cold water** into a cup. Sprinkle water, a tablespoon at a time (you'll use 4 to 5 in all), over flour mixture, stirring lightly and quickly with a fork just until all the flour mixture is moistened. (Mixture should be neither dry and crumbly, nor wet and sticky.) Stir with a fork until dough almost cleans sides of bowl.

Press lightly into a ball. Makes enough pastry for a double-crust 9-inch pie.

Streusel Topping. In a bowl, combine 1 cup **all-purpose flour,** ½ cup firmly packed **brown sugar,** and ½ teaspoon **ground cinnamon.** With your fingers, rub in 6 tablespoons **butter** or margarine until butter lumps are no longer distinguishable. Stir in ½ cup chopped **nuts,** if desired. Makes enough topping for a 9-inch pie.

	FRUIT in cups	SUGAR in cups	CORNSTARCH OR TAPIOCA in tablespoons	SEASONINGS in tablespoons (tbsp.) or teaspoons (tsp.)	BAKING temperature	minutes
APPLE (Granny Smith, Gravenstein, Jonathan, Newtown Pippin)—peel, core, and thinly slice						
9-inch double crust	8	¾–1	2½–3	1 tsp. ground cinnamon and ¼ tsp. ground ginger	425°	50–60
9-inch streusel top	6	½–¾	1½–2	¾ tsp. ground cinnamon and ¼ tsp. ground ginger	375°	60
APRICOT—use fully ripe; cut into quarters, remove pits, and slice, if large						
9-inch double crust	8	1¼–1½	3½–4	1 tbsp. lemon juice and 1¼ tsp. ground coriander	425°	55–60
9-inch streusel top	6	1–1¼	3–3½	1 tbsp. lemon juice and 1 tsp. ground coriander	425°	75–90
BERRY (blue, black, boysen, logan)—use whole berries						
9-inch double crust	6	1½–1¾	3½–4	1 tbsp. lemon juice (blueberry only)	425°	55–60
9-inch streusel top	6	1¼–1½	3½–4	1 tbsp. lemon juice (blueberry only)	425° (blueberry), 375° (others)	75–90 (blueberry), 55–60 (others)
CHERRY, SWEET—remove pits						
9-inch double crust	8	1–1¼	2½–3	2 tbsp. lemon juice and ¼ tsp. almond flavoring (optional)	425° for 15 min., then 350° for 30 min.	45 total
9-inch streusel top	6	¾–1	2–2½	1½ tbsp. lemon juice and ¼ tsp. almond flavoring (optional)	375°	40–45
PEACH or NECTARINE—peel (except nectarines), pit, and thinly slice						
9-inch double crust	8	¾–1	3–3½	2 tbsp. lemon juice and ½ tsp. ground nutmeg	425°	40–50
9-inch streusel top	6	½–¾	2½–3	1½ tbsp. lemon juice and ¼ tsp. ground nutmeg	425°	75
PEAR (Bartlett)—peel, core, and thinly slice						
9-inch double crust	8	¾–1	2½–3	2 tbsp. lemon juice and ½ tsp. ground ginger	425°	55–60
9-inch streusel top	6	½–¾	1¾–2¼	1½ tbsp. lemon juice and ½ tsp. ground ginger	375°	60
PLUM (Santa Rosa, Nubiana, prune)—pit and slice						
9-inch double crust	8	1½–2	6½–7	1 tsp. grated lemon peel and ½ tsp. ground cinnamon	425°	60
9-inch streusel top	6	1–1½	4½–5	¾ tsp. grated lemon peel and ¼ tsp. ground cinnamon	425°	65

Russian Cream

Snowy white and smooth as velvet, this simple, creamy gelatin dessert pairs perfectly with fresh strawberries. You can adjust the richness: use whipping cream for a mellow flavor, half-and-half for more tang and fewer calories—either way, it's delicious and refreshing. Serve it molded or not, as you like.

- ¾ cup sugar
- 1 envelope (1 tablespoon) unflavored gelatin
- ½ cup water
- ½ pint (1 cup) whipping cream or half-and-half (light cream)
- 1½ cups sour cream
- 1 teaspoon vanilla
  Strawberries
  Crisp vanilla or lemon-flavored cookies (optional)

In a small pan, blend sugar and gelatin. Add water, mixing well, and let stand for about 5 minutes; then bring to a full, rolling boil over high heat, stirring constantly.

Remove pan from heat and pour in whipping cream. In a small bowl, combine sour cream with vanilla and gradually beat into hot sugar mixture until smooth.

To make individual desserts, pour cream mixture into 8 small serving dishes or 8 metal ½-cup molds. Or pour mixture into a 4 to 5-cup serving bowl or mold. Cover and refrigerate for at least 4 hours or until next day.

To unmold, dip mold up to its rim in hot water for a few seconds or until edges of cream just begin to liquefy. Quickly dry mold and invert onto a serving dish; cream will slowly slip free (if not, return mold briefly to the hot water). If unmolded ahead, refrigerate; cover lightly when surface has firmed.

Accompany with strawberries and, if desired, cookies. Makes 8 servings.

Cranberry Pudding Squares

Rich and aromatic, this cranberry dessert may remind you of traditional steamed pudding. As a cool counterpoint to its hearty flavor, top each serving with a dollop of whipped cream or ice cream.

- 1 cup all-purpose flour
- 1 teaspoon baking soda
- ¼ teaspoon *each* salt and ground cinnamon
- 1 cup *each* raisins and chopped walnuts
- 2 teaspoons grated orange peel
- 1 cup *each* chopped cranberries and chopped pitted prunes
- 1 cup sugar
- 1 tablespoon butter or margarine, melted
- 1 teaspoon vanilla
- ¾ cup milk

In a large bowl, sift together flour, baking soda, salt, and cinnamon. Stir in raisins, nuts, and orange peel; set aside.

In another bowl, stir together cranberries, prunes, sugar, butter, and vanilla until well combined. Add to flour mixture along with milk, stirring until well blended.

Turn into a greased 9-inch square baking pan. Bake in a 325° oven for 1 hour or until a wooden pick inserted in center comes out clean. Let cool for about 30 minutes; cut into 3-inch squares. Serve warm or at room temperature. Makes 9 servings.

Golden Apple Crisp

Apples bake to sweet succulence under a crunchy cinnamon-crumb topping for a pleasant after-dinner offering.

- 4 to 5 medium-size Golden Delicious apples
  Butter or margarine
- ⅓ cup apricot nectar or orange juice
- ¼ cup granulated sugar
- ½ cup firmly packed brown sugar
- ¾ teaspoon ground cinnamon
- ¼ teaspoon salt
- ¾ cup all-purpose flour
- 4 tablespoons butter or margarine

Peel and core apples; cut into ½-inch-thick slices (you should have 6 cups). Distribute evenly in a well-buttered 7 by 11-inch baking dish.

In a bowl, combine apricot nectar with granulated sugar and pour over apples. Mix brown sugar, cinnamon, salt, and flour until well blended. Using a pastry blender or 2 knives, cut the 4 tablespoons butter into flour mixture until particles are about the size of peas. Sprinkle crumb mixture evenly over apples.

Bake in a 375° oven for 40 minutes or until topping is browned and apples are tender. Serve warm; or refrigerate and serve cold. Makes 6 to 8 servings.

Fresh Peach Crisp

A crunchy, nut-laced streusel topping accents sweet, juicy peaches in this simple dessert.

- 8 large, firm ripe peaches
- ¼ cup granulated sugar
- ¼ teaspoon salt
- 1 teaspoon lemon juice
- ¾ cup *each* all-purpose flour and firmly packed brown sugar
- ½ cup (¼ lb.) butter or margarine
- ½ cup chopped walnuts
  Whipped cream or vanilla ice cream (optional)

Peel and pit peaches; cut into ¾-inch-thick slices (you should have 5 to 6 cups).

In a small bowl, combine granulated sugar and salt. Arrange a layer of peach slices in an 8-inch square baking pan and sprinkle with some of the sugar mixture; repeat layers until all peaches and sugar mixture are used. Sprinkle with lemon juice.

In a bowl, combine flour and brown sugar. Using a pastry blender or 2 knives, cut butter into flour mixture until particles are about the size of peas; mix in nuts. Sprinkle crumb mixture evenly over peaches.

Bake in a 375° oven for 45 minutes or until topping is browned. Serve warm; or refrigerate and serve cold. Top each portion with whipped cream, if desired. Makes 6 to 8 servings.

Rhubarb Oat Crumble

Whether you grow the ruby stalks in your back yard or bring home a bundle from the market, rhubarb is sure to please no matter how you cook it. Here it mingles with a crunchy streusel mixture for a deliciously wholesome, easy-to-bake dessert.

1 **cup regular or quick-cooking rolled oats**
1 **cup** *each* **firmly packed brown sugar and all-purpose flour**
1 **teaspoon ground cinnamon**
½ **cup (¼ lb.) butter or margarine, softened**
4 **cups diced rhubarb (about 1¼ lbs.)**
1 **cup granulated sugar**
2 **tablespoons cornstarch**
1 **cup water**
1 **teaspoon vanilla**
   Red food coloring (optional)

In a large bowl, combine oats with brown sugar, flour, and cinnamon. With your fingers, rub in butter until lumps are no longer distinguishable. Press half the crumb mixture over bottom of a

9-inch square baking pan. Evenly distribute rhubarb over crumbs.

In a pan, combine granulated sugar and cornstarch. Add water and cook, stirring, over medium heat until thickened; let cool slightly. Add vanilla and a few drops of food coloring, if desired; pour over rhubarb. Sprinkle with remaining crumb mixture.

Bake in a 350° oven for 50 minutes or until richly browned. Serve warm or at room temperature. Makes about 9 servings.

Berry Roly-Poly

The British, who enjoy some silly-sounding but perfectly delicious sweets, have enriched the world's cuisine with a dessert called "jam roly-poly and custard." This juicy concoction is similar—but berries take the place of jam, and a dollop of ice cream, instead of custard, tops it off.

5 **cups fresh or frozen (unsweetened) boysenberries or blackberries**
1 **cup plus 6 tablespoons sugar**
1¾ **cups hot water**
2 **cups all-purpose flour**
3 **teaspoons baking powder**
1 **teaspoon salt**
6 **tablespoons solid shortening**
⅔ **cup milk**
4 **tablespoons butter or margarine, melted**
¼ **teaspoon ground cinnamon**
   Vanilla ice cream

If using frozen berries, let stand at room temperature for 30 minutes.

In a small pan over low heat, combine 1 cup of the sugar with hot water; simmer for 5 minutes; then pour into a greased 9 by 13-inch baking dish. Let cool.

Meanwhile, in a large bowl, combine flour, 2 tablespoons of remaining sugar, baking powder, and salt. Using a pastry blender or 2 knives, cut in shortening un-

til crumbs are as fine as cornmeal. Stir in milk and melted butter.

Gather dough into a ball and knead 10 times on a floured board. Roll out into an 8 by 12-inch rectangle. Distribute 2 cups of the berries evenly across dough and sprinkle with cinnamon and remaining 4 tablespoons sugar. Starting with a short end, roll up dough; pinch seam securely to seal in filling.

Cut roll into eight 1-inch-wide slices, and arrange, cut side up, in syrup in baking dish. Surround slices with remaining 3 cups berries, pushing berries down into syrup.

Bake in a 450° oven for 25 minutes or until top is richly browned. Let cool on a rack; serve warm or at room temperature, topping each portion with ice cream. Makes 8 to 16 servings.

Frozen Fruit Yogurt

(Pictured on page 138)

Here's a frozen dessert as deliciously creamy as ice cream, but with only half the calories. If you have an electric or hand-crank freezer, you can whip up a batch, liberally laced with your choice of fruit. Try any one—or all—of the fruit flavors offered.

   Fruit mixture (recipes follow)
3 **eggs, separated**
¼ **teaspoon** *each* **salt and cream of tartar**
¼ **cup sugar**
2 **quarts (8 cups) plain yogurt, homemade (page 85) or purchased**

To prepare fruit mixture of your choice, combine fruit and sugar (plus honey, if used) in a 3-quart pan over high heat. Bring to a boil, stirring; reduce heat to medium and cook, stirring constantly, until fruit softens and partially disintegrates (1 to 4 minutes, depending on ripeness of fruit); break up any large pieces with a fork.

(Continued on next page)

Remove from heat and stir in fruit juices, spices, and flavorings as indicated for fruit mixture.

In a small bowl, lightly beat egg yolks; stir in about ½ cup of the hot fruit mixture. Then stir egg yolk mixture into remaining fruit mixture; let cool to room temperature.

In a large bowl, beat egg whites until frothy. Add salt and cream of tartar, beating until soft peaks form. Gradually add the ¼ cup sugar and continue beating until stiff peaks form.

Turn yogurt into a 5-quart or larger bowl; use a wire whisk to smooth out any lumps. Fold fruit mixture into yogurt until well blended. Then gently fold yogurt-fruit mixture into egg whites. (At this point, you may cover and refrigerate for several hours.)

Transfer mixture to a gallon-size or larger hand-crank or electric ice cream freezer. Assemble freezer according to manufacturer's directions, using about 4 parts ice to 1 part rock salt. When hand-cranking becomes difficult or when electric motor stalls, remove dasher. Transfer frozen yogurt to rigid plastic containers and place a piece of plastic wrap directly on top of yogurt. Close containers and freeze for at least 3 hours. Makes 1 gallon.

APRICOT-ORANGE. Use 4 cups thinly sliced unpeeled ripe **apricots,** 2 cups **sugar,** 2 tablespoons **lemon juice,** ½ cup **orange juice,** 1 teaspoon grated **orange peel,** and 4 teaspoons **vanilla.**

BANANA-HONEY. Measure 4 cups thinly sliced ripe **bananas;** coarsely mash. Use 1¼ cups **sugar,** ¾ cup **honey,** 3 tablespoons **lemon juice,** and 2 tablespoons **vanilla.**

BLACKBERRY. Use 4 cups lightly packed whole fresh (or unsweetened frozen and thawed) **blackberries,** 2 cups **sugar,** and 4 teaspoons *each* **lemon juice** and **vanilla.**

BLUEBERRY. Use 4 cups whole fresh (or unsweetened frozen and thawed) **blueberries,** 1¾ cups **sugar,** 2 tablespoons **lemon juice,** and 1 tablespoon **vanilla.**

PAPAYA. Coarsely mash enough peeled and seeded **papayas** (2 or 3 of them) to make 2½ cups. Use 2 cups **sugar,** 2 teaspoons **vanilla,** and ¼ cup **lime juice.**

PEACH. Use 4 cups sliced peeled **peaches,** 2 cups firmly packed **brown sugar,** 3 tablespoons **lemon juice,** 2 tablespoons **vanilla,** and ¾ teaspoon *each* **ground nutmeg** and **ground cinnamon.**

RASPBERRY. Use 4 cups lightly packed fresh (or unsweetened frozen and thawed) **raspberries,** 2 cups **sugar,** and 4 teaspoons *each* **lemon juice** and **vanilla.**

Hot Papaya Boats

A cargo of cream cheese blended with chutney, raisins, and nuts emboldens halved and heated papayas for an unusual summertime dessert. Only mildly sweetened, these sumptuous creations also make a delicious side dish to serve with ham or barbecued chicken. Try it for a party, Hawaiian-style.

- 1 **large package (8 oz.) cream cheese, softened**
- 1 **egg yolk**
- 3 **tablespoons sugar**
- ¼ **cup Major Grey chutney, chopped**
- ⅓ **cup golden raisins, chopped**
- ⅓ **cup slivered blanched almonds**
- 3 **large firm papayas**
- 2 **tablespoons butter or margarine, melted**
- ½ **teaspoon ground cinnamon**

In a bowl, beat cream cheese with egg yolk and 1 tablespoon of the sugar until smoothly blended. Mix in chutney, raisins, and almonds.

Cut papayas in half lengthwise and scoop out seeds. Arrange halves on a baking sheet, skin side down. Spoon cheese mixture into cavity of each, mounding slightly, and brush cheese mixture and exposed fruit with butter.

In a small bowl, combine cinnamon and remaining 2 tablespoons sugar and sprinkle over top. Bake in a 375° oven for 20 minutes or until heated through. Serve immediately. Makes 6 servings.

Strawberries in Wine

Elegant-looking and easy on the waistline, this simple dessert celebrates the marriage of fresh strawberries with mellow, muscat-derived wine. Serve unadorned for lowest calorie count, or top with sour cream. Either way, you're sure to tempt everyone at the table.

- 8 **cups strawberries**
- 1⅔ **cups muscat grape wine or cream sherry**
- ¾ **cup sugar**
- 2 **tablespoons cornstarch**
  Sour cream or whipped cream (optional)

Hull strawberries and cut in half lengthwise. Place in a deep bowl and pour in wine; toss to coat. Cover and refrigerate for at least 2 hours.

In a small pan, stir together sugar and cornstarch. Drain strawberries, reserving wine; gradually add wine to cornstarch mixture. Cook, stirring constantly, over high heat just until mixture boils and thickens; let cool completely. Pour cooled wine mixture over berries, tossing to coat. Cover and refrigerate for at least 2 hours or until next day.

To serve, spoon berry mixture into serving dishes; top with a dollop of sour cream, if desired. Makes 6 to 8 servings.

A BONBON BOX
OF CANDY FAVORITES

For gift-giving or indulgence at home, we offer you a select assortment of our readers' favorite confections. Rapturous reviews have poured in for the tempting toffee with its milk chocolate and filbert topping. The two much-requested bonbons that follow it can pass the sternest inspection for no-nonsense nutrition (which doesn't in the least interfere with their good candy sparkle).

Filbert-topped Toffee

Chocolate candy bars make a quick coating for this caramel-flavored toffee.

- 1 cup (½ lb.) butter (do not substitute margarine)
- 1 cup firmly packed brown sugar
- 6 bars (1⅜ oz. *each*) milk chocolate
- ½ cup finely chopped filberts

Butter a 9-inch square baking pan and set aside.

In a deep pan over medium-high heat, combine the 1 cup butter and brown sugar; cook, stirring constantly, until mixture reaches 300° on a candy thermometer (hard-crack stage). Pour immediately into prepared pan. Lay chocolate bars evenly over hot candy. When softened, spread chocolate into a smooth layer. Sprinkle with nuts, pressing them in lightly with your fingers.

Refrigerate until chocolate is firm. Invert candy onto a flat surface and break apart into small pieces. Makes about 3 dozen candies.

Apricot Slims

Offer these sweets after dinner or as a nutritious snack any time of day. Unsweetened coconut is sold at health food stores and in some markets; if you wish, you can substitute sweetened flaked coconut.

- 1 cup (about 6 oz.) moist-pack dried apricots
- ⅓ cup unsweetened coconut
- 1 tablespoon orange juice
- 4 tablespoons finely chopped almonds

If apricots aren't moist, place in a wire strainer and steam over simmering water for 5 minutes.

Put apricots through a food chopper, using a fine blade. Combine them with coconut and put through food chopper again. Add orange juice, mixing well. Divide mixture into 4 equal portions, wrap, and refrigerate until thoroughly chilled.

Working with one portion at a time, roll back and forth on a board using the palms of your hands to form a 16-inch-long rope. For each rope, sprinkle board with 1 tablespoon of the nuts; roll rope in nuts to coat. To serve, slice diagonally into 2-inch pieces. Makes about 32 candies.

Pear Slims. Follow recipe for Apricot Slims, substituting 6 ounces (about 1 cup) **dried pears** for apricots; remove any bits of stem or core from pears. Instead of orange juice, use 1 tablespoon **lemon juice;** instead of nuts, use 4 tablespoons **unsweetened coconut.**

Fruit & Nut Slices

Tightly wrapped and stored in the refrigerator, these dried fruit candies keep well for several weeks.

- 8 ounces (about 1 cup) *each* dried figs and pitted dates
- 1 cup *each* raisins and unsweetened coconut
- 1½ cups chopped almonds, walnuts, or pecans
- 1 teaspoon grated lemon peel
- ¼ cup lemon juice
- 1 cup peanut butter (creamy or crunchy)

In a large bowl, combine figs, dates, raisins, coconut, and 1 cup of the chopped nuts. Using a food chopper fitted with a medium blade, put mixture through twice to blend thoroughly. Add lemon peel, lemon juice, and peanut butter; mix well with a wooden spoon.

Divide mixture in half and shape each portion into a log about 12 inches long. For each log, sprinkle ¼ cup of the remaining chopped nuts onto a piece of wax paper; roll log to coat with nuts. Wrap tightly and refrigerate for at least 3 hours. Using a thin, sharp knife, cut into ⅜-inch slices. Makes about 60 candies.

Fruit & Granola Slices. Follow recipe above, omitting nuts; instead, stir 1 cup **granola-type cereal** into fruits after grinding. Coat each log with about ⅓ cup of the cereal.

PICKLES & PRESERVES

Plus other provisions for the pantry

Sweet Freezer Pickle Chips

For the taste of homemade pickles without the trouble of canning, douse ice-cold cucumber and onion slices with hot syrup and freeze them. To serve, just thaw as many pickles as you plan to use.

2½ pounds (about 5 medium-size) cucumbers, cut into ⅛-inch-thick slices

1 medium-size mild white onion, thinly sliced

2 tablespoons salt

2 quarts ice cubes

4 cups sugar

2 cups cider vinegar

In a large bowl, combine cucumber and onion slices with salt; cover with ice cubes and refrigerate for 2 to 3 hours.

Drain water and discard any unmelted ice cubes; do not rinse. Pack cucumber and onion slices in freezer containers or jars, filling each to within 1½ inches of rim.

In a 2-quart pan over high heat, combine sugar and vinegar. Bring to a boil, stirring until sugar is dissolved. Pour just enough hot syrup over cucumber and onion slices to cover. Screw on lids and freeze for at least a week.

Let thaw in refrigerator for 8 hours before serving. Makes about 3 pints.

Bread & Butter Pickle Slices

Cooked quickly in a spicy mustard syrup, these refrigerator pickles perk up sandwich fare.

2½ cups sugar

2 cups cider vinegar

1 cup water

1 teaspoon *each* salt and celery seeds

1 tablespoon mustard seeds

1½ tablespoons whole mixed pickling spice

3½ pounds (about 8 medium-size) cucumbers, cut into ¼-inch-thick slices

In a 5 to 6-quart kettle over high heat, combine sugar, vinegar, wa-

152

ter, salt, celery seeds, mustard seeds, and pickling spice. Bring to a boil, stirring until sugar is dissolved. Add cucumber slices and return to a boil, turning cucumbers gently with a wooden spoon to coat with syrup. Boil for 1½ minutes.

Ladle hot cucumber slices and pickling liquid into hot clean jars; screw on lids. Let cool, then refrigerate for up to 3 months. Makes about 5 pints.

Green Tomato Refrigerator Pickles

Firm, garden-green tomatoes harmonize with a medley of other vegetables in this chunky and unusual pickle. If you can't find green tomatoes in the market and don't grow tomatoes yourself, a gardening friend may be willing to spare some.

One *Sunset* reader varies the recipe by adding cauliflower.

  3 large cloves garlic, quartered
  3 small dried whole hot red chiles, halved
  1 tablespoon whole mixed pickling spice
 10 to 12 medium-size green tomatoes
  3 or 4 large carrots
  2 or 3 stalks celery
  2 medium-size onions, cut into 1-inch cubes
  1 or 2 red or green bell peppers, cut into 1-inch squares
7½ cups water
2½ cups white vinegar
 ¼ cup salt

Evenly divide garlic cloves among 3 jars, each about 1-quart size. Drop 2 chile halves and 1 teaspoon of the pickling spice into each jar.

Core tomatoes; cut each into 6 to 8 wedges. Cut carrots in half lengthwise, then cut carrots and celery into 1½-inch lengths. Distribute tomatoes, carrots, celery, onions, and red bell peppers in jars.

In a 4-quart pan over high heat, combine water, vinegar, and salt. Bring to a boil; then pour into jars. Let cool; then cover and refrigerate for 3 weeks before sampling. Store in refrigerator for up to 3 months. Makes 3 quarts.

Zucchini Relish

When zucchini threaten to overrun your summer garden, use the overabundance for this relish, crisp and tart enough to stand up to meat entrées.

  5 pounds (about 15 medium-size) zucchini, chopped
  6 large onions, chopped
  ½ cup salt
     Cold water
  2 cups white wine vinegar
  1 cup sugar
  1 teaspoon dry mustard
  2 teaspoons celery seeds
  ½ teaspoon *each* ground cinnamon, ground nutmeg, and pepper
  2 jars (4 oz. *each*) diced pimentos, drained

In a large bowl, mix zucchini, onions, and salt; pour in enough water to cover mixture. Cover and refrigerate for 4 hours or until next day. Then drain, rinse under cold water, and drain again.

In a 5 to 6-quart kettle over high heat, combine zucchini mixture with vinegar, sugar, mustard, celery seeds, cinnamon, nutmeg, pepper, and pimentos. Bring to a boil, stirring. Reduce heat and simmer, uncovered, until reduced to about 3 quarts (about 20 minutes). Meanwhile, prepare 6 pint-size canning jars following step 1 below; fill jars and process according to step 2 (above right).

CANNING. You'll need a canning kettle, canning jars, lids, and ring bands.

Step 1: Wash jars; keep hot in dishwasher, or fill with hot water

until ready to fill with food. Immerse lids in boiling water until ready to use. Place rack in canning kettle and fill kettle about half-full with hot water. Cover and place on range. In a large teakettle or pan, heat water to add later.

Step 2: Fill hot jars, one at a time, with boiling hot food to within ¼ inch of rim. Run a narrow spatula between jar and food to release air bubbles; add more food, if necessary. With a clean, damp cloth, wipe rims clean. Place lids on jars and screw on ring bands as tightly as you comfortably can.

Place jars on rack in kettle, making sure they don't touch kettle's sides or each other. Add hot water, if necessary—water must cover jars by 1 to 2 inches.

Bring water to simmering (170° to 180°; use a thermometer to check) and process for 15 minutes (begin counting processing time when water begins to simmer and keep water simmering throughout processing).

Remove jars without disturbing seal and let cool on a folded towel away from drafts. To test seal, press lid with your finger; if lid stays down when pressed, jar is sealed. (Store any unsealed jars in refrigerator and use within a month.) Store sealed jars in a cool, dark, dry place and refrigerate after opening.

Quick Refrigerator Corn Relish

Corn is a truly native American food—the first white settlers of this country learned how to cook with it from the Indians, who called it "maize."

Here's a way to use corn that lets you enjoy summer flavor the year around. You can pile the zesty relish into hollowed-out tomato or green pepper shells for a festive salad, or sprinkle it over hamburgers or hot dogs.

(Continued on next page)

1¼ cups white vinegar
¾ cup sugar
2½ teaspoons salt
1¼ teaspoons celery seeds
¾ teaspoon mustard seeds
½ teaspoon liquid hot pepper seasoning
8 cups whole kernel corn, cooked and cut from cob, or canned corn, drained well
1 small green pepper, seeded and chopped
1 jar (4 oz.) diced pimentos, drained
3 green onions (including tops), chopped

In a 3-quart pan over high heat, combine vinegar, sugar, salt, celery seeds, mustard seeds, and hot pepper seasoning. Bring to a boil; reduce heat and simmer, uncovered, for 5 minutes. Let cool..

Stir in corn, green pepper, pimentos, and onions. Pour into jars, cover, and refrigerate for up to 4 weeks. Makes about 4 pints.

Spiced Onion Rings

Our readers went for hefty helpings of this crisp, marinated red onion relish. Refrigerated, it keeps well for 2 weeks. For longer storage, follow the canning instructions.

4 to 6 large mild red onions
4 whole cinnamon sticks
1 teaspoon whole cloves
4 cups white vinegar
2 cups water
1½ cups sugar
2 teaspoons salt

Thinly slice onions, then separate into rings (you should have 3 quarts). Break cinnamon sticks into pieces.

Use a large glass bowl, or if canning is desired, prepare 4 pint-size, wide-mouthed jars according to step 1 of canning instructions for Zucchini Relish (page 153). Layer onion rings with cinnamon and cloves in bowl or jars.

In a 3-quart pan over high heat, combine vinegar, water, sugar, and salt. Bring to a boil and pour over onions. Let cool; then cover and refrigerate for 24 hours or for up to 2 weeks. Or process according to step 2 of canning instructions for Zucchini Relish (page 153).

To serve, lift onions from marinade. Makes 4 pints.

Minted Pear Chutney

On its own, minted fruit chutney is a lively condiment for barbecued or roasted meats and poultry. Or stir it into mayonnaise or sour cream for a zesty fruit salad dressing.

¾ cup *each* sugar and white vinegar
½ teaspoon salt
¼ to ½ teaspoon crushed red pepper
2 tablespoons finely chopped fresh ginger
¾ cup raisins
4 to 5 large ripe Bartlett pears
1 lime
1 large orange, peeled and chopped
2 tablespoons finely chopped fresh mint leaves

In a 3-quart pan over high heat, combine sugar, vinegar, salt, pepper, ginger, and raisins. Bring to a boil; reduce heat and simmer for 5 minutes. Set aside.

Peel and core pears, then cut into ½-inch cubes (you should have 5 cups). Cut off and discard ends of lime; then finely chop.

Add pears, lime, orange, and mint to pan. Simmer, uncovered, stirring occasionally, until chutney is as thick as jam (about 40 minutes).

Pour into jars, cover, and refrigerate for up to a month, or preserve as directed below, using 4 half-pint canning jars. Makes 4 half pints.

PRESERVING. You'll need canning jars, lids, and ring bands.

Step 1: Immerse canning jars in water and boil for 15 minutes to sterilize; keep immersed in hot water until ready to use. Scald lids and ring bands; keep lids in scalding hot water until ready to use.

Step 2: Pour food into hot jars, skim off any foam, and fill with more food to within ¼ inch of rim. With a clean, damp cloth, wipe rims clean. Place lids on jars and screw on ring bands as tightly as you comfortably can.

Let cool on a folded towel away from drafts. To test seal, press lid with your finger; if lid stays down when pressed, jar is sealed. Store in a cool, dark, dry place.

Jalapeño Jelly

By removing some or all of the seeds in the jalapeños, you can adjust the level of "heat" in this sweet-hot pepper jelly to suit your taste. Serve the jelly with meats; it goes well with beef, chicken, or pork.

About 5 medium-size whole canned jalapeño chiles
½ cup chopped seeded green pepper
¼ cup chopped seeded red bell pepper or additional green pepper
6 cups sugar
2½ cups cider vinegar
1 bottle (6 oz.) liquid pectin

Prepare 7 half-pint canning jars according to step 1 of preserving instructions for Minted Pear Chutney (this page).

Discard stem ends of jalapeños, any bits of blackened skin, and half the seeds (or as desired). Chop jalapeños (you should have ¼ cup). In a blender or food processor, combine jalapeños, green pepper, and red bell pepper and whirl until finely chopped. Transfer to a 5-quart kettle and stir in sugar and vinegar.

Bring to a boil over high heat, stirring. Pour in pectin all at once, return to a boil, and boil, stirring, for 1 minute. Remove from heat and skim off foam. Proceed according to step 2 of preserving instructions for Minted Pear Chutney (page 154), filling jars to within ¼ inch of rim. Makes about 7 half pints.

Flavored Vinegar

Seal your favorite flavors in red or white vinegar for use at home or for gift-giving. Corked or capped and protected with sealing wax, the bottles can be adorned with hand-lettered labels and colorful ribbons.

If you want to use fresh corks, you'll need a corking device to insert them. Look for corking and capping supplies in wine-making departments or stores. Sealing wax is sold in stationery stores—or use leftover candles.

**Flavorings (suggestions follow)
Red or white wine vinegar**

Place flavorings of your choice in a clean bottle (each suggested flavoring combination is enough for one ⅘-quart bottle or two ⅖-quart bottles; double amounts for a half gallon). Fill with vinegar as directed, stopping an inch from rim if inserting a cork. Cap with screw caps or plastic-topped, push-in corks, or use fresh corks.

Place sealing wax in a tall, thin, juice-type can; set in a pan with a small amount of water over low heat until wax is melted.

To seal bottle top, run a short length of decorative ribbon up neck, over top, and down other side of each bottle and glue in place; then dip neck of bottle into melted wax to coat well (if using candle wax, you may need to dip several times).

Let bottles stand in a cool, dark place for 3 weeks to allow flavors to develop. To open, pull ribbon up to break wax. Vinegar keeps well for about 4 months.

SPICY CHILE VINEGAR. Poke into a bottle 4 **bay leaves,** 6 small **dried whole hot red chiles,** and 4 large cloves **garlic.** Fill with **red or white wine vinegar.**

GARLIC-LEMON-MINT VINEGAR. Put into a bottle 4 large cloves **garlic** and 4 long sprigs **fresh mint.** With a small sharp knife, cut a continuous spiral strip of peel about ¼ inch wide from 1 **lemon** (cut strip in half for small bottles). Place in bottle and fill with **white wine vinegar.**

GARLIC VINEGAR. Impale 6 large cloves **garlic** on a thin bamboo skewer (or put 3 cloves garlic on each of 2 skewers). Insert in bottle and fill with **red wine vinegar.**

TARRAGON OR DILL VINEGAR. Poke 4 sprigs (about 5 inches long *each*) **fresh tarragon** or dill into bottle. Fill with **red or white wine vinegar.**

Old-fashioned Strawberry Jam

Succulent and bright red, this classic jam not only looks beautiful, but also has a garden-fresh flavor.

4 **cups crushed fresh strawberries**
4 **cups sugar**

Place strawberries in a 4 to 5-quart kettle; stir in sugar until well blended. Bring to a boil over

high heat, stirring. Continue boiling, uncovered, stirring often, until thickened (10 to 15 minutes).

Meanwhile, prepare 4 half-pint canning jars according to step 1 of preserving instructions for Minted Pear Chutney (page 154). When jam is thickened, proceed according to step 2 on page 154, filling jars to within ¼ inch of rim. Makes 4 half pints.

Ginger Apple Marmalade

At the root of this potent apple marmalade is pungent fresh ginger, tempered by bits of orange and lemon. You can preserve the marmalade in canning jars or keep it in the freezer.

6 **ounces fresh ginger, peeled and finely chopped (about 1 cup)**
3 **pounds tart apples, peeled, cored, and chopped (about 9 cups)**
1 **small orange, unpeeled, seeded and finely chopped (about ¾ cup)**
2 **medium-size lemons, unpeeled, seeded and finely chopped (about 1 cup)**
2½ **cups water**
6 **cups sugar**

In a 6 to 8-quart kettle over medium-high heat, combine ginger, apples, orange, lemons, and water. Bring to a boil; cover, reduce heat, and simmer until fruit is very tender (about 45 minutes).

Stir in sugar, increase heat, and bring to a boil. Boil gently, uncovered, over medium heat, stirring often, until fruit mixture reaches desired consistency (20 to 30 minutes). To check consistency, remove pan from heat, place a spoonful of the marmalade on a plate, and refrigerate. Marmalade should jell in 10 to 15 minutes.

To preserve, prepare 5 pint-size canning jars according to step 1 of preserving instructions for Minted Pear Chutney (page

154). When marmalade is ready, proceed according to step 2 on page 154, filling jars to within ¼ inch of rim.

To freeze, let marmalade cool completely; then pour into freezer containers or jars, filling to within ½ inch of rim; cover and freeze. Makes about 5 pints.

Plum Honey Butter

You'll capture summer's bounty of ripe fruit with a whirl of your blender when you make this luscious plum spread. The butter is a cooked fruit purée sweetened with honey; try it on toasted English muffins.

About 5 pounds ripe plums (such as Satsuma, Santa Rosa, or Casselman), sliced and pitted

3 to 4 cups light mild-flavored honey

In a blender or food processor, whirl plums, a portion at a time, until puréed (you should have 2 quarts). Pour into a 5 to 6-quart kettle. Stir in 3 cups of the honey and bring to a boil over medium-high heat.

Reduce heat and simmer, uncovered, stirring more often as mixture thickens, until it reaches desired consistency (1½ to 2 hours). To check consistency, remove pan from heat, place a spoonful of the butter on a plate, and refrigerate. Butter should jell to proper thickness in 10 to 15 minutes (it should be thick, but not stiff). If butter is too stiff, gradually stir in water until it reaches desired consistency.

Add more honey, if desired. To preserve, prepare 6 half-pint canning jars according to step 1 of preserving instructions for Minted Pear Chutney (page 154). When butter is ready, proceed according to step 2 on page 154. Or let cool; then cover and refrigerate for up to 3 months. Freeze for longer storage. Makes about 6 half pints.

Fruit Leathers

To make fruit leathers—translucent sheets of sun-dried fruit purée —you'll need to get an early start. The fruit can take up to 24 hours to dry.

Fruit (suggestions follow)
Sugar

Prepare fruit (it should be fully ripe) as directed below, cutting away any blemishes. Measure fruit (you can use up to 5 pints for any one batch). Add sugar and heat as directed for each fruit.

In a blender or food processor, whirl hot fruit mixture, a portion at a time if necessary, until puréed (or put through a food mill or wire strainer). Let cool until lukewarm.

Have ready a smooth level surface, such as a table, outdoors in full sun. Tear off long strips of plastic wrap, stretch across drying surface, and fasten with tape.

Pour fruit purée onto prepared surface and spread ¼ inch thick (a 5-pint batch covers a 30-inch-long strip of 12-inch-wide plastic wrap). Let dry in sun. To keep fruit clean, stretch a piece of cheesecloth over it; secure cloth to two 2 by 4-inch boards on either side, taking care to keep it from touching fruit purée.

Fruit takes 20 to 24 hours to dry. At end of first day, fruit should be dry enough so you can loosen tape, slip a baking sheet underneath, and carry inside; return to sun the next morning.

When fruit is firm to touch, try peeling fruit sheet off plastic (fruit is sufficiently dry when whole sheet can be pulled off plastic with no purée adhering; don't leave in sun longer than needed).

In humid climates, finish drying indoors if necessary. Set sheets of fruit on pans in a 140° to 150° oven and leave door slightly open.

To store, roll up sheets of fruit leather, still on plastic, then cover with more plastic and seal tightly. Store for up to a month at room temperature, refrigerate for up to 4 months, or freeze for up to a year.

APRICOTS. Cut in half, remove pits, and measure; use 1½ tablespoons sugar for each cup fruit (1 cup sugar for 5 pints). In a pan over medium heat, combine fruit and sugar. Heat, crushing fruit, to just below boiling (about 180°).

BERRIES. Remove stems and measure whole; use 1 tablespoon sugar for each cup strawberries (½ cup sugar for 5 pints), 1½ tablespoons sugar for each cup raspberries (1 cup sugar for 5 pints), or 2½ tablespoons sugar for each cup blackberries (1½ cups sugar for 5 pints).

In a pan over medium heat, combine fruit and sugar. Bring strawberries just to a full rolling boil. Boil other berries, stirring, until liquid appears syrupy; then put through a food mill or wire strainer to remove seeds. Spread about 3/16 inch thick.

PEACHES AND NECTARINES. Choose yellow freestone peaches. Peel (do not peel nectarines), slice, and measure. Use 1½ tablespoons sugar for each cup fruit (1 cup sugar for 5 pints). In a pan over medium heat, combine fruit and sugar. Heat, crushing fruit, to just below boiling (about 180°). If liquid is thin, boil until syrupy.

PLUMS. Choose varieties with firm flesh; slice and measure. Use 2½ tablespoons sugar for each cup Santa Rosa plums (1½ cups sugar for 5 pints), about 1½ tablespoons sugar for each cup other plums (1 cup sugar for 5 pints).

In a pan over medium heat, combine fruit and sugar. Heat, crushing fruit, to just below boiling (about 180°). If liquid is thin, boil until syrupy.

INDEX

Metric Conversion Table

To change	To	Multiply by
ounces (oz.)	grams (g)	28
pounds (lbs.)	kilograms (kg)	0.45
teaspoons	milliliters (ml)	5
tablespoons	milliliters (ml)	15
fluid ounces (fl. oz.)	milliliters (ml)	30
cups	liters (l)	0.24
pints (pt.)	liters (l)	0.47
quarts (qt.)	liters (l)	0.95
gallons (gal.)	liters (l)	3.8
Fahrenheit temperature (°F)	Celsius temperature (°C)	5/9 after subtracting 32